The Writing of
Wole Soyinka

The Writing of Wole Soyinka

THIRD EDITION

▼▼▼▼▼▼▼▼▼▼▼▼▼▼▼▼▼▼▼▼▼▼▼▼▼▼▼▼▼▼▼▼

ELDRED DUROSIMI JONES
Professor of English
University of Sierra Leone

James Currey
LONDON
Heinemann
PORTSMOUTH N.H.

Heinemann Educational Books Inc
70 Court Street, Portsmouth, New Hampshire 03801, USA
James Currey Ltd
54b Thornhill Square
London N1 1BE, England

First published by Heinemann Educational Books & Twayne 1973
Reprinted 1975, 1978
Revised second edition 1983
Third edition 1988

Library of Congress Cataloging-in-Publication Data

Jones, Eldred D.
  The writing of Wole Soyinka / Eldred Durosimi Jones. —
  3rd ed.
    p.   cm.
  Bibliography: p.
  Includes index.
  ISBN 0-435-08021-0 (U.S.)
    1. Soyinka, Wole Criticism and interpretation. I. Title.
PR9387.9.S6Z7 1987
822-dc19   87-25167
ISBN 0-435-08021-0 (Heinemann)   CIP

British Library Cataloguing in Publication Data

Jones, Eldred Durosimi
  The writing of Wole Soyinka.—3rd ed.
  1. Soyinka, Wole—Criticism and interpretation
  I. Title
  828   PR9387.9.S6Z/
  ISBN 0-85255-503-2 (James Currey)

Printed and bound in the United States of America

For W. S. Our W. S.

Contents

▼▼▼▼▼▼▼▼▼▼▼▼▼▼▼▼▼▼▼▼▼▼▼▼▼▼▼▼▼▼▼▼▼▼

viii

Preface to first edition

▼▼▼▼▼▼▼▼▼▼▼▼▼▼▼▼▼▼▼▼▼▼▼▼▼▼▼▼▼▼▼▼

A BIOGRAPHY or a definitive edition of Soyinka's work at this time would be as premature as the accounts of Mark Twain's funeral. He is at the height of his productive powers, and will no doubt add considerably to the existing corpus of his work. This book pretends to be neither complete nor definitive. Rather it is a tentative offering of one man's reading of a writer whose work has intrigued and fascinated him. It cannot be final even for me since successive readings of the author's work continue to produce new insights. Phrases like 'for me' in my interpretations convey the only sort of authority claimed for my readings.

I have of course benefited in my reading from such criticism as there is of Soyinka's work, and have acknowledged direct indebtedness to particular critics. I have discussed Soyinka in conferences and seminars with colleagues and students in Africa, in Europe, in the U.S.A. and Canada, and many of these discussions have given me fresh insights and points of departure for which I am grateful.

Some people have given me help of a personal nature which I gratefully acknowledge. Wole Soyinka himself has always kindly sent me unpublished material when I have asked him; but I have deliberately refrained from questioning him about his intentions in any work of art, preferring to take the works as offered even at the risk of misreading them. This is a risk every reader has to take, and a danger every writer runs. Mrs Valerie Land while she was in Lagos, and Mr Martin Banham, both helped me with local material in Nigeria. Mrs Anne-Marie Heywood very generously showed me some unpublished notes on the author which I found most illuminating. Friends like Ulli Beier and 'Goke Olubimmo have driven me over many miles to Yoruba sites and ceremonies. Professor Bernth Lindfors sent me copies of some published but little-known short stories of Soyinka as well as copies of the two radio plays. For all this help I am enormously grateful.

For the actual writing of the book I am specially indebted to the Council of Canadian Universities for a totally unlooked for and generous fellowship which enabled me to take time off from teaching while I wrote it. My own College Council of Fourah Bay, with the enthusiastic support of my Principal, Canon Harry Sawyerr, gave me leave of absence on generous conditions. Without the help of these two bodies this book would still have been in the form of notes. My thanks to them are deep and sincere. As usual, my wife typed the manuscript of this book. For her loving care and valuable suggestions I am eternally grateful.

For the section on *Poems from Prison* I have used material which appeared in my review of these poems in *African Literature Today*.

Eldred D. Jones
New College, Toronto
and
Fourah Bay College
Freetown

Preface to the third edition

▼▼▼▼▼▼▼▼▼▼▼▼▼▼▼▼▼▼▼▼▼▼▼▼▼▼▼▼▼▼

Aké: The Years of Childhood in which Soyinka records his recollections of the first eleven and a half years of his life, appeared when the revised (second) edition of this work was already with the printers, and was therefore only glancingly referred to in a footnote. This work, which illuminates the author's later life and work, receives fuller attention in this third edition. In the last few years, as Soyinka has felt the need to stir the social conscience of the ordinary citizen and voter, he has produced a number of topical works ranging from popular music – he has a long playing record, *Unlimited Liability Company* – and pieces for street theatre, to *Opera Wonyosi* (an adaptation of Brecht's *Threepenny Opera*) and *Requiem for a Futurologist*. The last two having been published are also examined here.

This edition coincides with the award to Soyinka of the Nobel Prize for Literature, the crowning achievement so far of a literary career which has now topped a quarter of a century.

My wife on whose eyes I now almost totally depend, worked even harder on this edition than on the earlier ones and deserves most of the credit for its having appeared at all.

The enthusiasm of Soyinka's many admirers, including his publisher Rex Collings, James Currey, Abiola Irele and Kole Omotoso, have also been sustaining influences.

Leicester Village
Freetown 1987

Acknowledgements

▼▼▼▼▼▼▼▼▼▼▼▼▼▼▼▼▼▼▼▼▼▼▼▼▼▼▼▼▼▼▼▼▼

We are grateful to the following publishers for permission to quote extracts from the work of Wole Soyinka:

Autobiography:
The Man Died: Prison Notes of Wole Soyinka (Rex Collings Ltd, London, 1973); *Aké: The Years of Childhood* (Rex Collings Ltd, London, 1981).

Plays:
A Dance of the Forests, *The Lion and the Jewel*, *The Swamp Dwellers*, *The Trials of Brother Jero*, and *The Strong Breed* (published under the title of *Five Plays*, Oxford University Press, London, 1964); *The Road* (Oxford University Press, London, 1967); *Madmen and Specialists* (Methuen, London, 1971); *Jero's Metamorphosis* (published in *The Jero Plays*, Eyre Methuen, London, 1973); *The Road* (Oxford University Press, London, 1965); *The Bacchae of Euripides* (Eyre Methuen, London, 1973); *Death and the King's Horseman* (Eyre Methuen, London, 1975); *Opera Wonyosi* (Rex Collings Ltd., London, 1981); *Requiem for a Futurologist* (Rex Collings Ltd, London, 1985).

Poetry:
'Of the Road', 'Lone Figure', 'Of Birth and Death', 'For Women', 'Grey Seasons', 'October '66', 'Idanre' (published under the title of *Idanre, and Other Poems* Methuen, London, 1967); *Poems from Prison* (Rex Collings Ltd, London, 1969); 'Requiem' appeared in the first edition of Gerald Moore and Ulli Beier's *Modern Poetry from Africa* (Penguin, London, 1963) but was not included in their revised edition of 1968; *A Shuttle in the Crypt* (Rex Collings/Eyre Methuen, London, 1972); *Ogun Abibimang* (Rex Collings Ltd., London, 1976).

Fiction:
The Interpreters (Andre Deutsch, London, 1965; also Heinemann, London, African Writers Series, 76, 1970); *Season of Anomy* (Rex Collings Ltd., London, 1973).

Biographical Outline

▼▼▼▼▼▼▼▼▼▼▼▼▼▼▼▼▼▼▼▼▼▼▼▼▼▼▼▼▼▼▼▼

NOTE: Only first or specially notable productions of plays are given.

1934   Born in Abeokuta of Ijegba parentage

1938–1943   Primary Education – St Peter's School, Ake, Abeokuta

1944–1945   Abeokuta Grammar School

1946–1950   Government College, Ibadan

1952–1954   Student at University College, Ibadan (now The University of Ibadan)

1954–1957   Student at the University of Leeds, obtained B.A. (Honours English). Short Stories published: *Madame Etienne's Establishment* and *A Tale of Two Cities*
Another story also called: *A Tale of Two Cities*

1957–1959   Attached to the Royal Court Theatre, London as Play Reader *The Invention* (never published) performed at the Theatre on Nov. 1, 1959. On the programme were also excerpts from *The House of Banigeji*, and *A Dance of the African Forests*

1959   *The Swamp-Dwellers* produced in London

1959   *The Swamp-Dwellers* and *The Lion and the Jewel* produced in Ibadan, Nigeria

1960   Langston Hughes' *African Treasury* published, containing Soyinka poems

1960   Lagos. Formed 'The 1960 Masks', drama company

1960   *A Dance of the Forests* produced in Lagos. The play won *Encounter* independence play award

1961–1962   Rockefeller Research Fellow, Ibadan University

1962–1964   Lecturer – University of Ife

1963   Satirical revue – *The Republican* performed by 'The 1960 Masks'. Later in the same year *The New Republican* performed

1963   *The Lion and the Jewel* published

1963   *A Dance of the Forests* published

1963   *Three Plays* published by Mbari

1963	Gerald Moore and Ulli Beier's *Modern Poetry from Africa* (Penguin) published, containing Soyinka poems
1964	Orisun Theatre (drama group) formed
1964	(March) *The Strong Breed* – A twenty-five-minute adaptation filmed in Nigeria for American television (Esso World Theatre)
1964	(December) *The Strong Breed* and *The Trials of Brother Jero* produced at Greenwich Mews Theatre (U.S.A.)
1964	*Five Plays* published
1965	(March) *Camwood on the Leaves* (radio play) broadcast – B.B.C. Overseas Service
1965	(September) *The Detainee* (radio play) broadcast – B.B.C. Overseas Service
1965	*Before the Blackout*, satirical revue, produced
1965	(September) *The Road* directed by David Thompson at Theatre Royal, Stratford East, London
1965	(October) – Soyinka arrested in connection with a 'pirate' broadcast made from the Western Region Studios of the Nigerian Broadcasting Corporation following the disputed Western Region elections (December) – Acquitted
1965	*The Road* published
1965	*Kongi's Harvest* directed by author at the Federal Palace Hotel, Lagos
1965–67	Senior Lecturer, University of Lagos and Acting Head of Department of English
1966	*Kongi's Harvest* performed at Dakar Festival of Negro Arts
1966	*Rites of the Harmattan Solstice* celebrated at University of Lagos (6th June)
1966	(June) *The Trials of Brother Jero* produced at Hampstead Theatre, London
1966	(December) *The Lion and the Jewel* produced at Royal Court Theatre, London
1967	*Kongi's Harvest* published
1967	*Idanre and Other Poems* published
1967	(August) Detained by the Federal Military Government of Nigeria
1968	Received Jock Campbell/*New Statesman* Award
1968	*The Forest of a Thousand Daemons*, Soyinka's translation of D. O. Fagunwa's Yoruba novel *Ogboju ode ninu Igbo Irunmale*, published

1969	*Three Short Plays* published and *Poems from Prison* published
1969	Appointed head of the Department of Theatre Arts, U of Ibadan
1969	(October) Released from detention
1970	(August) *Madmen and Specialists* produced at the Eugene O'Neill Theatre Centre, Waterford, Connecticut, U.S.A.
1971	(January) *Madmen and Specialists* performed in Ibadan, Nigeria
1971	*Before The Blackout* published
1972	*A Shuttle in the Crypt* and *The Man Died* published
1973	Soyinka's version of Euripides' *The Bacchae* published and performed in London at the Old Vic by the National Theatre
1973	Visiting Professor at the Department of English, U of Sheffield. Overseas Fellow, Churchill College, U of Cambridge
1973	*Collected Plays*, vol. I, published
1973	*Jero's Metamorphosis* published
1973	*Season of Anomy* published
1973	*Camwood on the Leaves* published
1974	*Collected Plays*, vol. II, published
1975	*Death and the King's Horseman* published
1976	*Myth, Literature and the African World* published
1976	*Ogun Abibiman* published
1976	Visiting Professor, Institute of African Studies, U of Ghana
1976	Professor of Comparative Literature, U of Ife
1977	Festac (The International Festival of Negro Arts and Culture), Lagos, at which in his public lecture Soyinka advocated the adoption of Swahili as the common language of the continent
1980	Visiting Professor, Yale University
1980	(December) Delivered inaugural lecture, University of Ife, on "The Critic and Society: Barthes, Leftocracy & Other Mythologies".
1981	*Opera Wonyosi* published
1981	*Ake: The Years of Childhood* published
1982	(August) Delivered a lecture, Stratford-on-Avon on "Shakespeare and the Living Dramatist"
1982	(December) *Die Still Rev. Dr. Godspeak*, a radio play broadcast BBC African Service
1983	*Requiem for a Futurologist* produced and directed by the author
1983	(July) long playing record *Unlimited Liability Company* released
1984	Film, *Blues for a Prodigal*, shown at Ife
1985	*Requiem for a Futurologist* published
1986	Awarded the Nobel Prize for Literature
1986	Awarded Nigerian Order – Commander of the Federal Republic (CFR), Nigeria's second highest award

Part 1

Soyinka, the Man
and his Background

Soyinka, the Man
and his Background

▼▼▼▼▼▼▼▼▼▼▼▼▼▼▼▼▼▼▼▼▼▼▼▼▼▼▼▼

WOLE SOYINKA has his roots in Yoruba culture, as even a cursory reading of his works soon shows, but his experience extends far wider; his formal education and his working experience have brought him into contact with ideas from the whole modern world. This other half of his experience is also represented in his work. His imagery ranges from tropical yam roots to the falling acorns of Tegel. But he starts as a Yoruba.

Apart from having been born a Yoruba and thus being naturally a part of the culture, Soyinka has taken a deep and scholarly interest in the culture of his people. His interest in the language is strikingly illustrated by his thoughtful translation of one of the most popular works of Yoruba literature, D. O. Fagunwa's *Ogboju ode ninu Irunmale* under the title *The Forest of a Thousand Daemons*. In a very significant Translator's Note prefixed to the work, Soyinka demonstrates the linguistic discretion he had to exercise. His explanation of his choice of the word 'daemon' is illustrative of the point. He writes: 'The spelling is important. These beings who inhabit Fagunwa's world demand at all costs and by every conceivable translator's trick to be preserved from the common or misleading associations which substitutes such as *demons, devils* or *gods* evoke in the reader's mind. At the same time, it is necessary that they transmit the reality of their existence by the same unquestioning impact and vitality which is conveyed by Fagunwa in the original.'[1] Some of the results of the translator's ingenuity are new words like Ghommids, dewild, Gnom (without an e) and kobold, It is worth noting that these beings from Yoruba tradition found in Fagunwa's world (and in the forests of Tutuola) are also found in Soyinka's own forests in his play *A Dance of the Forests*. The Crier's summons in that play is:

> To all such as dwell in these Forests; Rock devils,
> Earth imps, Tree demons, ghommids, dewilds, genies
> Incubi, succubi, windhorls, bits and halves and such

[1] *The Forest of a Thousand Daemons* (Nelson, London, 1968), p. 4.

Sons and subjects of Forest Father, and all
That dwell in his domain . . .[2]

Soyinka shares in this respect the same mythological world as Fagunwa
and Tutuola.

His scholarly interest in this world is further demonstrated in his essay
'The Fourth Stage'[3] in which he develops a theory of Yoruba tragedy by
examining the ideas underlying the Yoruba concepts of being, and in
particular, the ideas underlying Yoruba theology. The effect of this deep
scholarly interest in Yoruba culture endows Soyinka with a base of ideas
from which his works flow. Indeed some knowledge of Yoruba culture is
necessary for any serious study of this author's work.

YORUBA CULTURE

The Yoruba are one of Africa's most remarkable peoples. Their culture is
not only rich, but shows a remarkable capacity for survival in areas far
removed from its original home. Yoruba culture survives robustly for
example in Brazil and other parts of South America, the Caribbean, and in
Sierra Leone, areas which centuries ago, largely through the slave trade,
came into contact with Yoruba of the diaspora.

The original home of the Yoruba is of course Western Nigeria. G. J.
Afolabi Ojo, himself a distinguished Yoruba scholar defines their cultural
area thus: '. . . the area where Yoruba culture is typical coincides with the
six western provinces of Western Nigeria [Oyo, Ibadan, Abeokuta, Ijebu,
Ondo, Lagos]; Ilorin Division of Ilorin Province; and Kabba Division of
Kabba Province'.[4]

Soyinka was born in Abeokuta, an area which still retains the highest
density of Yoruba speakers – over 90 per cent of the population, according
to Ojo.

GODS, SPIRITS, ANCESTORS

Traditional Yoruba life is dominated by religion. The Yoruba are
surrounded by gods and spirits with whom the lives of mortals interact. In
what is more an idiomatic expression for the idea of multiplicity than an
actual count, the Yoruba ascribe to themselves four hundred and one
gods. (Soyinka prefers to translate a similar expression *Irunmale*, not
literally as four hundred deities but as 'a thousand and one'.)[5] The total

---

[2] *Five Plays* (O.U.P., London, 1964), p. 50.
[3] D. W. Jefferson (ed.), *The Morality of Art* (Routledge and Kegan Paul,
London, 1960).
[4] *Yoruba Culture* (Ife University Press and London University Press, 1966), p. 20.
[5] *The Forest of a Thousand Daemons*, p. 3.

count of deities probably can never be given since local areas have some deities peculiar to them. There are of course major deities who are recognized and worshipped all over Yorubaland. Olodumare (Olorun) is the supreme god – 'Creator, king, Omnipotent, All-wise, All-knowing, Judge, Immortal, Invisible and Holy'.[6] He is worshipped through minor deities, and although constantly invoked in oaths, the Yoruba do not represent him physically or build shrines to him. In deference to Yoruba tradition (and because he would not know what he looked like anyway) Kola, the artist in Soyinka's novel *The Interpreters*, does not represent Olodumare in his painting of the Yoruba Pantheon. (He appears as Forest Head in *A Dance of the Forests*.) The gods represented in Kola's canvas are Orisa Nla, the principal deity under Olodumare, Esu, the spirit of disorder, evil and change, Sango, god of lightning and electricity, Sopona (Obaluwaiye) of smallpox, Erinle, Esumare, and Soyinka's favourite god, Ogun. The duality of this last god, the seeming contradiction in his nature – he is both the creative and the destructive essence – makes him an enigmatic symbol both in Soyinka's own creative work and in his criticism. Man in his capacity both for creation and destruction is a reincarnation of this contradictory god of the forge. In *'The Fourth Stage'* for example Soyinka writes thus about Ogun:

> As for Ogun, he is best understood in Hellenic values as a totality of the Dionysian, Apollonian and Promethean values. Nor is this all. Transcending even today, the distorted myths of his terrorist reputation, traditional poetry records him as 'protector of orphans', 'roof over the homeless', 'terrible guardian of the sacred oath'; Ogun stands in fact for a transcendental humane but rigidly restorative justice.[7]

Below the deities, in Yoruba belief, are numerous spirits of the ancestors and of things. Some of the gods in fact are ancestors who have been elevated into deities. Thus Sango was once the third Alafin (king) of Oyo. Gods and the spirits of the ancestors are thus very close to each other. Trees, peculiar land formations, rivers etc., all could become imbued with spirits which make them sacred. Human life itself is regarded as part of a continuum of life stretching from the spirits of unborn children through bodily existence to the spirits of departed ancestors. The abiku child who appears as a symbol at the end of *A Dance of the Forests* and is also the subject of a poem is a manifestation of a restless child spirit who is constantly shuttling back and forth between the land of the unborn spirits and this life, causing itself to be born over and over again by the same mother only

[6] Ojo, *Yoruba Culture*, p. 182.
[7] Jefferson, *The Morality of Art*, p. 120.

to plague her by its death. These are the gods and spirits which make up the teeming population of Soyinka's forests in *A Dance of the Forests*.

The ancestors are worshipped through the *egungun*, masked figures who, if the ceremonies are duly observed, become possessed by the spirits they represent, and are able to speak with unearthly wisdom. Soyinka makes use of this idea of possession in both *A Dance of the Forests* and *The Road*, two of his most important plays. In contrast to this proper use of masks, he offers the travesty of the District Commissioner and his wife in *Death and the King's Horseman*, prancing about in the 'fancy dress' of captured *egungun* regalia, ironic symbols of a tragic alienation. The carving of masks and other objects for the worship of these numerous ancestors and deities has made the Yoruba probably the most prolific as well as the most artistic wood carvers in the world. A good impression of both their skill and sheer output (it must be remembered that the light wood used is highly perishable necessitating constant replacement) can be gained from Ulli Beier's illustrated booklet, *The Story of Sacred Wood Carvings From One Small Yoruba Town*.[8] The carver is central to Yoruba life and worship; this central position is reflected in the symbolic role of Demoke the carver in *A Dance of the Forests* who becomes a representative of humanity.

YORUBA OCCUPATIONS AND FESTIVALS

Farming is the most important occupation of the Yoruba although quite interestingly they are also an urban people, their farms being situated a long way from their homes. Hunting, fishing, weaving, dyeing and trading are other occupations, but it is the regular rhythm of farming – clearing the farm, hoeing it, sowing it, and reaping the harvest – which dictates the larger patterns of life. A failure of crops is a disaster of the greatest magnitude. In Soyinka's symbolism such a failure becomes a symbol for destruction and the very negation of life, while the image of a successful and plenteous harvest represents the positive forces of life. The big Yoruba festivals predominantly come at the time of harvest when there is plenty to eat and drink. Harvest thus has associations of both piety and joy, as is reflected in Soyinka's poem 'Idanre'.

Some trees and crops have come to be prominent in the culture and assume symbolic stature. Dr Ojo lists among these, yam, kola, oil palm, and maleguetta pepper. These appear in this symbolic role in Soyinka's works; indeed all of them appear in a single poem 'Dedication'. Palm wine, one of the products of the oil palm, is the universal drink; thirst quencher as well as drink of ceremony and celebration. Tutuola's most famous character, the Drinkard, undertakes his perilous pilgrimage to the

[8] Published by *Nigeria Magazine*, Lagos, 1957, 1959.

land of the dead in pursuit of his dead palm wine tapster without whose services life was insupportable. Palm wine assumes almost a mystical role in Soyinka's work. It is the wine of Professor's special version of the rite of communion in *The Road*. Egbo has to have a gourd of the best on his visit with the unnamed girl to his shrine in *The Interpreters*. Soyinka's special interest in palm wine (artistic and gastronomic) is exemplified by a celebration of the rites of the Harmattan solstice which he organized at the University of Lagos and for which he composed poems both in Yoruba and English, all around the theme of palm wine.[9]

Yoruba culture is rich in ceremonies ranging from the simple ceremonies of regular worship (the principal deities are worshipped every four days) through family ceremonies associated with birth, marriage, death, to the big annual festivals of particular gods, and special ceremonies relating to the crowning and the rule of Obas (kings). Ulli Beier in his booklet *A Year of Sacred Festivals in One Yoruba Town*[10] describes with pictures eleven of the major festivals celebrated in this town of six thousand inhabitants. His list is limited to the big town festivals and does not include the more numerous smaller family and personal celebrations.

The principal external features of these festivals are drumming, singing, dancing, feasting and sacrifice. Poetic praise songs (oriki) and prayers are recited, mimetic dances re-enact events whose originals are lost in mytho-logical gloom, sacrifices, often of freshly killed animals, are offered, and pent-up spirits are released in general dancing. Oyin Ogumba has pointed out how the Yoruba festival has influenced Soyinka's plays:

> But by far the most significant traditional element in these plays is the overall design of a festival. This is particularly true of the plays, namely *Kongi's Harvest*, *The Strong Breed* and *A Dance of the Forests*. In each of these plays, the prevailing mood is that of the preparation for or celebration of a great event which produces so much excitement or tension in the whole populace that everybody thinks of nothing but the great event. This is, in fact, the atmosphere that prevails when important ceremonies are performed in traditional Africa, and Soyinka in these plays very often catches the essence of the festival mood with the drumming, bustle and other manifestations of a holiday.[11]

The head of Yoruba government is the Oba. He is a king who rules

---

[9] Mr Soyinka kindly gave me a copy of the mimeographed pamphlet which records the occasion.

[10] Published by *Nigeria Magazine*, Lagos, 1959.

[11] 'The Traditional Content of the Plays of Wole Soyinka' *African Literature Today*, 4 (Heinemann Educational Books, London, 1970), p. 8.

surrounded by ceremony, and combines both political and priestly functions. The Oba's spiritual authority is exemplified in *Kongi's Harvest* in which, even when the Oba's political authority has been eroded by the new regime of Kongi, he still has reserves of moral and spiritual authority with which to compel deference from the functionaries of the new regime. Baroka, the wily Bale of Ilujinle, is another of Soyinka's evocations of the Yoruba traditional ruler.

All Yoruba culture is enshrined in the language, a highly tonal and musical language which gives the impression of being chanted rather than spoken. These rhythmic and tonal qualities do not come over into English, which is a language of a very different type. What does flow over into Soyinka's English is the wealth of imagery and proverbial formulas which he uses with remarkable effect. Soyinka thinks in images, and his poems in particular are elaborate formulations of imagery which only reveal their full meaning when the image code is broken. His fondness for puns, which sometimes seems over-indulged in English, is also probably an overflow from the word puzzles, tongue-twisters and other verbal tricks of his original language.

CHRISTIAN INFLUENCES

His Yoruba traditional background provides the key to one part of Soyinka, but it is well to remember that there are other influences as well, so universal that they cannot be so easily identified. Although Soyinka received his basic formal education up to university level in Nigeria, the content of this education was essentially Christian-European. He has declared that he is no longer a practising Christian,[12] but the influence of Christianity on his work is quite apparent. He has a facility of Biblical reference which could only come of years of early Bible study. A complete list of Biblical references in Soyinka's work would be impressive, but only a few illustrations are given here.

In *The Interpreters*, Dehinwa who deliberately slams the door to aggravate Sagoe's already splitting headache becomes Jael (*Judges* 4, 21) who drove a tent pin through Sisera's temples. In the same novel, Joe Golder, dissatisfied with his complexion (too light for a Negro) felt 'like Esau cheated of my birthright', a reference to the well-known story of Esau and Jacob (*Genesis* 27, 36). The Life of Christ must have made a deep impression, for there are Christ figures all over Soyinka's work, often with verbal links with the Bible. 'The Dreamer' is an obvious example. He hangs

> Higher than trees a cryptic crown
> Lord of the rebel three

[12] Interview, *Spear* (Dar-es-Salaam, May 1966), p. 19.

> Thorns lay on a sleep of down
> And myrrh; a mesh
> Of nails, of flesh
> And words that flowered free

This picture obviously derives from Christ on the Cross.[13] There are parallels too between Eman in *The Strong Breed* and Christ. Both men are victims of people for whom they worked, and each died high on a sacred tree leaving the people stunned by their deaths.[14] Willing sacrifice is one of Soyinka's recurrent themes

The miracle of the feeding of the five thousand (*Mark*, 6), is ironically recalled in the last section of the poem 'Ikeja, Friday, Four O'clock' in the words: 'Let nought be wasted, gather up for the recurrent session/Loaves of lead, lusting in the sun's recession.' There are undertones of Christ's entry into Jerusalem in 'Easter'. Some of the references are so natural that they could have been unconscious. Quite obviously, like Dehinwa, Sagoe, and Egbo in *The Interpreters*, Soyinka had large doses of Sunday School.

OTHER INFLUENCES

His higher education, started at Ibadan, was continued at Leeds where he read English. The Leeds syllabus is very wide in scope, and must have brought Soyinka into contact with the whole range of modern European and American literature. He was one of G. Wilson Knight's memorable pupils. The great literary critic in his preface to *The Golden Labyrinth*, acknowledges his debt to Soyinka's interpretation of the character of King Lear, which in turn influenced his conception of the work. The English poet Thomas Blackburn, after whom Soyinka wrote his poem 'By Little Loving', was another Leeds contact. Describing his other experiences in Britain and continental Europe Soyinka himself said: 'I worked in a night-club partly as a barman and partly as a bouncer. During one of the long vacations, I worked as a bricklayer in Holland. Then I taught in a variety of schools in Britain. From very good grammar schools to those which qualify to be called borstals.'[15] An interest in and facility of reference to other mythologies, but particularly Greek mythology, is obvious in his later work. *Shuttle in the Crypt*, his essay 'The Fourth Stage' and, of course, his adaptation of *The Bacchae* of Euripides copiously illustrate this.

Perhaps even more significant was Soyinka's attachment to the Royal Court Theatre, the home of the English Stage Society, where he was a play

[13] For a fuller discussion, see pp. 130–31 below.
[14] See pp. 60–61 below.
[15] *Spear*, May 1966, p. 16.

reader. Some of his early pieces were tried out there. 'The Invention' and excerpts from other works formed the programme at the Sunday night productions of that theatre on November 1, 1959. The attachment to the Royal Court put him in contact with the work of the *avant-garde* European playwrights as well as the work of traditional dramatists. (English reviewers of his plays have seen influences on his work ranging from Ben Jonson, through Wycherley, Ibsen and Chekov to Wesker and Pinter.) Soyinka has travelled widely since over a vast area of the world, and no doubt being a sensitive man has been influenced. His work is, however, a truly original manifestation of his whole vast range of experiences. Certainly this range of experiences has given him a world-wide view of mankind, even though he naturally chooses to treat man mainly through the African environment.

He is primarily an African writer and whatever influence his work has on the rest of the world – he is now performed in Britain, continental Europe and America[16] – his primary audience is in Africa where his works should be read and performed a great deal more there than they are. Among the plays, the shorter works, particularly the comedies, are performed fairly often, but the major plays far too seldom. The main reason for this is that the major plays do make considerable demands on the skill of actors and the ingenuity of directors, and tropical Africa does not have professional companies which can put on the plays with the degree of professional skill that they require.

SOYINKA AND THE STAGE

Soyinka himself is conscious of the need for companies which would keep a body of players together under expert direction long enough for them to develop the necessary skills for the production of the new African drama which draws on African traditional methods of presentation as well as the techniques of European and other traditions of theatre. On his return from England he formed 'The 1960 Masks', the company which put on *A Dance of the Forests* in Nigeria's independence year. Later he formed Orisun Theatre. His hope for permanent theatre groups is still far from fulfilment, but he has used university theatre groups as the nuclei of acting companies which have performed his plays both within and outside Nigeria.

Soyinka is himself a skilled actor and director whose productions of his own plays demonstrate the fact that a professional production is not necessarily an elaborate production. He directed the première of *Kongi's Harvest* on the floor of the conference hall of the Federal Palace Hotel in

[16] *The Bacchae* of Euripides, having been actually commissioned by the National Theatre Company of Britain for performance in that country, could be said to have been addressed primarily to a non-African audience, but Soyinka brought his Yoruba background to the Greek story. See my note on this play on p. 113 below.

Lagos without benefit of a proper stage, but by expert lighting, and the sensitive use of music and movement he pulled off an excellent production. Not every director is a Soyinka, and it must be admitted that plays like *A Dance of the Forests* present formidable problems of staging. Conversely, elaborate facilities may not in themselves effect a successful production. At least one critic suggests that the direction of *The Bacchae* failed to respond adequately to the demands of the text: 'Faced with a text that calls for precise and meaningful gesture, for narrative clarity, and for a theatre language based on ritual, the director has opted for imitation orgies, fake horror, and whooped-up excitement.'[17]

Soyinka's other work, particularly the poetry, has the reputation of being difficult. What this really means is that it demands close and sensitive reading – as does his novel *The Interpreters*. Very few writers, however, repay this attention more copiously than Soyinka does. However complex he may be, though, it seems ludicrous that in Africa reading lists which include T. S. Eliot's poetry with its background of classical European mythology and mysticism, should exclude Soyinka on grounds of difficulty.

BASIC CONCERNS

Soyinka's life is inseparable from his work, much of which arises from a passionate, almost desperate, concern for his society. This concern is apparent in his poetry, drama and essays, but is not merely literary. It shows itself in his letters to the Nigerian papers which can always be relied upon to rouse enthusiastic support or bitter opposition. Indeed it is this very concern, and the speed with which he translates ideas into action that puts him so often at odds with institutions and governments. His dramatic resignation from the University of Ife, the celebrated Radio Station episode, and his detention during most of the Nigerian Civil War are all examples of Soyinka in uncomfortably exposed positions as a result of deeply held convictions. And yet, Soyinka constantly insists that he is not a 'committed' writer. All that this really means, as he explains in the *Spear* interview, is that he is 'not committed to any ideology'. There can be few writers who believe more deeply in freedom and are prepared to sacrifice as much for it. In his own words:

> I believe there is no reason why human beings should not enjoy maximum freedom. In living together in society, we agree to lose some of our freedom. To detract from the maximum freedom socially possible, to me, is treacherous. I do not believe in dictatorship benevolent or malevolent.[18]

[17] Albert Hunt, 'Amateurs in Horror', reprinted in James Gibbs (ed.), *Critical Perspectives on Wole Soyinka* Three Continents Press, Washington, DC, 1980).

[18] *Spear*, May 1966, p. 20.

It is from deeply held convictions like these that the 'works' both literary and social flow. Soyinka is a unified personality; the artist and the man are one.

The essential ideas which emerge from a reading of Soyinka's work are not specially African ideas although his characters and their mannerisms are African. His concern is with man on earth. Man is dressed for the nonce in African dress and lives in the sun and the tropical forest, but he represents the whole race. The duality of man's personality, his simultaneous capacity for creation and destruction which makes him almost at every moment a potential victim of his own ingenuity, is a universal trait of *homo sapiens* who has been given by his creator the gift of free will. In *A Dance of the Forests*, the Yoruba style deity, Forest Father, represents the creator, and Demoke the Yoruba carver represents man. Any universal god or any abstraction for the source of life could take Forest Father's place just as any man of sensibility could take the place of the Yoruba artist.

SALVATION AND THE INDIVIDUAL WILL

Soyinka sees society as being in continual need of salvation from itself. This act of salvation is not a mass act; it comes about through the vision and dedication of individuals who doggedly pursue their vision in spite of the opposition of the very society they seek to save. They frequently end up as the victims of the society which benefits from their vision. The salvation of the society then depends on the exercise of the individual will. Thus the act of Atunda, the Yoruba slave who fragmented the unified essence and produced many individual essences or gods, is celebrated in 'Idanre' as are other individual deities or inspired men (prophets) who by the exercise of their individual will transformed the lives of men. The Yoruba figure then is paralleled by figures from all universal religions. Atunda is a symbol for a universal idea which Yoruba mythology and religion conveniently supplies.

If the individual will is so important, society must enable it to be exercised freely. For Soyinka any form of political repression is a suppression of this individual will, which is the force through which new ideas and new life proceed. The suppression of the individual will is thus a suppression of the very forces of life. This is the point of the play *Kongi's Harvest*, to give just one prominent example of the theme. This is not a Yoruba or an African idea. If it has validity, this is a general validity. The clash between the individual and the society which Soyinka so often portrays in African terms is a universal phenomenon; the martyr who is the positive product of the clash is also fortunately (I reproduce Soyinka's irony) universal.

The individual with a vision for society has to communicate this vision and to disseminate it if society is to be improved by it. The tragic irony which appeared in a number of Soyinka's works was that the visionary remained misunderstood and isolated, and often died before his message was understood. Soyinka's own experience, as he saw men whose views and attitudes he thought held promise for Nigeria – Victor Banjo[19] and Major Fajuyi,[20] for example – die without seeing their ideas reach any fulfilment, would have confirmed how often this circumstance attended human affairs. It was still the duty of the visionary to pursue his course, lonely or not, since as in the case of his dreamer in the poem of that name, the ideas once sown may sprout even after the death of the sower. False prophets, by contrast, seem to produce more instant growths, like seeds on stony ground. In works like *Kongi's Harvest* the focus is turned a little on *groups* of faithful followers of reformist leaders. Segi and Daodu had their groups of women and young farmers in opposition to the tyranny of Kongi's rule in *Kongi's Harvest*. In *The Man Died* Soyinka is impressed by the strength conveyed by the song of the group of Ibo prisoners,[21] and his post-prison novel, *Season of Anomy*, portrays a community with a philosophy and a corporate vision as a catalyst for reform. This is a shift of emphasis. The leaders are still there, still dreaming and daring often alone – Ofeyi, like Orpheus, has to take the decision to make his journey through Hell alone – but attention is also given to the supporting group of ordinary men and women who are the society.

CONCERN FOR LIFE

Soyinka's work celebrates life, and deprecates its opposite. This opposite includes minor internal repressions, but it also embraces the general wastefulness of war. This is an aspect of Soyinka's work that is more obviously relevant to the whole modern world. Again he finds Yoruba mythology handy with the enveloping images. Ogun, temporarily maddened by drink, and indiscriminately killing friend and foe, is a personalization of the idea of the senseless waste that war brings. The message of 'Idanre' is a universal one, equally applicable (only more so) to those who are armed with nuclear weapons as to those who have only swords. The Nigerian Civil War, a national catastrophe gloomily foreshadowed in *A Dance of the Forests*, was thus to Soyinka an awful and unnecessary waste, a negation of the principle of life. Since to him literature was only one manifestation of life, he involved himself totally in efforts to frustrate the pursuit of the war, with results in terms of personal suffering which are only too well-known.[22]

[19] See *The Man Died* (Rex Collings, London, 1973), p. 174.
[20] See *The Man Died*, p. 155–6, and *Idanre*, p. 54.
[21] *The Man Died*, p. 110–2.
[22] Soyinka's *The Man Died* and *A Shuttle in the Crypt* give a prose and poetic record of his experiences in detention.

A minor variation on the destruction of human potential, is man's destruction of the environment. This is a theme – pollution – which has become popular in recent years in the industrialized world. In many parts of Africa it still seems remote. Indeed Africa is at the stage when it is actually clamouring for the factors of pollution as fast as it can obtain them. In one of his earliest plays (and funniest, so that the point is often missed) Soyinka gives the 'backward' Oba of Ilujinle a plea for the environment:

> And the wish of one old man is
> That here and there,
> Among the bridges and the murderous roads,
> Below the humming birds which
> Smoke the face of Sango, dispenser of
> The snake-tongued lightning; between this moment
> And the reckless broom that will be wielded
> In these years to come, we must leave
> Virgin plots of lives, rich decay
> And the tang of vapour rising from
> Forgotten heaps of compost, lying
> Undisturbed . . .[23]

Human life presents constant challenges and constant choices, and man has to thread his way through all the contradictory alternatives. Soyinka himself seems to prefer the personality of Ogun who has always lived a life amidst the challenges and the risks of wrong choices. Ogun (unlike the eternal penitent Obatala who forbids wine to his worshippers), 'in proud acceptance of the need to create a challenge for the constant exercise of will and control, enjoins the liberal joy of wine'.[24] A similar characteristic of Dionysos is no doubt one of the reasons why Soyinka found Euripides' play *The Bacchae* an interesting one to adapt. It is in response to the challenges that man moves towards true wisdom, battered and bruised by his experiences. This is the kind of pilgrimage through all life's opportunities and hazards that Soyinka gives the young interpreters in his novel.

These are the kinds of huge concerns which remain in the mind when the particular mannerisms through which they are expressed in individual works have been forgotten. These are the sorts of ideas which give Wole Soyinka his universal appeal.

[23] *Five Plays* (O.U.P., London, 1964), p. 144.
[24] D. W. Jefferson (ed.), *The Morality of Art* (1960), p. 133.

Part 2
Autobiography

The Man Died

▼▼▼▼▼▼▼▼▼▼▼▼▼▼▼▼▼▼▼▼▼▼▼▼▼▼▼▼▼▼▼▼▼▼▼▼▼

THE MAN, a victim of the tyrannical brutality which for Soyinka was typical of the style of the Gowon military regime, died and thus became a metaphor for the death of justice and of any claim to legitimacy of the regime. The simple report provided a convenient title to a book which combines personal testimony, personal accusation, with broader reflections on the preconditions for a viable state, on the responsibilities of the individuals and groups whose acquiescence makes the continuance of any system possible and the organized opposition of whose will is the eventual escape route from an intolerable regime.

The theme had been explored in imaginative works before by Soyinka himself, most explicitly in *Kongi's Harvest*, but the coincidence between the imagined foreshadowing and the actual experience, must have struck Soyinka with the wryness of its irony; when for instance, he found himself (as his Captain of the Soldiers had been before Mata Kharibu in *A Dance Of The Forests*)[1] being interrogated as a traitor, for (in Soyinka's case) opposing and acting, however quixotically, to prevent a war he thought unnecessary. Soyinka reconstructs the exchanges between himself and 'Mallam D' during the early stages of his detention:

> You say here that you formed a committee to campaign internationally against the importation of arms to Nigeria – you realize by the way that that is a very disloyal thing to do?
> I don't accept that.
> You don't think it helps the rebels? How is a war to be fought without weapons?
> The rebels would use the same argument with justice to prove my antagonism to their cause.
> We are not particularly concerned with the views of the rebels.
> I am. I have declared already that this war is morally unjustified.
> Are you a pacifist?
> Certainly not.
> You would accept some other wars?
> Depends. And always as a last resort.

[1] For a discussion of this play, see pp. 43–59 below, particularly p. 52. Also p. 183.

What kind of wars would you support for instance?

Any war in defence of liberty.

And what of the Rivers people who have been forcibly brought into the so-called Biafra? You think we have no obligation to give them their liberty.

I do not support Biafran secessions, so I am clearly for the statehood of the minority groups.

How then do you want the secession brought to an end?

Not by this particular war.[2]

In so far as literature can prepare one for life – one's own literary output and one's own life – Soyinka may have anticipated the general consequences of his failure to achieve a short-circuiting of the Civil War and of being judged disloyal by the side with whom his lot naturally lay, that is, by birth – though Soyinka would be the first to assert that by birth he was a human being! What he perhaps could not have anticipated, for the details were sometimes more bizarre than fiction, were the directions which the interrogations took, the adventures which developed out of seemingly routine incidents like medical examinations, sinister scenarios for shot-while-trying-to-escape episodes, the quirks of the human personality revealed in both prisoner and captor by the process of confinement, the resources of the mind in the interest of survival – ranging from low cunning to abstract mental athletics – and the devious routes to the survival of the human spirit over affliction, which all contribute to the subject matter of a book which will be many things to many men.

The purely literary scholar will see numerous links with other works, particularly with *Season of Anomy* (the key word of whose title is only the most obvious and elementary of the links) and *Shuttle in the Crypt*, whose metaphor occurs frequently in the prison narrative. If the links are pursued with sensitiveness and imagination, the search could be fruitful, but it could also degenerate into the compilation of a barren balance sheet.

The value of *The Man Died* to the biographer of Soyinka is immense because it contains an intensely personal account of a crucial period in the man's life when his eventual survival must have been a matter of doubt, and he was thus faced with the ultimate reality of death. It is impressive that in this situation the ideals for which Soyinka has always fought and suffered emerge only more sharply defined, not drastically changed – a tribute to his essential moral stability as distinct from his overt mannerisms, which may be unpredictable.

The most controversial aspect of the book must be Soyinka's reading of

[2] *The Man Died; Prison Notes of Wole Soyinka* (Rex Collings, London, 1973), pp. 48–49.

the whole Nigerian situation, of the post-independence years of the country's history, particularly of those just preceding the January 1966 coup, right on to the secession and the Civil War. That the war was a tragedy, which should have been avoided at all costs, few would deny. Soyinka has provided in his book his own account of his activities in an effort to abort it, and there has never been a published official account denying his version. He denied any confession implied in an official release, even while he was still imprisoned. The alleged confession therefore must be discounted.

Soyinka's position on the question of 'genocide' – was there a deliberate attempt to wipe out the Ibos or an official attitude to condone this crime? – is unequivocal: 'Genocide *was* the chosen cure for assets probes'. (p. 176, italics his.) Also baldly asserted more than once is the complicity of the Gowon regime in this, and the general prostitution of justice. For Soyinka, the coup of 15 January 1966 had flaws – 'I did and still wish that the revolt in the West had achieved victory as a people's uprising (pp. 160–1) – but it was, even so, a basis for a national struggle. (p. 161.)

The Man Died is a personal testimony written for a public purpose and addressed to 'the people to whom I belong', that is, the ordinary citizens who do not belong to or enjoy the privileges of the power group. Indeed, the book is a first step towards the unseating of such a group, for, as the author writes in this prefatory letter to his compatriots, 'a first step towards the dethronement of terror is the deflation of its hypocritical self-righteousness.' Soyinka reiterates the evidence of the terror and of the regime's complicity in it. The unnecessary cruelty and viciousness of the conditions of Soyinka's own imprisonment, much of it in solitary confinement, deprived of books, both his mental and his bodily health massively assaulted, amount to a powerful indictment; but the author is even more concerned to put this in perspective against the backdrop of a larger evil, the total sacrifice of justice mainly for personal financial gain. His own particular case then becomes an item, albeit a prominent one, in a catalogue. For if he can be treated in this way, how about the thousands of nameless people picked up and detained without even being properly identified? Soyinka chronicles encounters with such ordinary people at various points in his story, to bring out not only their personal suffering and the injustice of their treatment, but also a bond which seems to be strengthened with each such encounter between himself and his ordinary suffering countrymen.

Both he and the unarmed Ibo woman who is casually thrown into a cell with him seem to derive strength from their brief meeting. I have opted to quote this episode extensively, since it is illustrative of the immediate point but is also typical, I think, of Soyinka's narrative style, gradual and oblique in its approach and carrying much of the moral commentary in the gradual unravelling of the details. The woman is brusquely thrown into the room in a state of shock and terror, and at first she mistakes her fellow prisoner for an officer, even a possible torturer; but she soon catches sight of his chains – an unnecessary humiliation inflicted on him – and the narrative continues:

> I saw her body go lax, sympathetic. She came forward, her hand patting the table as if to engage some reassurance of concrete things. I watched her silently. She needed no further comforting from me; the sight of my chains had done more than words could have done for her, calmed her down. But then I saw yet a new change in her face. She stood suddenly still, unbelieving. Recognition. I saw it even before she spoke. Are you not . . . are you not Wole Soyinka? I nodded. From my face, to my legs, back to my face. A pause to take it in. Then she broke down in tears.
>
> The guard – he must have gone off briefly to help with the new influx – looked in a minute and gasped. What is she doing here? He screamed down the corridor for the officer on duty. No one is supposed to go in the room with that suspect! When they all rushed in she had stopped crying. The duty officer was all regretful; he had not known there was anyone in there. They led the woman away, calmer, stronger. She turned round at the door looked at me in a way to ensure that I saw it, that I knew she was no longer cowed, that nothing ever again would terrorize her. I acknowledged the gesture. I wondered if she knew what strength I drew from the encounter.
>
> (pp. 41–2.)

It is significant that both prisoners draw strength from the encounter. Soyinka's belief in the potential strength of ordinary, even of disadvantaged folk seems to have been strengthened by his imprisonment. The Nsukka student who in protest against injustice led a hunger strike, knowing it to be a futile gesture, strikes an answering chord in Soyinka's mind: 'I needed to do something in protest no matter how vague or irrelevant.' (p. 109.) There is also a reassuring strength in the song of the Ibo prisoners. Yon da kilo, no Ibo, brokenly puts into words the peculiar influence that comes out of such unpromising sources – 'muck' to which they have been reduced: 'Strength, that was it. Strength. It has such strength, you know. It gave me strength, even while it hurt me.' (p. 112.)

These are the 'orphans of the world', who are still to discover and use their strength in delivering themselves from tyranny. Nor are all of them prisoners. Even among the lowlier servants of power there are those altruistic hounds of justice who, conscious of the evils of the system in which they are trapped, engage in surreptitious acts of decency and mercy and even support opposition to the regime. In an alliance of such people lies hope for 'the revolutionary changes to which I have become more than ever dedicated'. (p. 12.)

The restoration of justice (a just system of rule) would be the aim of the 'revolutionary changes', just as it is the denial of justice that is the central indictment of the regime in *The Man Died*. Soyinka saw this in the harsh and inhuman treatment of Ibo detainees and the lenient treatment given to soldiers suspected of killing Ibos. He was unable to remain indifferent when he saw two such suspects given privileged treatment and later released without trial or further punishment. He saw this as final proof of condonation. His letter from prison exposing this is betrayed into the hands of authority, and he nearly loses his life in reprisal. Soyinka sees the case of the two soldiers primarily as a perversion of justice to which he at the time thought the Judiciary of the West acceded (he later found out that the judges protested, and he acknowledges this in a footnote) and therefore makes two suggestions, both of which are directed at a reform of the judicial position of the West. He writes:

> *I suggest: First and foremost, that the judiciary of the West be declared independent. I do not know what this implies in our relationship with the Federal Courts nor do I particularly care. I only demand that one way or the other, the Western Judiciary place itself in such a position that no power within or without the region can ever again interfere with its judicial processes and render it, as it is today, accomplices by default in the doctrine of justifiable genocide.*
> *Two: That some form of law be passed in the region which makes it a crime for any man or group to molest or in any way interfere with another for reasons of tribe, or practise any form of discrimination based on tribe. (Add religion, etc. etc. if you wish to make it comprehensive.)*

(pp. 21–2.)

The abject disintegration of an apparently spineless judge, as narrated by Fajuyi (whom Soyinka admired),[3] is recorded with some relish. (p. 156–7.) 'For me, justice is the first condition of humanity.' The deprivation of justice is thus potentially dehumanizing both for the tyrant and for his victim.

With the denial of justice, all other human rights can be violated with impunity by those in control, and liberty, respect for human dignity and life go by the board. The evil that is thus generated becomes an organic

[3] See 'For Fajuyi', *Idanre and Other Poems*, Methuen, London, 1967.

force which has to be actively resisted and it becomes not only right but a compelling duty to resist such evil. In his judgement, the combination of interests presided over by the Gowon regime represented such an evil. The needless cruelty that he saw around him, given point by his own personal mistreatment, sharpened his views on the subject:

> These men are not merely evil, I thought. They are the mindlessness of evil made flesh. One should not ever stumble into their hands but seek the power to destroy them. They are pus, bile, original putrescence of Death in living shapes. They surely infect all with whom they come in touch and even from this insulation here I smell a foulness of the mind in the mere tone of their words. They breed themselves, their types, their mutations. To seek the power to destroy them is to fulfil a moral task.   (p. 225.)

The suggestions in the language of an active infection leading to widespread contamination and death is not casual. It is consistent with Soyinka's image patterns in earlier works, though the tone is more personal here.

The defence of liberty is one of the justifications for war that Soyinka admits during his interrogations by 'Mallam D' (p. 48), and such a civil war is frequently referred to as a means of removing domestic tyrants. The novel *Season of Anomy*, one of the fruits of Soyinka's imprisonment, is concerned with an underground movement with such a purpose, harnessing the latent strength of ordinary men and women against their tyrannical rulers.

The Man Died was eagerly read when it first came out in 1972 because it gave the personal views of a remarkably interesting and controversial man and a distinguished author on a topical and highly controversial issue; but the work has survived that initial interest and has been published in an American edition and an English paperback edition. Its capacity for survival will remain high while the Biafran secession and Civil War retain their interest, but it is also compelling in the way personal and national issues are related to broader questions of liberty and justice, and because of the manner of the telling. Soyinka's control over material which could have induced and been overwhelmed by paranoia (he is conscious of the threat at points in the narration), his employment of dialogue, perceptive description and scene setting (he seems capable of total recall), his character portrayal and mastery of the vignette all contribute to the literary value of a book that is likely to survive as a feature of the unfortunately growing genre of prison literature.

Aké:
The Years of Childhood

▼▼▼▼▼▼▼▼▼▼▼▼▼▼▼▼▼▼▼▼▼▼▼▼▼▼▼▼▼▼▼▼

IT IS POSSIBLE to read *Aké* for clues on the chronological growth of the writer. How old was he for instance when, despairing at the levity which his requests to start school provoked, he one day collected a few previously selected books from his father's bedroom, and surreptitiously followed his older sister to the infant school? He was less than three years old and from that day on neither his enthusiasm nor his progress faltered; he was soon helping his sister with her lessons and was in Abeokuta Grammar School at the age of nine-and-a-half. His greatest concern, when soon after starting school he broke his head and lost a lot of blood, was that the blood be carefully retrieved and poured back into his head – a vital organ for the business of progressing at school – so that he would not lose a day's attendance! How old was he when for the first time he ventured alone out of the walled protection of the mission compound which enclosed home, school, church and a whole world of play and adventure, and, in the wake of the police band, inducted himself into Abeokuta and the wider world? He was four-and-a-half and could already in addition to his native Yoruba, speak and understand English except when it was spoken with the highly nasalised accent of the white police officer. When exactly did he enter Government College, Ibadan? When did he run those errands for Beere (Auntie Fumilayo) and the Women's Movement?[1] The chronology would quickly reveal an extremely precocious boy with a sharp intellect and a quick argumentative mind.

It is even more fascinating to observe how the various influences, some of them opposed and contradictory, coalesced to feed his imagination from which later the poems, plays and novels flowed; to detect the seeds which later flowered into ideas, themes, and metaphors; to see the first stirrings of a social conscience – his resentment, for instance, at the humiliation of his elder sister for being slower than her clever brother. The development of arguments by his father and his cronies into practical demonstrations with

---

[1] Prof. 'Molara Ogundipe-Leslie examines this chronological puzzle in her review of *Aké* in *African Literature Today*, ed. Eldred Jones & Eustace Palmer, London, Heinemann, no. 14, 1984, p. 141.

dangerous implements may have shown the direct link between thought and action; his early ability to link seemingly unconnected objects or to imbue abstractions with life may have led to that dense metaphorical style of later years. All these make *Aké* an extraordinarily rich quarry. It is also, being a product of Soyinka's maturity, a piece of fine literature in its own right, one of the most sensitive childhood recollections ever written.

Some of the influences were clearly discernible in the works themselves. What the autobiography does is to document them and recreate them more fully. So effortlessly do biblical allusions flow from Soyinka's pen that it was easy to deduce his Christian up-bringing. But *Aké* fills out the details of life in the Parsonage, the walled compound which had once housed the venerated Bishop Samuel Ajayi Crowther. Church and school – his father was headmaster – were only a few paces from his home, and Soyinka received large doses of Sunday school in addition to the Arabian Nights and other romances from the storehouse of Christian colonial education:

> . . . it was at the Sunday School that the real stories were told, stories that lived in the events themselves, crossed the time-border of Sundays or leaves of the Bible and entered the world of fabled lands, men and women. The pomegranate was most niggardly in producing. It yielded its outwardly hardy fruit only once in a while, . . . yet even the tiniest wedge transported us to the illustrated world of the Biblical Tales Retold. The pomegranate was the Queen of Sheba, rebellions and wars, the passion of Salome, the siege of Troy, the Praise of Beauty in the Song of Solomon. This fruit, with its stone-hearted look and feel unlocked the cellars of Ali Baba, extracted the genie from Aladdin's lamp, plucked the strings of the harp that restored David to sanity parted the waters of the Nile and filled our parsonage with incense from the dim temple of Jerusalem.   (p. 3.)

Within the home itself where his mother Wild Christian presided, the Christian influences were reinforced. He and the other children could trace his father's progress home from the schoolhouse by watching his reflection on the glass fronts of a succession of framed biblical texts placed (and duly adjusted by the children) at strategic intervals. The Chirstian influence was not however unadulterated. Wild Christian had herself been brought up in the household of Great Uncle, the Reverend J.J. Ransome-Kuti and thus was the product of the best Christian tradition. But was not her own brother Sanya an *oro* whose spirit companions had to be placated with a feast?

No, there was no question about it, our Uncle Sanya was an *oro*; Wild Christian had seen and heard proofs of it many times over. His companions were obviously the more benevolent type or he would have come to serious harm on more than one occasion, J.J.'s protecting Faith notwithstanding. (p. 11.)

And did not the Reverend J.J. himself confront these spirits from the depths of the Yoruba background and command them to retreat? *Aké* itself contrasted with the old Mr Soyinka's home at Isara, where the traditional religion and practices dominated.

Such were the contradictions which were reconciled in a pious Christian life and which Soyinka inherited. The Parsonage itself bristled with spirits in one form or the other. Soyinka's playmate Bukola, the daughter of the Bookseller, was an 'Abiku', a figure which recurs in the poetry and drama later. Bukola, like the child in the poem, was weighted down with bangles and other charms in a vain hope of earthing her to this world:

> ... Bukola, was not of our world. When we threw our voices against the school walls of Lower Parsonage and listened to them echo from a long distance, it seemed to me that Bukola was one of the denizens of that other world where the voice was caught, sieved, re-spun and cast back in diminishing copies. Amulets, bangles, tiny rattles and dark copper-twist rings earthed her through ankles, fingers, wrists and waist. She knew she was *abiku*. The two cicatrices on her face were also part of the many counters to enticements by her companions in the other world. Like all *abiku* she was privileged, apart. (pp.15–16.)

Later this real childhood friend emerges in the generality of art:

> In vain your bangles cast
> Charmed circles at my feet
> I am Abiku, calling for the first
> And the repeated time.
>
> Must I weep for goats and cowries
> For palm oil and the sprinkled ash?
> Yams do not sprout in amulets
> To earth Abiku's limbs.
>
> So when the Snail is burnt in his shell
> Whet the heated fragment, brand me

Deeply on the breast – you must know him
When Abiku calls again.

I am the squirrel teeth, cracked
The riddle of the palm; remember
This, and dig me deeper still into the god's swollen foot.

Once and the repeated time, ageless
Though I puke, and when you pour
Libations, each finger points me near
The way I came, where

The ground is wet with mourning
White dew suckles flesh-birds
Evening befriends the spider, trapping
Flies in wine-froth;

Night, and Abiku sucks the oil
From lamps, Mothers! I'll be the
Suppliant snake coiled on the doorstep
Yours the killing cry.

The ripest fruit was saddest;
Where I crept, the warmth was cloying.
In silence of webs, Abiku moans, shaping
Mounds from the yolk.[2]

Another of Wole Soyinka's playmates and regular lunchtime companion
was not a Christian at all. Osiki lived in a compound with its own *egúngún*, and he not only regularly watched it come out of the earth, but
generously invited his friend to come and witness this phenomenon. The
horrified Wild Christian sternly forbade such total regression into
paganism: 'Better not even let your father hear you' (p. 32.)
    The grounds of the compound with its rock formations and thick
vegetation giving out into bush and forest, not only provided mushrooms,
snails and small game, but *inwin* and other spirits – the denizens of the
forest in *A Dance of the Forests*. The large rock in the school yard which
Soyinka had all to himself at weekends and school holidays was only
diminished in his eyes when the Sunday School teacher lighted on it as a
comparison in size with Jonah's whale; the young Soyinka had long

[2] Wole Soyinka, 'Abiku', *Idanre and other Poems*, London, Methuen, 1967, pp. 28–30.

peopled it with more exciting beings! Nothing was ordinary. Bishop Crowther long dead, nevertheless popped up everywhere. His venerable face appeared among the bushes. To the awed fascination of the little boy, he took out his pocket watch from the fob of his waistcoat and flicking it open let his eyes fall, one by one, from their sockets into its faceless case while the rest of his features were transformed into a skull. (p. 5.)

Abstractions and inanimate objects were imbued with a spirit of their own. Soyinka conveys this by using words like 'Birthday', 'Temperature' and 'Change' without either article or inflection to make them stand as pure concepts. The little boy, having ticked off the days on the calendar, invited his friends home and sat down with them expecting 'Birthday' to happen! 'Temperature' similarly attached itself in appropriate moments – or was induced to do so almost as though it had an independent bodily existence. 'Change' came and went, sometimes with forewarning, and sometimes without. What the maid Nubi sees as Wole's lack of enthusiasm for what she regarded as a proper bath, elicits the comment from Wild Christian 'I don't know what he has done to water but they don't appear to get on very well'. (p. 53.) Overwhelmed by the almost infinite variety of commodities in the market, the boy muses 'I never thought there was so much *thing* in the world'. No grammatical solecism this; this is how it struck the boy and the adult author gladly accepts the suggestion. To the poet's eye, things merge with other things, and ordinary objects yield unlikely emanations; thus the Canon, because of his features, 'was a chunk from those rocks, black huge, granite head and enormous feet' (p. 12.); his title, Canon, was quickly associated in the boy's mind with guns outside the residency at Ibara: '. . . I had already found my own answer. It was the head, Pa Delumo's head was like a cannon ball, that was why Father called him Canon.' (p. 13.) The Bookseller carries about with him the aura of the domestic animals he keeps and so contrasted is he in stature and temperament with his ample, ebullient wife, that when the slight man disappears for several days young Wole thinks that the large lady had merely swallowed up her little husband.

The bookseller brought into the house that aura of guinea-fowl, turkeys, sheep and goats all of which he raised in his abundant compound. The sheep were always being rounded up; either the gates had been left carelessly open by a visitor or the stubborn animals had found yet another gap in the stone-and-mud walls. Thin and peppery, leather-taut cheekbones thrust out restlessly, he punctuated his discourse with bird-like gestures. Even at his most aggressive his shoulders slouched, his fingers refused to release the cloth-cap which, outside, never left his head perhaps because he was completely bald. We could tell his laughter apart, shrill and raspy, revealing gapped teeth which imparted to his face, finally, the look of an old wicker-chair.

The bookseller's wife was one of our many mothers; if we had taken a vote on the question, she would be in the forefront of all the others, including our real one, with bovine beauty, jet-black skin and inexhaustible goodness, she nevertheless put disquieting thoughts in my head, and all because of her husband. By contrast to him, she was ample, and sometimes when the bookseller disappeared for days, I felt certain that she had just swallowed him up.   (p. 15.)

God himself strode the Aké landscape mingling with men and things to give Sunday a special aura in the boy's imagination.

On a misty day, the steep rise towards Itoko would join the sky. If God did not actually live there, there was little doubt that he descended first on its crest, then took his one gigantic stride over those babbling markets –which dared to sell on Sundays – into St Peter's Church, afterwards visiting the parsonage for tea with the Canon. There was the small consolation that, in spite of the temptation to arrive on horseback, he never stopped first at the Chief's, who was known to be a pagan; certainly the Chief was never seen at a church service except at the anniversaries of the Alake's coronation. Instead God strode into St Peter's for morning service, paused briefly at the afternoon service, but reserved his most formal, exotic presence for the evening service which, in his honour was always held in the English tongue. The organ took on a dark smoky sonority at evening service, and there was no doubt that the organ was adapting its normal sounds to accompany God's own sepulchral responses, with its timbre of the *egúngún*, to those prayers that were offered to him.   (p.1)

Soyinka's metaphorical style owes much to his ability to make quick and unexpected associations and leads to the denseness which has given him the reputation of being difficult. The stained glass window in St Peter's Church bore the figures of two white missionaries with St Peter himself in the middle. If ancestral spirits could come out of the earth in the form of *egúngún*, why could not St Peter be similarly conjured up into the novel manifestation of a saintly christian *egúngún*? This was beyond the comprehension even of Osiki to whom the incarnation of pagan spirits was a common occurrence. For young Soyinka the logic of the situation was obvious. Thus, saintly Bishops, Canons of the church, Apostles and even the Almighty merged with imps, *ghommids*, *òrò*, *abiku*, *egúngún*, spires, market places and palaces to the accompaniment of organs, brass bands, drumming, dancing, singing and chanting to coalesce in a fervid imagination.

Numerous episodes that had a later influence are narrated in the course of *Aké* but the march through Abeokuta in the wake of the police band is specially significant both in its portrayal of the boy's first encounter with the real world – 'I had, in some way, become markedly different from whatever I was before the march' (p. 50.) – and in its illustration of the author's method of narration; moving from the immediate object in the boy's vision, linking it up with something out of view, and showing the light of understanding dawning on him as he makes the essential connection. In this way a multi-dimensional picture is constructed. As he marches along, he catches sight of the wayside corn grinding meal, links it with the *ogi* which was made out of it at home, and a whole slice of domestic life is revealed. Soyinka's lifelong enthusiasm for good Nigerian cooking celebrated in the essay 'Salutations to the Gut'[3] is evident here as in several other passages in *Aké*:

> Every week, sometimes more often, Lawanle or Joseph would go off with a large basin of corn and return with it crushed, a layer of water over it. Then would begin a series of operations with the calabashes, strainers, baskets and huge pots. It ended with those pots being placed in a dark corner of the kitchen, covered. As the days passed they would give off an ever ripening smell of fermentation. A week would pass and after several tests, tasting and sniffing, one pot would emerge from the darkness, and from it was scooped the smooth white paste which in turn was stirred in hot water to provide the morning *ogi*, a neutral mixture which everyone seemed to enjoy but I. The *akara* which went with it, the *jogi*, *moinmoin* or *leki* was a different matter. My mouth was watering even as I thought of it. But I could not understand how *ogi* which took so much mysterious labour, could appeal to any taste. (pp. 38–9.)

Similarly the sight of the photographer's studio, 'Miss McCutter's Maternity Clinic' (Miss Makota in the boy's mind until this moment), the establishment of 'Mrs T. Banjoko, London-Trained Sewing Mistress' and other sights take us back through the boy's growing awareness into some aspect of social and domestic life. But it is in the market-place that the conrucopia overflows; the vast world explodes in the boy's consciousness:

[3] *Reflections*, ed. Francess Ademola, African Universities Press, Lagos, 1962.

it did not seem possible that there was so much *thing* in the world! . . . I
turned into the market, wide-eyed. Peppers of all shapes and sizes rose
in profusion from wooden and enamel trays. There were mounds of gari
which beggared those cupfuls that were brought out at cooking-time to
be turned to *eba* in hot water. The earthy smell of yam powder assailed
my nostrils long before I came on it, piled high in calabash trays. And
SALT! Nobody surely, not even the whole of Aké could eat so much salt
in a hundred years, yet I came on the piles stall after stall. It gave way to
a variety of tubers, vegetables, dried fish and crayfish, then the stalls of
meat with men flashing long, two-edged knives among slabs of meat,
brushing away flies with one hand or hitting a small boy on the head for
dozing off while flies landed on the meat. . . .

It seemed a long time before the goods stopped altogether, giving way
to clothes, sewing materials, toys, even small bookstalls with pens,
rubbers, inkwells and notebooks neatly laid out.

And then I came to a sudden stop and backed away. Staring me in the
eye was a shrunken head of an animal, dangling from a low wooden
shelf beneath a stall.   (pp. 41–2.)

Surely, the two old women of *Madmen and Specialists* came out of this
market, to be transformed later by the poet's imagination. Coming upon
them alone at the age of four-and-a-half, sitting behind their piles of leaves,
roots and bundles of bark, their heads shrunk almost to the basic
dimensions of the hollow skulls of animals – and who knows of children? –
that they sold, he had fled in terror even when one smiled at him:

> . . . I experienced shock at their flat, emptied breasts and remembered
> suddenly that it was wrong to stare. I looked away.
>
> Were these the witches we heard so much about? No breast that I had
> seen before had appeared so flat, it did not seem human. Yet when I
> looked in the trays again I recognized barks and roots similar to those
> which were bought by Father, stuffed into bottles and jars where they
> were left to soak for days.   (p.42)

Recollected later in tranquility, they were to become the custodians of the
life force as they accumulated roomfuls of herbs, guarding a humane
tradition against the brutal incisiveness of the specialists' inhumane regime
in the play. The suggestions of plenitude and vitality in the market merge
into the mystery and numinous tradition of the neighbouring Alake's
palace to provide the ambience for the dilemma of the King's horseman in
Death and the King's Horseman.

A.O. Ransome-Kuti and his wife Fumilayo etched themselves into

Nigerian history, the former for his contribution to education as Principal of Abeokuta Grammar School and a member of the Elliott Commission on Higher Education in West Africa – the reason for his braving Hitler's submarines – and the latter, for her leadership of the Women's Movement and her consequent participation in pre-independence politics. Soyinka obviously idolised both and his intimate glimpses into their domestic life are charming as well as historically valuable. They were quite probably hovering just below the top level of his consciousness when he created 'Daodu' (Reverend Ransome-Kuti's nickname) and 'Segi', the social reformers in *Kongi's Harvest*.

There are more tenuous, scarcely discernible relationships between sights, sounds and impressions in *Aké*, and their reappearance, transformed by imagination and art, in the author's other work. The impact of the death of his sister, Folasade, on the first anniversary of her birth was traumatic but its full meaning as yet unrealised:

> Folasade was laid out in a long white dress which covered her plaster and stretched over her feet. Her eyes were closed and she was just as still as she had been for several weeks past. . . .
>
> Suddenly, it all broke up within me. A force from nowhere pressed me against the bed and I howled. As I was picked up I struggled against my father's soothing voice, tears all over me. I was sucked into a place of loss whose cause or definition remained elusive. I did not comprehend it yet, and even through those tears I saw the astonished face of Wild Christian, and heard her voice saying, 'But what does he understand of it? What does he understand?'
> (pp. 97–8.)

Comprehension, or at least a groping towards it, came later:

> We triumphed then upon the wails of birth
> And felt no fears. By mute assertion
> Of the later year, she marked *her* victory.
> Grief has long receded, yet the wonder
> Stays.
>
> Truly, it was a deed of grace, this death
> At the first teething, contrary
> Precision of her first birthday, almost
> On the hour.
>
> Knowledge as this growth's diffusion
> Thins, till shrouds are torn from swaddlings.

She was not one more veil, dark across
The Secret; Folasade ran bridal to the Spouse
Wise to fore-planning – bear witness, Time
To my young will, in this last breath
Of mockery.[4]

Aké's primary value is for the light it throws on the young Soyinka's
view of the world and the early impressions which formed the imaginative
storehouse that was to produce the later works, all of this recollected by the
adult Soyinka, well past his 'first three white hairs' in some of his best
writing. Its value as social history, though incidental, is perhaps greater for
being seen essentially through the eyes of the child. Professor Ogundipe-
Leslie has raised questions on how much the adult Soyinka intervenes in
such passages – especially in the author's account of the activities of the
Egba Women's Union – and his role in it.[5] When he records the rise of the
Egba Women's Union, he is the omniscient observer first from the railings
of the verandah above the courtyard, then as a 'teacher', errand boy, and
general 'limpet'. As the narrator reconstructs the rise of the movement
from a meeting of *onikaba* – a rather upper class group of women – into a
formidable force for social and political change, there is a coherence and
flow which must have been imposed. Most of the dialogue recounted here
and throughout the work took place in Yoruba and so even the
reproduction in English is an editorial act which must have been
accompanied by others of organisation. The result, however is a unique
view of one of the most significant moments in Nigerian history, told with
a keen eye for detail. The drama of the encounter between Madam Amelia
and the Alake, Mrs Ransome-Kuti and the District Officer, the
discomfiture of the *ogboni*, the birth of a child in the midst of the siege, all
give an unusual angle to a piece of important history.

Inevitably, the adult Soyinka intervenes in the role of editor
reconstructing myriad events and giving them form and order. The
narrative is, in any event, not continuous; there are jumps where one idea
leads to another as when, for instance, he suddenly jumps from Aké to
Isara and keeps both locations in view using the rafters as a linking
image:

But the walls have retained their voices. Familiar voices break on the
air, voices from the other side of the rafters. Isara was second home –
Essay's natal home. all the grandparents were Father and Mother – and

---

[4] Wole Soyinka, 'A first Deathday', *Idanre and Other Poems*, London Methuen, 1967,
p. 26.
[5] See note 1.

somehow we said these as if with capital letters. There the rafters were
smoky, bare of the usual ceiling mat. . . .

I could not understand why Father's rafters in Isara should be so
bare, yet so full of surprises, while the ceiling at the parsonage, though
sealed up was beyond the scuttling of mice, devoid of mystery.

(pp. 66–7.)

This brief extract scarcely does justice to a passage which contains some of
Soyinka's most evocative writing. The total effect is of a series of
impressions, some more sustained than others. His father's orgy of
photography and valedictory injunctions are isolated in the middle of other
matters and remains more or less as it struck the mystified child, a vivid
episode, not fully understood at the time. When the day dreamer's straying
finger absentmindedly pulls the trigger of his father's gun, he is only
conscious of a certain disorientation and the adult narrator pieces together
the steps by which realisation came to the child:

A loud, truly deafening noise was the first awareness I had that anything
was wrong. It brought the world to an end. Something smacked against
the mat, an instant later another sound, dull yet crisp announced that
something had passed through and hit the metal sheeting of the
roof.

But the definition of those sounds came much later, for I was at this
point on the floor, the explosion having startled me off my chair. I
believed also that I was paralysed and refused to move: I had been shot
to death, there was no other explanation for the suddenness of my
descent to earth, none other for the lack of pain or the full clarity of my
senses. Obviously, I had attained a heavenly dimension. Moreover, HM
was in his bedroom at the time; I was waiting for him to emerge when it
happened. There was no motion, so it could not be his bedroom whose
door still seemed so plain to the eye.

The preceding moments regained focus. Yes, I had been sitting in the
front room, under the porcelain clock. I occupied the chair where
visitors sat who had business with my father. His air-gun leant against
the wall and I sat in the chair by the door, waiting for him to come out
so as to accompany him, as usual.

. . . I had drifted off perhaps into a frequent reverie while caressing
the stock of the rifle. My hand must have found the trigger. Then it
became clear to me that I was not dead, so, naturally, a different terror
took its place. Indeed only then did any fear intrude. Acceptance of my
death had come easily: very different was the thought of my father's
reaction to my carelessness.

(pp. 67–8.)

Characteristically between the two excerpts quoted above Soyinka interjects a cameo of hunting expeditions with his father.

Although Soyinka's father lived and worked in Egbaland, that was his wife's home. He himself was an Ijebu from the royal house of Isara to which he took his family for the New Year. Compared with the more urban Abeokuta, Isara was rural, casually insanitary in its ways, touchy about traditional etiquette, versed in farm and forest lore, and deep in traditional mystery and ritual. Isara complemented Aké in Soyinka's education. 'Broda Pupa' introduced him to real farming on an exciting day which included among its thrills, the killing, cooking and eating of a snake – this was never mentioned to Wild Christian! – the theory and practice of avoiding being stung to death by hornets and other details of rural life went into a crash course.[6] Grandfather, again without the knowledge of Mrs Soyinka who was never really relaxed in this wild territory, arranged for ritual incisions round the boy's ankles, to protect him from being poisoned, a fate Mrs Soyinka dreaded on these visits, and to strengthen him for taking on opponents bigger than himself:

> '. . . anyone offers you food or drink, if your mind does not hesitate, go ahead. It is I that say so. If however, you experience even one moment of doubt turn your back on that place and never go back. Next, don't ever turn your back on a fight. Where you are going maybe next year, maybe the year after the next, I don't know. For all I know they may not let you back here before you go to that school but it does not matter. Wherever you find yourself, don't run away from a fight. Your adversary will probably be bigger, he will trounce you the first time. Next time you meet him, challenge him again. He will beat you all over again. The third time, I promise you this, you will either defeat him, or he will run away. Are you listening to what I am telling you?'   (p. 147.)

Soyinka must have believed in the efficacy of the rite if he is to be judged by his willingness to take on tough opposition. Soyinka's father's people were quite visibly different from his mother's; she was also royally connected, but more distantly, to the Alake. The author describes the itinerant traders who trudged the weary forty miles between Isara and Abeokuta on market days arriving worn out at dead of night:

[6] This is one of the passages in which Soyinka slightly modifies standard English to suggest that the speaker was using Yoruba. The exchanges between 'Kemberi' and the Alake is another instance; Paa Adatan the eccentric of the market place uses pidgin.

They frequently arrived late at night like a weather-beaten caravan, heavy-laden baskets and fibre sacks on their heads. (p. 128.)

They departed at dawn the day after, leaving behind a tang of smoke and indigo. (p. 129.)

These are the originals for the traders pictured in 'Death in the Dawn':

> ... burdened hulks retract,
> Stoop to the mist in faceless throng
> To wake the silent markets – swift, mute
> Processions on grey byways. . . .[7]

The childhood scenes strike the adult eye differently and on later revisitations lose their wonder and shrink even in size:

> The Mission left the parsonage just a vicar and his catechist; Aké was no longer worth a bishop. But even the Vicar's 'court' is a mere shell of itself. The orchard has vanished, the rows of lemon grass have long been eaten by goats. . . . Stark, shrunk with time is that white square monument which, framed against the rocks dominated the parsonage, focussing the eye on itself as a visitor entered the parsonage gate. (p. 12.)

The society itself changes and the children of the new breed of bureaucrats and professionals lick ice creams from cones and eat *moin-moin*, now naked of leaf in strange machine-shaped chunks to the accompaniment of western pop, immersed in cheap imported culture! In more senses than one, shades of the prison house have closed in on Ake and its growing boy:

> The hawkers' lyrics of leaf-wrapped *moin-moin* still resound in parts of Aké and the rest of the town but, along Dayisi's Walk is also a shop which sells *moin-moin* from a glass case, lit by sea-green neon lamps. It lies side by side with McDonald's hamburgers, Kentucky Fried chicken, hot dogs and dehydrated sausage-rolls. It has been cooked in emptied milk-tins and similar containers, scooped out and sliced in neat geometric shapes like cakes of soap. And the newly-rich homes stuff it full of eggs, tinned sardines from Portugal and corned beef from the Argentine. The fate of *wara*, among others, is however one without even

---

[7] Wole Soyinka, 'Death in the Dawn', *Idanre and other Poems*, London Methuen, 1967, p. 10.

this dubious reprieve. The vendor of milk-curds, floated in outsize gourds has been banished by chromium boxes with sleek spouts which dispense yellowish fluids into brittle cones....

Our teeth were cut on *robo*, hard-fried balls of crushed melon seeds, and on *guguru-and-epa*, the friend and sustainer of workers on the critical countdown towards pay day.   (p. 156.)

For the Soyinka scholar, *Aké* has an extra fascination as a window into the mind of a child who grew up into the man of the literary works. It has value also for the social historian for its portrayal of life in Abeokuta and Isara, and in the case of Abeokuta, how the city changed over the years. The unique glimpse into politics throughout the history of the Egba Women's Union which merged with the great N.C.N.C. party provides valuable material for the political historian. Perhaps even more valuable is the picture of the combination within the Alake's palace of traditional politics rooted in the *Ogboni* and modern colonial wiliness in both of which styles the Alake participates. Equally illuminating insights into education emerge from the contrast between the white-ruled Government College, Ibadan – no pockets, no shoes and no corporal punishment – and Abeokuta Grammar School under A.O. Ransome-Kuti whose discipline involved open court sessions but also the cane.

Aké is primarily, however, a piece of literature – an artistic deployment of words to reveal character incident and atmosphere. It presents the tragedy and comedy of life through a parade of characters. His parents, Wild Christian and Essay emerge rounded and full-blooded, supported by a whole cast of characters, some of whom are only vignettes, but are memorable for all that, sometimes with the aid of a clinching line. 'Broda Pupa' etched himself into memory when to Wole's bewildered question as to what he was to do if the quiescent snake turned awkward tersely replied 'Speak English to it'. 'You-Mean-Myself' and Mr 'Lè-móo' are also fixed by telling phrases. The canvas is wide – his father's argumentative cronies, the commune of children whose individual patterns Wild Christian could mysteriously distinguish from the tell-tale pools on the urine-soaked sleeping mats, Osiki, Grandfather at Isara, the Bookseller, his wife and their Abiku child, even the fringe characters in the market place, Paa Adatan, the mad woman and her lover, figures which subtly influence later portrayals are given form and substance. Ultimately, *Aké* is not the property of the scholar; it is a remarkable piece of literature for all who care to read. Its evocations of places, characters and dramatic encounters give it value as a highly satisfying and skilful piece of fine writing.

Part 3
Plays

The Swamp-Dwellers

▼▼▼▼▼▼▼▼▼▼▼▼▼▼▼▼▼▼▼▼▼▼▼▼▼▼▼▼▼▼▼▼

The Swamp-Dwellers had its first performance in London in 1959 and that same year featured with *The Lion and the Jewel* in a double bill at the Arts Theatre in Ibadan. In a writing span which covers over twenty years this could be called an early Soyinka play. Although its tone is graver than that of its near-contemporary, *The Lion and the Jewel* (it too has its share of humour) it is, like the lighter play, an examination of a society in a state of change.

For such a short play, *The Swamp-Dwellers* covers a remarkable range of themes. The village in the swamps which is the setting of the play seems to be poised on the edge of change. It had survived within its strictly sanctioned borders without much threat from outside influences, but now these outside influences have begun to make steady encroachments so that a point of near crisis has been reached. The drain of the youth away to the city no less than the predatory swamps threatens the continued existence of the village. Soyinka infuses into the play a sense of physical danger which reflects the precarious state of the society. Its youth has been vanishing into the city – into the unknown – with a suddenness and a finality which is well pictured in Alu's concern for the safety of her second son Igwezu who has stayed out too long on his visit to his ruined farm:

> I'm going after him. I don't want to lose him too. I don't want him missing his foothold and vanishing without a cry, without a chance for anyone to save him.

> I'm going out to shout his name until he hears me. I had another son before the mire drew him into the depths. I don't want Igwezu going the same way. (*Five Plays*, p. 161.)[1]

The all-threatening swamp supplies a physical image for spiritual death. For it turns out that Awuchike who is pictured in the second passage as having been swallowed by the swamps is not only alive, but is prospering

[1] Page references for *The Swamp-Dwellers, The Lion and the Jewel, A Dance of the Forests, The Strong Breed* and *The Trials of Brother Jero* are to *Five Plays* (O.U.P., London, 1964).

in the city. But for all the contact he has with his home, he might just as well have been swallowed by the swamp: 'Awuchike is dead to you and to this house. Let us not raise his ghost.' This spiritual death by which the young sever all familial and indeed all human ties with the village and commit themselves to a totally new life in the towns is one of the main threats to the society of the village. It is also a threat to the humanity of the emigrants, for the city tends to dehumanize them. One has to develop new ways – a city heart – in order to survive in the city.

Although Awuchike does not appear in person in the play, his shadow is always evident. There is an implicit comparison of him with his less successful brother throughout the play. Sometimes it comes out explicitly as in this exchange between Igwezu and his father: 'Father. Tell me, father, is my brother a better man than I?/No son. His heart is only more suited to the city.' (p. 192.) Awuchike has buried himself in the city and has sacrificed the responsibilities of family ties for success in the city. Igwezu on the other hand is always looking back to the village – to his parents, and to his farm which for him represented the last prop when all else failed. His first act as soon as he has made a little money in the city is to send his father a barber's chair which he had promised him when he left home – 'He's a man for keeping his word.' (p. 176.) He has religiously performed all the sacrifices required by the Priest of the Serpent, he kept his mask in the village – a concrete symbol of his spiritual attachment – indeed is a model son and citizen. Yet he meets with humiliating failure in the city and a spiritually more devastating failure when he returns home and finds his farm totally destroyed by the floods. But Awuchike who has 'died' to his roots has become a very successful timber merchant in the city. This is one of the ironies of the play.

This total failure does inevitably raise questions in Igwezu's mind. In order to articulate these questions, however, he has to have help from outside. This is the role which the blind beggar from the North fulfils in the play. He introduces a completely new force, a new way of thinking into the hidebound society of the village. He comes from the dry North into the flood-prone riverine swamps. He comes from a different religious tradition – he is a Moslem – and is therefore not inhibited by the religious taboos of the village. He has come from such a tradition of barrenness, has seen such total frustration of his own hopes that almost anything offered a chance of hope. In his unshakeable faith in the face of adversity the beggar shows a spiritual superiority to Igwezu which qualifies him to be Igwezu's mentor. Although the beggar is a Moslem, he is another of Soyinka's Christ-figures. Soyinka's work contains many biblical references, but few are more pointed than the tableau in this play in which Alu washes and anoints the feet of the beggar:

[. . . Alu squats down and washes his feet. When this is finished, she wipes them dry, takes a small jar from one of the shelves, and rubs his feet with some form of ointment.]

This vividly recalls the washing of Jesus' feet described in *St Luke*, 7, 37–50. The beggar is also Christ-like in that he enters a hidebound traditional society and makes men begin to think again. He gives himself selflessly and unasked for the good of others: 'How have I deserved so much of you that you would beg for me?' (p. 196.)

This play is sometimes seen as a rebellion or at least a questioning of tradition by the young – this element is certainly there – but the influence of the not-so-young beggar from outside the society should not be minimized. That he is a threat to the established order is seen in the unspoken antagonism between himself and the pillar of the old order – the Kadiye. At the mention of 'Allah' in the beggar's greeting, the stage directions require the Kadiye to be *'startled'*. (p. 175.) He recognizes the threat from another religion immediately. His mechanical gift of money is wordlessly spurned by the beggar who 'turns his bowl upside-down' when the Kadiye's servant offers to drop a coin into it. There is indeed a contrast between the representatives of the two religions which reflects adversely on the Kadiye. The man from the North is ascetic and abstemious while the village priest lives by the flesh-pots. The physical contrast is required to be shown on the stage:

[*The blind man is tall and straight. It is obvious from his dress that he is a stranger to these parts. He wears a long tubular gown, white, which comes below his calf, and a little skull cap. Down one ear hangs a fairly large earring, and he wears a thick ring on one of his fingers. He has a small beard, which, with the skull cap, accentuates the length of his face and emphasizes its ebony-carving nature.*] (p. 168.)

The Kadiye is a dramatic contrast:

a big, voluminous creature of about fifty, smooth-faced except for little tufts of beard around his chin . . . He is bare above the waist. At least half of the Kadiye's fingers are ringed. He is followed by a servant, who brushes the flies off him with a horse-tail flick. (p. 175.)

The grossness of the Kadiye's figure in the midst of a disastrous harvest is an index of his lack of concern for the fate of his flock. The beggar whose perceptions are keener in compensation for his blindness, senses his size from his voice. He asks Igwezu – the question is a teaser which further stimulates Igwezu's doubts about the role of the priest:

Is he fat, master? When he spoke I detected a certain bulk in his
voice.

IGWEZU: Ay, he is fat. He rolls himself like a fat and greasy porpoise.

(p. 184.)

The beggar's contempt for the Kadiye is already affecting Igwezu – the
contempt is obvious in the porpoise simile.

The beggar then is a threat to the hitherto unquestioned role of the
Kadiye. But the beggar is not just a mischievous sower of discontent; his
history is one of extraordinary fortitude in the face of disaster. His march
from the North is itself epic. He has not only overcome his blindness, but
has liberated himself from his own tradition which made begging the only
occupation open to the blind. This blind man is looking for work, and the
insistence with which he demands it startles Makuri. The beggar has
credentials of a moral and spiritual nature which qualify him to raise
questions about more complacent regimes.

So intertwined is religion with all life in the village, that this questioning
comes close to blasphemy. The beggar's startling ideas on land reclamation
constitute, in traditional thinking, an invasion of the territory of the
Serpent. Such words are 'profanities' as the horrified Makuri points out.
He explains:

The land that we till and live on has been ours from the beginning of
time. The bounds are marked by ageless iroko trees that have lived
since the birth of the Serpent, since the birth of the world, since the
start of time itself. What is ours is ours. But what belongs to the
Serpent may never be taken away from him.   (pp. 173–4.)

It is obvious from Makuri's reaction that he and his generation are totally
unreceptive to new ideas. They have achieved a resigned compromise with
their surroundings, a fatalistic acceptance of good and evil which is a kind
of peace. They seem to be the last for whom the village would give that
total security and happiness to which they look back in their reminiscences
early in the play. If there is to be change, then it has to come from
somewhere else. His double failure in spite of all his efforts makes the
youthful ear of Igwezu more receptive to the beggar's influence. Makuri's
attitude is interesting because there are occasional signs that he too has
doubts about both Priest and Serpent. His near-blasphemy may have been
an unconscious slip brought on by Alu's perversity – 'The serpent be . . .
Bah! You'll make me voice a sacrilege before I can stop my tongue.'
(p. 162.) His pique at the Kadiye's slights loosens his tongue a little more
and he calls the revered Kadiye (behind his back of course) 'The pot-bellied

pig'. (p. 179.) He is not, however, ready to question any further, and contents himself with such occasional mutterings.

The relationship between the beggar and Igwezu is central. In a play in which entrances and exits are so organized that they become thematically significant, Igwezu's entrance for his meeting with the beggar is well timed. Indeed, the dialogue from the beginning seems to lead up to this meeting. When he does appear, he comes in unobserved by the others at a crucial point in the beggar's narration of his last disappointment – a ruined harvest. This is thematically apt. Igwezu has just returned from viewing and contemplating a similar catastrophe. Makuri in an earlier speech indicates the extent of Igwezu's disaster:

> Not a grain was saved, not one tuber in the soil . . . And what the flood left behind was poisoned by the oil in the swamp water . . . It is hard for him, coming back for a harvest that isn't there.   (pp. 172–3.)

It is a total disaster, but not unprecedented. The beggar – he is blind to boot – has suffered with his people a similar disappointment in the dry North, and it is the narration of this disaster that Igwezu, unseen, hears. The beggar's tale is particularly poignant because the expected harvest seemed to have brought a new humanity to the village. The disaster was therefore a defeat not only for their bodies, but for their very souls:

> Nothing could keep us from the farms from the moment that the shoots came through the surface, and all through the months of waiting. We went round the plantains and rubbed our skins against them, lightly, so that the tenderest bud could not be hurt. This was the closest that we had ever felt to one another. This was the moment that the village became a clan, and the clan a household, and even that was taken by Allah in one of his large hands and kneaded together with the clay of the earth. We loved the sound of a man's passing footsteps as if the rustle of his breath it was that gave life to the sprouting wonder around us. We even forgot to beg, and lived on the marvel of this new birth of the land, and the rich smell of its goodness . . . But it turned out to have been an act of spite. The feast was not meant for us – but for the locusts.   (pp. 181–2.)

Igwezu hears not only this but also the beggar's resolute response to this total collapse of his hopes: 'I headed away from my home, and set my face towards the river.' For the beggar, the man from the dry North, water was life. He was spiritually thirsty for water – any kind of water: 'But let there be water, because I am sick of the dryness.' Water had been the cause of Igwezu's ruin – the very water for which the blind man craved.

The beggar's narration establishes his credentials in Igwezu's mind, although he has yet to relive his disaster and come to terms with himself. He too has had a bitter 'feast' (the beggar too uses the word 'feast' somewhat ironically in his narration) 'I have had my feast of welcome. I found it on the farm where the beans and the corn had made an everlasting pottage with the mud.' (p. 183.) When the beggar makes the surprisingly hopeful proposal he arouses a new interest in Igwezu who looks up at him 'as if seeing him for the first time'. (p. 184.) Once the beggar catches Igwezu's attention he plies him with questions, the answers to which would make all the difference between Igwezu's continued acceptance of the old ways of living and some attempt to discover new paths. He repeats, for example, to a more hopeful ear his earlier question about the obstacles in the way of a new approach to the land: 'Do you serve the Serpent, master? Do you believe with the old man – that the land may not be redeemed? That the rotting swamps may not be purified?' (p. 185.) He prods more sensitive areas – the well-fed priest and, glancingly, the god himself – 'Does the priest live well? Is the Serpent well kept and nourished?' (p. 185.) Receiving the right sort of response he moves directly at the god: 'How does the Serpent fare in times of dearth? Does he thrive on the poisonous crabs? Does he drink the ooze of the mire?' This is too much for Makuri who interrupts this dangerous line of questioning – 'That borders on sacrilege.' (p. 186.) The beggar's work is half done, however. He retires gracefully and hands the role of questioner neatly to Igwezu: 'It is for the master to question, not the slave.' How well the beggar had done his work is seen in the encounter between Igwezu and the priest when for once the latter loses his superior position and lies helpless in the barber's chair looking up at the razor in Igwezu's hand.

When Igwezu challenges the priest and subjects him (in the manner of the beggar) to a series of searching questions, he is challenging the whole conservative basis of life in the village by which the Kadiye, acting on behalf of the Serpent, sets the bounds of human conduct, and swallows their offerings with little regard to their fates. All this contempt for the Kadiye's venality comes out in his question: 'Why are you so fat, Kadiye?' The priest stands exposed as a false prophet. There is no mistaking the pun on 'lie' in Igwezu's verdict on the priest: 'You lie upon the land, Kadiye, and choke it in the folds of a serpent.' (p. 195.) Igwezu has emancipated himself mentally through his questions, from the tyranny of the Kadiye and the Serpent. He realizes that essentially he is now on his own. This is a hard discovery:

If I slew the fatted calf, Kadiye, do you think the land might breathe again? If I slew all the cattle in the land and sacrificed every measure of goodness, would it make any difference to our lives, Kadiye? Would it make any difference to our fates? (p. 195.)

Igwezu's mood is one of despair. He has shaken off the old shackles but he still has to work out something as positive as the beggar's resolute search for a new life. He himself is bewildered by the new-found strength with which he has challenged the Kadiye. Has it an abiding, positive quality?

I wonder what drove me on.

Do you think that my only strength was that of despair? Or was there something of a desire to prove myself? (p. 196.)

Igwezu's departure for the city after all this is not a decisive gesture. He does not see any new hope there. The analogy between the city and the swamp recurs in his despairing question: 'Is it of any earthly use to change one slough for another?' He has to leave the village because he has challenged the basis of its existence and 'must not be here when the people call for blood'. (p. 197.) His departure then is forced, and is thus for the time being a negative reaction. Nor is there any hope in his words of a return in due course: 'Only the children and the old stay here, bondsman. Only the innocent and the dotards.' (p. 197.) In this mood there is no hint of a return. But Igwezu has gone through an experience which has shaken all his old beliefs, and so when he sets out, it is without the old props afforded by the Kadiye and the Serpent. The question is whether he is strong enought to go through life on his own. We do not know, and he does not know. The beggar watches and waits. 'I shall be here to give account.'

In a brilliant arrangement of exits, the beggar is left symbolically alone on the stage. Alu and Makuri, the two dried-up representatives of the old life had opened the play, taunting each other with gibes at their own decrepitude. They are a failing generation, and have symbolically faded from the scene. The Kadiye, the bastion of the old life, has been shown in a vulnerable moment, and his venality has been exposed. After his triumph over the Kadiye, the beggar had called Igwezu 'slayer of Serpents'. The Serpent and all he represents has not been completely slain, but his regime has been shaken for the first time; it is vulnerable. The discomfited Kadiye would no doubt organize a temporary rally, a holding operation, but that regime too will crumble. It would have been easy to see the young Igwezu completing the rout of the old forces, but Soyinka, as he does time and time again, shuns such easy solutions. The forces of tradition are not so easily routed. Igwezu is certainly not strong enough to oppose the Kadiye – at least not yet – so he has to flee. Any hope of change within the village is represented by a blind beggar who is, in spite of his handicap, a spiritually strong force. He is the only hope in a village of innocents and dotards. But some seeds once sown have a way of thriving in the most unpromising surroundings. Sometimes, on the other hand, they just die. This is the kind of open situation that we have at the end of *The Swamp-Dwellers*.

The Lion and the Jewel

▼▼▼▼▼▼▼▼▼▼▼▼▼▼▼▼▼▼▼▼▼▼▼▼▼▼▼▼▼▼▼▼▼▼

The Lion and the Jewel, like *The Swamp-Dweller*, is set in an African village which is facing the challenge of rapid change. Soyinka gives a visual image of the state of the village in the opening set which is 'dominated by an immense "odan" tree', with the 'bush school' only flanking the stage on the right. The bush school is yet to occupy centre stage in village life and cannot yet provide, with its mechanical chanting of the 'Arithmetic times', a substitute for the established traditional basis of village life. This is in fact the crux of the play – what would happen to the village of Ilujinle if by a kind of magic the Bale and Lakunle were to change places and the latter was able to put his ideas into practice? There is little doubt that the result would be total confusion. Viewed in this way, the play would be seen to be not a contrast between progress and reaction – represented by Lakunle and the Bale – but between a muddle-headed sloganeering, and a hard-headed conservatism. Conservatism (it is certainly not held up as an ideal) wins because it has a clearer view of life, and in the prevailing state of the contest is more likely to succeed. Within the context of the play a victory for Lakunle would have been against the evidence, just as outside the context of the play the results of his confused leadership would be disastrous.

Lakunle is half-baked where both Sidi and the Bale are sound. The stage directions describe Sidi as *'a true village belle'*. 'True' is indicative of her genuine quality. *'She balances the pail on her head with accustomed ease. Around her is wrapped the familiar broad cloth which is folded just above her breasts, leaving the shoulders bare.'* (This 'exposure' causes the self-conscious Lakunle acute embarrassment.) Lakunle in contrast to Sidi is ridiculous in the costume by which he vainly strives to hold on desperately to the coat-tails of a fashion he does not understand. His appearance, *'in an old-style English suit, threadbare but not ragged, clean but not ironed'* etc. signals a man of unformed values, incompetently imitative. His words soon confirm the visual image.

Soyinka's portrayal of Lakunle is subtle. He emerges as a comic character, but there is an underlying pathos arising from the recognition that he has a split personality, the two separate halves of which are clearly visible. He is engaged in doing violence to his 'true' nature. Although he loudly denounces the Bale for his backwardness – chief among the Bale's sins is his practice of polygamy – Lakunle secretly envies the man just this. It is with a start that he has to recall himself to his 'civilized' duty when his mind wanders off in unconscious admiration of the Bale. (His true nature sometimes gets the better of him and he indulges in a little bottom-pinching himself.) His speech in criticism of the Bale demonstrates both the real Lakunle which he tries to suppress and the bloodless substitute which he holds in front of himself:

> Voluptous beast! He loves this life too well
> To bear to part from it. And motor roads
> And railways would do just that, forcing
> Civilization at his door. He foresaw it
> And he barred the gates, securing fast
> His dogs and horses, his wives and all his
> Concubines . . . ah, yes . . . all those concubines
> Baroka has such a selective eye, none suits him
> But the best . . .
> [*His eyes truly light up* . . .]
> . . . Yes, one must grant him that.
> Ah, I sometimes wish I led his kind of life.
> Such luscious bosoms make his nightly pillow.
> I am sure he keeps a time-table just as
> I do at school. Only way to ensure fair play
> I don't know what the women see in him. His eyes
> Are small and always red with wine. He must
> Possess some secret . . . No! I do not envy him!
> Just the one woman for me. Alone I stand
> For progress, with Sidi as my chosen soul-mate, the one
> Woman of my life . . .   (*Five Plays*, pp. 117–18.)

The unresolved split in Lakunle's personality is signalled by a subtle change in style within the speech. When he slips from his conscious posturing into an almost subconscious musing, the playwright eases him into a more natural linguistic register. 'Luscious bosom' is the sort of phrase he shuns in his conscious posturing. (In his first encounter with Sidi he had had recourse to the euphemistic 'shoulders' as a substitute for breasts:

> How often must I tell you, Sidi, that
> A grown up girl must cover up her . . .
> Her shoulders? I can see quite . . . quite
> A good portion of – that!)

During his reverie his guard comes down, and the honestly appreciative phrase 'luscious bosoms' comes tumbling out from his smothered soul. The syntax too gradually eases up to approximate to normal coloquial speech: 'I am sure he keeps a time-table just as I do at school.' The comparison with his school time-table is natural and apt. Once he recovers himself however and the prudish sentinel takes over, he returns to a rhetorical style studded with the clichés from his book-learning. The inverted syntax signals the return of the respectable veneer: 'Alone I stand/For progress, with Sidi as my chosen soul-mate, the one/Woman of my life.' This is an example of Soyinka's subtle use of linguistic register to highlight Lakunle's total unfitness for the role of reformer with which he flatters himself. An examination of any of his speeches of more than a line or two in length usually reveals a potentially disastrous mental confusion. The ideas which come pouring out are so undigested as to become comic. Even when these ideas have some appearance of worth, the way in which they are presented shows that in Lakunle's mind they really have no meaning. Soyinka usually provides the deflating device within the speech itself so that by the time it is over Lakunle has succeeded in emptying his own ideas of any validity they may have seemed to have.

He rejects the traditional form of marriage – the bride-price in particular – as 'a savage custom'. In its place he would put a 'civilized' institution. But the very form of address 'Ignorant girl' with which his speech begins signals both his dangerous conceit and an impetuous lack of control. Phrases like 'To buy a heifer off a market stall' (with 'heifer' standing out like a sore thumb), 'chattel', and the stilted 'wed' suggest his books rather than Lakunle himself as the real speaker. As the speech proceeds and Lakunle triumphantly makes each proposition for the wrong reason, he isolates himself from both his society and the sympathy of the audience, so that he becomes an object of ridicule, and the butt of his own missiles:

> Ignorant girl, can you not understand?
> To pay the price would be
> To buy a heifer off the market stall.
> You'd be my chattel, my mere property.
> No, Sidi! [*very tenderly*]
> When we are wed, you shall not walk or sit
> Tethered, as it were, to my dirtied heels.   (p. 100.)

Even at this stage, and in spite of the danger signals which have been pointed out, the speech still manages only to skirt total disaster. But it continues:

> Together we shall sit at table
> – Not on the floor – and eat,
> Not with fingers, but with knives
> And forks, and breakable plates
> Like civilized beings.

The end of the statement completely destroys any worth the beginning may have had. The proposition that eating off 'breakable plates' is civilized is a prime example of Lakunle's thinking. Quite obviously by isolating the most irrelevant and least valuable attribute of a certain type of plate, and using this as the mask of civilization, Lakunle shows that he does not understand anything either about plates or about civilization. The technique of deflation is repeated as the speech continues:

> I will not have you wait on me
> Till I have dined my fill.
> No wife of mine, no lawful wedded wife
> Shall eat the leavings off my plate –
> That is for the children

Apart from the mechanical crib from the Prayer Book: 'lawful wedded wife' which signals the imitator rather than the reformer, the proposition seems acceptable until Lakunle brings it all crashing down with – 'That is for the children.' The resulting proposition is ridiculous, for it becomes something like 'Civilized parents feed their children on the leavings of their plate.'

Of course by this point of the play Lakunle's fate is sealed, and no minute examination of his speeches is needed to throw audiences into convulsions of laughter almost every time he opens his mouth. His very appearance, so carefully detailed at the beginning of the play, serves as an ever-present deflating device. When he assumes the weary pose of the prophet crying out in vain in the wilderness, or of the great man of ideas casting his pearls before swine, the effect is hilarious; because that is just what he is not:

> [*wearily*] It's never any use
> Bush-girl you are, bush-girl you'll always be;
> Uncivilized and primitive – bush-girl!
> I kissed you us all educated men –
> And Christians – kiss their wives.
> It is the way of civilized romance.[1]   (p. 101.)

[1] The resemblance between Lakunle and Joyce Cary's *Mr Johnson* is striking.

It is clear then, that this ridiculous figure does not represent any kind of progress. (The contrast between him and Eman in *The Strong Breed* is total.) He is a self-proclaimed prophet, but as he himself follows a false trail, he cannot lead his society anywhere but to disaster.

The Bale is quite different. He is conservative, resists the building of roads and railways, and tries to keep his society largely insulated from 'progress'. If progress is represented by Lakunle's vapid descriptions of it, then it can be said without hesitation that the village of Ilujinle would be better off without it. According to Lakunle, the Bale has deprived the village of 'Trade,/Progress, adventure, success, civilization/Fame, international conspicuosity'. (p. 116.) (He could have gone on to itemize cocktail parties, a school of ballroom dancing, a modern park for lovers, 'High-heeled shoes for the lady, red paint/on her lips', breakable plates, etc., as he does elsewhere.) All these, merely for their own sake, Ilujinle could happily do without.

The Bale fears progress, and in this he can be credited with the foresight of anticipating some of the disasters of progress which 'civilized' societies have only discovered by hindsight. His statement on progress is a far more controlled utterance than Lakunle's, and thus has some integrity:

> I do not hate progress, only its nature
> Which makes all roofs and faces look the same.
> And the wish of one old man is
> That here and there,
> Among the bridges and the murderous roads
> Below the humming birds which
> Smoke the face of Sango, dispenser of
> The snake-tongue lightning; between this moment
> And the reckless broom that will be wielded
> In these years to come, we must leave
> Virgin plots of lives, rich decay
> And the tang of vapours rising from
> Forgotten heaps of compost, lying
> Undisturbed . . .   (p. 144.)

There is wisdom here in that the Bale sees the reverse side of the coin of progress, which in Soyinka's work is frequently symbolized by the motor road which not only speeds things up, but can also be justly described by the Bale's term, 'murderous'.

Of course the mere apprehension of danger is not in itself constructive. The Bale's reaction to progress is conservative in a negative way. (It must be remembered that in the speech just quoted the Bale is doing some word-spinning in the process of subduing Sidi to his will. His own view of himself is therefore most attractively presented.)

The Bale has made two very strange concessions to progress. Fascinated by the idea of postage stamps he has designed a pathetically inefficient stamp machine so that Ilujinle 'Will boast its own tax on paper, made with/Stamps like this. For long I dreamt it/And here it stands, child of my thoughts.' (p. 142.) That this strange machine which does not work – 'All is not well with it' – has the immediate effect of impressing Sidi with the Bale's ingenuity, should not blind us to the fact of its total incongruity in an illiterate society. The Bale has also allowed his servants to form a trade union – 'The Palace Workers Union' – and has conceded them a day off, 'in keeping/With the habits – I am told – of modern towns'. There is an element of whim in both the Bale's gestures to progress, rather than any deliberate selection of desirable items from the package of progress. He is in reality a conservative under whom the village is likely to remain exactly as it has always been, if he has his way. Even so, he is certainly the lesser of two evils. No doubt change is inevitable. The village school itself is an index of this. With the intrusion of the photographer too the village is shown to be vulnerable. The Bale would, in spite of himself, have to yield to change. He would not however have started the slide himself, and he at least knows what he does not want. He also has some idea of what he wants for himself, and how to get it. While Lakunle plies his barren rhetoric and tries vainly to suppress his natural feelings, the Bale enjoys his harem, his wrestling, and his favourite delicacy – a mixture of 'ground corn and pepper'. The Bale in short lives, while Lakunle frustrates his own vitality. They represent opposing values which in more sombre works are equated with the opposed principles of life and death.

The winning of Sidi by the Bale is only logical in the play, since Lakunle's concern is for rhetoric and the Bale's concern is for life. It is clear that Lakunle desires Sidi more with his head than with his heart. He wants to rescue a poor 'bush-girl' and 'civilize' her with marriage. He must do this on his own terms: 'I obey my books . . . "Man takes the fallen woman by the hand"/And ever after they live happily.' (p. 153.) Sidi's feelings and wishes do not enter into the business at all. His is not a wooing; it is a piece of misguided social evangelism.

The Bale on the other hand is a past-master in the practical arts of wooing, and while Lakunle only succeeds in irritating Sidi, the Bale, once by his strategem – even the worldly-wise Sadiku is completely deceived – he gets her into his palace, succeeds in first dazzling the girl, then eventually compelling her admiration. Nor are his intentions merely intellectual as Sidi soon finds out! The Baroka is as virile as he is wily. By comparison, Lakunle is as trivial and emasculated as Sidi's contemptuous comparison implies:

> I who have felt the strength,
> The perpetual youthful zest
> Of the panther of the trees?
> And would I choose a watered-down,
> A beardless version of unripened man?   (p. 155.)

There is an interesting side glance in the play at the sex war; the opposition of male and female which explodes into a victory dance when Sadiku believes that the Bale has become impotent. Up to this point in the play Sadiku has appeared as the ideal head wife in a polygamous household. Not only does she not complain about the institution of polygamy, she is an enthusiastic wooer of new wives for her husband. So totally is she immersed in the system that Sidi's contemptuous rejection of the Bale's offer of marriage, and her very assumption that she has any choice once she is asked, totally scandalizes Sadiku who can only pray for a restoration of Sidi's wits: 'May Sango restore your wits. For most surely some angry god has taken possession of you.' (p. 115.) Sadiku just cannot contemplate the consequences of Sidi's attempt to assert this independent role. It would appear however that under her obedient conformity seethes a basic resentment against her prescribed role. The Bale's impotence (or her belief in it) releases her suppressed feelings, and she invites Sidi to celebrate with her the victory of their sex over the dominating male:

Not me alone, girl. You too. Every woman. Oh my daughter, that I have lived to see this day . . . To see him fizzle with the drabbest puff of a misprimed 'sakabula'.
    Take warning my masters . . .
    We'll scotch you in the end.   (p. 125.)

So much then for the comfortable male doctrine of the contented, uncomplaining, compliant female who totally accepts the system of polygamy. Unfortunately for Sadiku, and even more for Sidi, the victory celebration is premature. There is still plenty of life left in the old lion.

The play is a harmonious blend of words, song, dance, and mime. Soyinka's use of mime and dance in particular is worth some notice. Twice in the play, once to represent the first visit of the photographer and again to represent the Bale's bribing of the railway surveyor, mime and dance are used structurally to recall past events. This use of the flashback technique, more commonly associated with the cinema, gives the play historical depth. In this play the scene for each of these flashbacks is obviously set and we know we are being given a glimpse of the past. In *The Strong Breed* there is an even bolder breaking up of time divisions so that at moments the play seems to be suspended in a fusion of past and present. A similar scrambling of time is seen also in the technique of narration used in *The Interpreters*.

Because *The Lion and the Jewel* is a comedy, the follies of Lakunle result only in his own mild discomfiture. He is a false leader, but fortunately no one follows him. Indeed the play ends on a note of hope for Lakunle himself when he seems to be on the verge of giving his heart a chance as he is seen fascinated by the buttocks of the dancing girl. One feels that if he can only let himself really dance without being prompted, he might yet be saved. Other false prophets in Soyinka's works – the Kadiye in *The Strong Breed* for example – represent a more sinister threat to their society.

A Dance of the Forests

▼▼▼▼▼▼▼▼▼▼▼▼▼▼▼▼▼▼▼▼▼▼▼▼▼▼▼▼▼▼▼▼▼▼▼

A Dance of the Forests presents a comprehensive view of man over a massive span of history; it even – in the highly symbolic chorusing of the future – looks into the future. For Soyinka, history is a nearly cyclical movement, any progress being represented by a kink after an evolution and at the start of a new cycle. 'Idanre' invokes the image of the snake swallowing its own tail and that of the 'mobius strip', a figure of interlocking rings – to represent this idea:

> multiform
> Evolution of the self-devouring snake to spatials
> New in symbol, banked loop of the 'Modius Strip'
> And interlock of re-creative rings, one surface
> Yet full comb of angles, uni-plane, yet sensuous with
> Complexities of mind and motion.
>
> (*Idanre and Other Poems*, p. 83.)

A Dance of the Forests is an attempt to represent the complexities of the human personality and its consequences within this cyclical pattern of history. The result is a very complex play with tremendous possibilities for staging as well as for interpretation; it is a warning against moral complacency and escapism.

The play is set at a crucial point in a particular evolutionary pattern – the completion of a cycle. Since it was written for Nigeria's Independence, the end of an era and the beginning of another, this is apt. The Crier who announces the ceremony of 'the welcome of the dead' invites only those of the dead who have completed a cycle:

> only such
> May resume their body corporeal as are summoned
> When the understreams that whirl them endlessly
> Complete a circle. Only such may regain
> Voice auditorial as are summoned when their link
> With the living has fully repeated its nature, has
> Re-impressed fully on the tapestry of Igbehinadun
> In approximate duplicate of actions, be they

Of good or of evil, of violence or carelessness;
In approximate duplicate of motives, be they
Illusory, tangible, commendable or damnable.

(Five Plays, p. 50.)

Another cycle has been completed, and characters who took part in the cycle represented by the Court of Mata Kharibu eight centuries earlier are now present at the beginning of another cycle, represented at the social level by the 'Gathering of the Tribes', which could be taken to represent independence and the ceremonies celebrating it. At another and more important level, this is also an opportunity for stocktaking, self-examination, self-confession, and possible self-regeneration. While all are involved in the social celebration, only a few humans – representatives of the race – take part in the process of introspection, and even these represent different levels of feeling and different capacities for understanding what they see – Demoke is obviously far more capable of feeling and understanding than Adenebi for example.

Although a particular geographical and social setting is selected for what amounts to a trial, it is important to remember that it is not just Nigerian man who is under examination but *homo sapiens* as a whole. The use of gods and spirits, the backward plunge into history, as well as the peering into the future with the aid of possessed humans, all combine to give the play an archetypal quality and an application broader than any confining parcel of space or time.

Numerous themes appear – some only momentarily – in this vast drama, but they are all contained under a broad enveloping theme of the contradictions of man's nature and the consequences of such contradictions (both as it involves the single man and as it varies from man to man) for the whole race of man and his environment. The environment involves not only other men and trees and rivers and minerals, etc., but also gods and the spirits of the dead who act as prodders and stimulators to the human conscience. Within this vast framework there is room for a great variety of sub-themes – the nature and functions of art, political corruption, the destruction of the natural environment, war, changes in values brought about by 'modernization', the consequences of free-will – there is a profusion of themes which arise naturally from Soyinka's treatment of the overall theme. No wonder then that as Margaret Laurence comments, 'There are some parts of *A Dance of the Forests* which seem overloaded. There are moments when the multiplicity of themes creates the feeling that there are a few too many plates spinning in the air – some of them speed by without being properly seen, and some crash down'.[1] Margaret

[1] *Long Drums and Cannons* (Macmillan, London, 1968), p. 45.

Laurence's own interpretation of the play is most sensitive and points a path through all these complexities, thus proving that the play is complex, but not confused. Indeed the problems arise mainly over the precise interpretation of the significance of the drama of the Half-Child at the end. Each succeeding reading produces insights which suggest a complete vision on the part of the author. It thus seems very likely that Margaret Laurence's expectations of the play will be fulfilled, namely that what is obscure to us 'may seem perfectly plain to the next generation of readers and play-goers'.

In addition to the multiplicity of themes, there is a multiplicity of symbols. One of the difficulties of interpretation may arise not merely from the multiplicity of symbols, but from the use of different symbols to reinforce the same idea. Man is the central figure in the play, and man is represented by living men and women – Demoke, Adenebi, Rola, Agboreko, The Old Man, etc. Some of these have a dual existence in that they also appear as historical characters in the court of Mata Kharibu. (This device conveniently establishes the essential continuity of human nature.) The Dead Man and Woman also represent man – man as victim of other men – and history as an indictment of man's past actions. The ants also represent man or rather men – the mass of men who are the victims of those in power – the manipulated masses. Man is also represented by the Half-Child, that ambiguous symbol of man's future. One has to be prepared for these changing symbols for different aspects of the same thing and respond to them. A perfectly coherent interpretation of the play is possible with a little care, though there will always be questions and disagreements over particular details.

The Gathering of the Tribes, the central social event, is celebrated in the town (sometimes called village), but its sounds and its effects penetrate into the forest which is the scene of the spiritual exercise of introspection. At the end of the play, just after Demoke's crucial restoration of the Half-Child to his mother, there is a silhouette of the rejoicings in the town which emphasizes the isolation of the social celebration from the deeper spiritual action which is taking place in the Forest:

> *A silhouette of Demoke's totem is seen. The village people dancing round it, also in silhouette, in silence. There is no contact between them and the Forest ones.* (*Five Plays*, p. 82.)

This tableau underlines one of the themes of the play – the insensitivity of the generality of men to the deeper spiritual concerns, and their preoccupation with the mere externals of life. Here as in other works of Soyinka, it is given to a few – often a lonely individual – to seek and find the vision for the community as a whole. This is the opportunity which the play gives to the three human protagonists Demoke, Rola, and Adenebi. These characters are clearly distinguished from each other, and their differences must be appreciated for a satisfactory interpretation of the play.

Adenebi is the least sensitive of the three. He is Council Orator in this life, and in an earlier existence had produced the play's most rhetorical speech in defence of Mata Kharibu's indefensible war. (Rhetoric of Adenebi's kind is frequently a mark of insincerity or hollowness in Soyinka's work.) Adenebi is given a thin surface respectability signalled by his rhetoric but also by his consciousness of his social position and his reluctance to be *seen* in the wrong company. When Rola's notorious identity as a prostitute becomes known, his one worry is that he would be contaminated by 'scandal': 'The whole horrible scandal. How did I ever get in your company?' (*Five Plays*, p. 22), and more explicitly:

> Oh yes, and I found that the woman who was with us was that notorious lady they call Madame Tortoise. That was really why I left. Think, if I, a councillor, was discovered with her!   (p. 36.)

Underneath this respectable exterior is concealed an involvement with petty municipal corruption exemplified by the 'Incinerator' episode.

Adenebi's insensitivity is even more clearly demonstrated by his general lack of taste. In his enthusiasm for a new civilization, he is curiously without firm values. He has forsaken the humane, hospitable ways of the past, and cloaks his lack of generosity under his responsibilities to 'a proper family life', 'privacy', etc. But there is indecision even in his expression of his new creed, signalled here by 'I suppose', 'you know' and his hesitant delivery:

> It is rather difficult. I suppose one has to be firm. You start your own family, expect to look after your wife and children, lead – you know – a proper family life. Privacy . . . very important . . . some measure of privacy.   (*Five Plays*, p. 5.)

He is incapable of appreciating art, his mind having been sealed off by a rule of thumb by which anything 'pagan' is bad:

> I really ought to tell you how disappointed I was with your son's handiwork. Don't you think it was rather pagan? I should have thought that something more in keeping with our progress would be more appropriate.   (*Five Plays*, p. 33.)

His whole attitude is one of respectable philistinism. In this spirit he had supported the Old Man's proposal for an invitation to the ancestors to join in the celebration, and had enveloped the whole scheme in his characteristic rhetoric. His picture of the ancestors is dangerously romantic: 'Purple robes. White horses dressed in gold. Processions through the town with communion and service around our symbol.' (p. 33.) This shallow, insensitive man is Council Orator, and in an earlier existence, Court Historian. In this earlier role he had silenced the common sense of the unwilling Warrior in the flood of rhetoric with which he supported the causeless war of Mata Kharibu and branded the Warrior as a traitor. (pp. 57–8.) In return for a bribe he had testified to the soundness of the slave dealer's boat which he had never seen. Adenebi in both existences represents the insensitive, corrupt, philistine trimmer who is always loud in support of power and of doctrines conducive to his own convenience. He is a clearly delineated person and is at the same time a manifestation of a type.

Rola is an odd mixture. In both existences she is a woman with a fatal attractiveness whose path is littered with dead lovers whom she has callously sent to their death. In her current existence, she too has repudiated the traditional ways, and finds family hospitality a burden: 'This whole family business sickens me. Let everybody lead their own lives.' (*Five Plays*, p. 6.) The implied selfishness and lack of human feeling is given a more sinister expression in her attitude to men whose lives have no value beyond their role as ministers to her own convenience. They are expendable pawns in her business. Her fierce defence of her position carries incidentally an ironic satirical comment on a society which is indifferent to human life in its pre-occupation with money-making:

> When your business men ruin the lesser ones, do you go crying to them? I also have no pity for the one who invested foolishly. Investors, that is all they ever were – to me. (*Five Plays*, p. 24.)

Rola's attitude in an earlier existence had exactly paralleled this one. A rejected lover who committed suicide has been selected, 'just as I select a new pin every day. He came back again and could not understand why the door was barred to him. He was such a fool.' (*Five Plays*, p. 64.) Rola represents in this side of her nature a destructive force. The Dead Woman excludes her from womanhood as a source of new life: 'I am certain she had no womb, but I think/*It* was a woman.' (The last pronoun, italics mine, is significant.)

About all that can be said for Rola in either existence is that she shows some appreciation of art. She is not quite the philistine that Adenebi is in this regard. The expression with which she is to say these lines to Demoke (according to the stage directions) suggests an awed appreciation of the carver's skill: '[*with unexpected solemnity.*] And you did not even cut it down. Climbing the king of trees and carving it as it stood – I think that was very brave.' (p. 7.) (It would perhaps be carping to observe that Rola's admiration is rather more for the carver's daring than for the resulting work of art.) This quality in Rola would not have been worth mentioning had not art and the appreciation of art as an index of moral sensitiveness been so important in Soyinka's work. The words of Obaneji (who is really Forest Head – the chief of the gods) in appreciation of Demoke's art are significant, particularly since his speech is a rejoinder to Rola's own remark last quoted: 'It is the kind of action that redeems mankind.'

Because of this sensitivity, the significance of the ceremony of the welcome of the dead is not entirely lost on Rola. She comes out of the experience looking (in the words of the stage directions) '*chastened*'. And Demoke (she herself is too overawed to speak) yokes her with him in the experience. She is no longer what she had been, the heartless 'Madame Tortoise': 'Not any more. It was the same lightning that seared us through the head.' (*Five Plays*, p. 85.) (It is significant that Adenebi just fades out of the play, being incapable of taking any significance from the vision he has just seen.) Rola/Madame Tortoise is rather more complex than appears on the surface. She is certainly capable of redemption and is thus nearer to the most sensitive of the three human protagonists, Demoke.

Demoke is the artist. (The redemptive role of art and the artist in Soyinka's work has been remarked on before.) In his earlier existence – as the Court Poet – he had also lived as an artist. Yet he too involves a contradiction. Being human, even this extraordinary artist is susceptible to jealousy and vertigo; he is capable of destruction as well as creation; of murder as well as the production of an extraordinary work of art – 'the kind of action that redeems mankind'. In the scenes showing his earlier existence, his work as a poet is not highlighted – except in the fulsome poetic phrases with which he praises Madame Tortoise – but his dual nature is even there suggested by the contrast between the deep contempt (revealed in asides) which he feels at Madame Tortoise's callousness, and the flattery which he lavishes on her in her hearing:

> Your hair is the feathers my lady, and the breast of the canary – your forehead my lady – is the inspiration of your servant. Madame, you must not say you have lost your canary – [*aside*] unless it be your virtue, slut!   (*Five Plays*, p.52.)

He is bold enough to defy Madame Tortoise and forbid his novice to go on the hazardous errand to recover the canary – 'I forbid him to go' (p. 53) –

and his innuendoes almost bring down the wrath of his callous mistress on his head: 'And look out, my poet: sometimes, you grow wearisome.'[2] (p. 63.) But it is Demoke the carver (not the earlier Court Poet) who has the greater significance for the play.

Demoke combines the destructive and the creative capabilities of man. His very act of creation involves destruction. The majestic *araba* has to be destroyed in order to produce the totem. This is a necessary act, however, and a limited one. The further destruction of the forest by the townspeople, and the resulting vulgarization of his work, disgusts Demoke:

> When I finished it, the grove was cleared of all the other trees, the bush was razed and a motor road built right up to it. It looked different. It was no longer my work. I fled from it. (p. 8.)

Unlike the destruction of the *araba* tree, the murder of Oremole is not necessary; it is a crime, and the memory of it plagues Demoke's soul until he confesses it. At first he skirts round his crime. He mentions the death of his apprentice as though it had nothing to do with him: 'And one man fell to his death.' (p. 7.) The growing uneasiness of his conscience is dramatized by his compulsive urge to question the dead – he is the only one of the protagonists who takes any real interest in them. But what begins as an anxiety that his crime might be revealed by the voices of the dead, becomes – with the help of Forest Head's gentle prodding – an irresistible urge to make an open confession which leaves the way open for the regeneration which is Forest Head's purpose in ordering the welcome ceremony. Soyinka dramatizes the murder in a verbal flashback heightened by poetry. The narration highlights the mixture of jealousy and humiliation which motivated Demoke to murder his apprentice because he could climb higher than his master:

> I plucked him down
> Demoke's head is no woman's cloth, spread
> To receive wood shavings from a carpenter.
> Down, down I plucked him, screaming on Oro.
> (*Five Plays*, pp. 27–8.)

This act of murder is immediately succeeded by a frenzied act of creation no less vividly-described:

[2] I differ here from Margaret Laurence who writes of the poet: 'The poet lets his novice fall to his death in rescuing the queen's canary from the roof-top' (*Long Drums and Cannons*, p. 57.)

Before he made hard obeisance to his earth,
My axe was executioner at Oro's neck. Alone,
Alone I cut the strands that mocked me, till head
And boastful slave lay side by side, and I
Demoke, sat on the shoulders of the tree,
My spirit set free and singing, my hands
My father's hands possessed by demons of blood
And I carved three days and nights till tools
Were blunted, and these hands, my father's hands
Swelled big as tree-trunks.

Both acts – of destruction and creation – are essentially Demoke's. (In spite of Ogun's attempts to take over the responsibilities of his protégé's crime: 'In all that he did, he followed my bidding. I will speak for him.' (p. 66.)

Demoke's open confession of his crime (as well as a triumphant assertion of his act of creation) is in contrast to the reactions of both Adenebi and Rola to the proddings of Forest Head. Adenebi, for ever shoring up the façade of respectability which covers his real nature, never admits anything. We can only deduce his complicity in municipal corruption. He staves off the questions of Obaneji (Forest Head) with a show of sensitive anger. (p. 17.) He is equally furious at the same questioner's attempt to get him to say what sort of death he would like to die (the answers of both Rola and Demoke are self-revelatory). Adenebi misses the opportunity of self-examination and confession offered by Forest Head, and hence disqualifies himself from benefiting from the significance of the welcome of the dead.

Rola's reaction is different again. Once pushed to the corner she fiercely turns against her accusers. (It is significant that Adenebi baits her mercilessly: 'What! No shame. No shame at all,' (p. 22), while Demoke is almost protective.) Indeed she seems at one point to lay the blame for her conduct on her nature: 'I owe all that happened to my nature.' But she also admits her own responsibility in a defiant, satisfied way: 'I only know I am master of my fate. I have turned my training to good account. I am wealthy, and I know where my wealth comes from.' (p. 24.) There is some honesty here which is totally absent from Adenebi's hypocritical reactions. Rola could thus take some meaning from the vision at the end. These then are the three living human protagonists who witness the welcome of the dead.

The dead, variously called by uneasy humans 'accusers', 'executioners' and other derogatory names have been invited by Aroni to trouble the conscience of the living. Their appearance does have this effect. Demoke's father is the most concerned to drive them back. He wants to keep the part of the past which these dead represent, hidden. To him in particular they bring memories of his son's crime which he would not have revealed. But he really speaks for men in general when he says that these particular dead 'have come to undermine our strength. To preach to us how ignoble we are.' The Old Man is here resisting the truth about himself and the rest of mankind; he is denying his true history and his true nature. It was he and Adenebi who had put the proposal to the Council to invite representatives of the ancestors as guests at the Gathering, but they only wanted guests who would flatter their ideas of themselves. They only wanted the noble, not the ignoble side of their history and their nature represented. 'We were sent the wrong people. We asked for statesmen and were sent executioners.' (p. 30.) and 'If we can drive them away from here, it will be sufficient.' (p. 29.)

This refusal to face the fact that man is capable of both creation and destruction, of both nobility and meanness, and the consequent failure to take this into good account in national thinking, constitute a dangerous romanticism. It makes men totally unprepared when the results of this other side – the evil side – of their natures suddenly overtake them. For Soyinka even outside this play, Africans (particularly writers) who indulge in this kind of myth-making are lulling their people into a dangerously false sense of virtue out of which a sudden discovery of their own viciousness rudely wakes them and finds them unprepared:

> We, whose humanity the poets celebrated before the proof, whose lyric innocence was daily questioned by the pages of the newspapers, are now being forced by disaster, not foresight, to a reconsideration of our relationship with the outer world. It seems that the time has now come when the African writer must have the courage to determine what alone can be salvaged from the recurrent cycle of human stupidity.
>
> The myth of irrational nobility, of a racial essence that must come to the rescue of the white depravity, has run its full course. It never in fact existed, for this was not the problem but the camouflage.[3]

The Old Man in trying to hunt the Dead Man and Woman away from earth, to smoke them out with petrol fumes, is involved in a game of 'camouflage'; of smothering the truth under a pall of smoke. Fortunately the Old Man's son – Demoke – acknowledges the presence of the dead, and through this, acknowledges the duality of man's nature so that (as apparently happened to him when he murdered his apprentice) man's viciousness will not take him by surprise. Unfortunately for most men it is the camouflage, the racial myth, that is important. Conscience and the unpleasant parts of

[3] Soyinka, 'The Writer in a Modern African State', in Per Wastberg (ed.), *The Writer in Modern Africa* (Uppsala, 1968) p. 20.

the truth, represented by the dead, must be suppressed. Eventually the truth comes out; the ancestors cannot be so easily got rid of and the Old Man's efforts prove futile. As the Elder Agboreko asks: 'Will you never believe that you cannot get rid of ancestors with the little toys of children . . .' (p. 41.)

The historical section of the play, the Court of Mata Kharibu, is an evocation of the truth of the past. Such a court had been in the minds of the Old Man and Adenebi when they made their proposal for the invitation – 'Mali, Songhai. Perhaps a descendant of the great Lisabi. Zimbabwe. Maybe the legendary Prester John himself . . . I was thinking of heroes like they.' (*Five Plays*, p. 33.) The court shown in the play has the external trappings of what Adenebi wanted. Mata Kharibu is powerful and keeps a glittering court but he is also vicious. He is surrounded by learned men, but they do not have the courage to speak the truth. The one man in the court who has the courage to speak the truth is emasculated and sold as a eunuch. The Court Scene is beautifully balanced. The brutal tyranny of Mata Kharibu on one side of the stage is complemented by the coquettish cruelty of Madame Tortoise on the other. The results are the same – the condemnation of human beings to death in fulfilment of a whim. Both violate the sanctity of human life for trivial purposes. The Court contained not only prostituted academics and distinguished bribe-takers, but also that sinister figure (usually pictured as an alien but here pictured as one of the nation) the slave dealer – a man who thrives on the miseries of others. All the characters are recognizable in our own times. Soyinka underlines this by giving the Historian, the Poet and Madame Tortoise a contemporary existence, as well as by bringing the dead man and woman from this court into the contemporary world to witness against the living.

The whole play moves towards the 'welcome of the dead' which Aroni has organized on behalf of Forest Head. This is the real climax. The earlier sections prepare the minds of the mortal characters for the experience and inexorably draw all the participants to the scene of welcome.

The human characters have been looked at, but a glance at some of the Forest dwellers – the gods – is necessary. Forest Head is the supreme deity; the creator who has endowed man with free will, and now has to endure the pain of watching his creation perversely choosing the wrong path over and over again.

Interfering would be to deny man his free will and Forest Head will not do this. All he can do is every so often – at the completion of a cycle – to give man an opportunity of looking into his real self 'pierce the encrusta-tions of soul-deadening habit, and bare the mirror of original nakedness – knowing full well, it is all futility'. (*Five Plays*, p. 82.) It is to this end the welcome ceremony is staged.

Aroni, who acts on behalf of Forest Head and who like an Elizabethan 'Presenter' gives a prologue to the play, is an embodiment of wisdom and justice. His role then is to bring men to justice and make public what is hidden. In the words of Agboreko:

Aroni is Widom itself. When he means to expose the weaknesses of human lives, there is nothing can stop him. And he knows how to choose his time.   (*Five Plays*, pp. 34–5.)

Agboreko's reference to 'the scales of Aroni' (p. 35) emphasizes his judicial role. He does not however pass judgement. He only 'exposes' the evidence in the hope that the right self-verdict will be given by man himself. 'Let the future judge them by reversal of its path or by stubborn continuation.' (p. 67.)

Ogun and Eshuoro, although Forest Dwellers (gods), are curiously linked to men, not only by the fact that they are respectively patrons of Demoke and Oremole, but also by their human-like conduct. Forest Head who has to come between them as they spring at each other's throats, comments: 'Soon, I will not tell you from the humans, so closely have their habits grown on you.' (*Five Plays*, p. 67.) They are contrasted one with the other, but they are also shown (as are the humans) as embodying contradictions within themselves. (It is probably wise to take these two beings as they are defined within the play rather than to bring too much from external knowledge of the Yoruba Pantheon. In any case Eshuoro is a special creation for the play of a combination of two deities Eshu and Oro.) The two deities are introduced by Aroni in his opening 'testimony':

Eshuoro is the wayward flesh of ORO – Oro whose agency serves much of the bestial human, whom they invoke for terror. OGUN, they deify, for his playground is the battlefield, but he loves the anvil and protects all carvers, smiths, and all workers in metal.
            (*Five Plays*, p. 2.)

Eshuoro (also described in the list of characters as a wayward cult-spirit) comes out in the play as an enemy of man, particularly of the noble part of man's nature. His attitude to Demoke's totem seems to bear this out. He is unable to see the work of art; he is so obsessed with the desecration of his tree and the insult to his dignity that this implies:

The totem, my final insult. The final taunt from the human pigs. The tree that is marked down for Oro, the tree from which my follower fell to his death . . . But my body was stripped by the impious hands

of Demoke, Ogun's favoured slave of the forge. My head was hacked
off by his axe. Trampled on, bled on, my body's shame pointed at the
sky by the edge of Demoke, will I let this day pass without vengeance
claimed blood for sap?   (*Five Plays*, pp. 47–8.)

This is the voice of pique. Eshuoro's anger seems to spread over all men –
'the human pigs' – and transcends the single act of Demoke. It is as a
general enemy of man that he functions in the final pageant of the play.
His inability to see the work of art reminds us of the philistinism of
Adenebi. Murete is infuriated by Eshuoro's attitude to the totem and his
speech points to the place of art in Forest Head's scheme of things:

that is
an offering which would have gladdened the heart of Forest Father
himself. He would have called it adulation. Did he not himself teach
them the arts, and must they be confined to little rooted chips which
fall off when Eshuoro peels like a snake of the previous year . . .?

This restores the balance. For Eshuoro appears as something of the
protector of the forest. He quite rightly resents the indiscriminate
deforestation and pollution which has taken place: 'Have you seen how
much of the forest has been torn down for their petty decorations?' (p. 45),
and 'The whole forest stinks. Stinks of human obscenities.' (p. 46.)
(Indiscriminate deforestation is often a signal of human vandalism – in *The
Lion and the Jewel*, for example.) In extending his wrath to the totem and
condemning it, however, Eshuoro shows a lack of discrimination and
taste. He acts out of mere pique and ruins his case. In any event his pique
leads him to work his rage out on Murete's tree thus neutralizing
somewhat his role as protector of the Forest. (pp. 44–5.) Eshuoro also
seems to be incapable of seeing the heroism of the Warrior's conduct: 'The
soldier was a fool. A woman. He was a woman.' (p. 65.) He obviously
preferred the bloodthirsty self-destructive path of man. His general
malevolence to man is seen even more clearly in the final dance.

Ogun is prominent in the play as the god of creativity and of art. He is
Demoke's patron and champion. He defends everything Demoke does
and accepts responsibility for his crime. 'I, Ogun, swear that his hands
were mine in every action of his life.' (p. 67.) This is of course an excessive
claim as Forest Head's rejoinder implies. But it at least establishes his
complicity in, and condonation of, the crime. He too, like his protégé,
combines both the elements of creativity and destruction – 'His playground
is the battle-field' as well as the studio. He and Demoke seem to be on the
same side of the struggle for the Half-Child at the end. He is thus identified

with man in the struggle against the merely bestial which Eshuoro represents.

These qualities of the gods are important in an interpretation of the complex dance which is the climax of *A Dance of the Forests*. From the very opening of the play attention is directed to a trial at the end. The dead man and woman come out of the ground looking for human advocates to take their 'case'. It soon becomes clear that a trial is to be organized by Forest Head: 'Forest Father, masquerading as a human,/Bringing them to judgement.' (p. 29.) The nature of this judgement is further revealed as a process of self-judgement and self-condemnation to be undertaken by the humans themselves. It is Aroni's purpose 'To let the living condemn themselves'. (p. 37.) Later Forest Head himself gives out that he has summoned the welcoming 'for ends of my own' (p. 67), which in the words of Aroni are to give man an opportunity for regeneration. 'It is enough that they discover their own regeneration.' The particular cases of the Dead Man and Woman become involved with a more general case involving all mankind. It is ironical that at first the Dead Man and Woman look at Demoke to take their case until they discover that he too is on trial: 'What is this? The one who was to take my case – has he sent another down? Into the pit?' (p. 26.)

The hearing of the particular cases of the Dead Man and Woman becomes mixed up in the general trial at the end. In the more general case of man which soon emerges, the Dead Woman speaks not just for herself. Her question is 'For all the rest':

> Say someone comes
> For all the rest. Say someone asks –
> Was it for this, for this,
> Children plagued their mothers? (p. 69.)

The question suggests a consciousness of the ultimate futility of human life. Was it worth it all? In her particular case – she is accused of depriving her unborn child of life by herself committing suicide – she pleads weakness. She did not see the point of continuing either her own or the child's life. She had in fact tried to save the child the futility of life. But this is wrong. The suffering cannot be escaped, as Forest Head points out: 'Child, there is no choice but one of suffering.' This point having been established, interest shifts from the Woman to the Dead Man. His appearance establishes that all his three existences (the other two are not indicated) have entailed unjustified suffering, and like the Dead Woman he wants rest: 'I have come to sleep.' (p. 70.) The Questioner (Eshuoro in disguise) accuses him of having learnt nothing. He had let power (in the Court of

Mata Kharibu) slip through his fingers. He is to be condemned to wander a hundred years more. Eshuoro is merely repeating his earlier opinion which encourages man's degeneracy. At this inconclusive stage of his particular case the Dead Man is ushered off and never appears again. The two particular cases seem to be dropped but the Dead Woman features prominently in the drama of the Half-Child later.

A new drama is introduced when the three human protagonists are masked and become possessed so that they speak, not in their own voices, but for the various spirits who now appear. Into this drama is woven the drama of the Half-Child, the details of which have caused readers of this play most trouble.[4] The chorus of the spirits by comparison is fairly straightforward. The spirits together symbolize the total environment of Africa – all its resources and all its potentialities. To what purpose will they all be used? The suggestions are that they will be used unwisely, even destructively. The spirit of the palm whose sap is ordinarily life giving – it 'suckles' – will turn to blood, because of the evil in man's nature – 'blackened hearts'.

> White skeins wove me, I, Spirit of the Palm
> Now course I red.
> I who suckle blackened hearts, know
> Heads will fall down
> Crimson in their bed!

The imagery indicates a violation of the processes of life; a contamination of the sources of nourishment for life. (Soyinka frequently portrays this idea through images of an aborted harvest.) Each spirit speaks in a similar vein, showing man doomed through a perverse exploitation of his resources. The pollution of the sources of life so that they become the sources of death is clearly imaged in the chorus of the waters:

> Let no man then lave his feet
> In any stream, in any lake
> In rapids or in cataracts
> Let no woman think to bake
> Her cornmeal wrapped in leaves
> With water gathered of the rain
> He'll think his eye deceives
> Who treads the ripples where I run
> In shallows.   (pp. 75–6.)

[4] For a summary of the different readings of Ulli Beier and Una Maclean, and Margaret Laurence's own interpretation see the latter's *Long Drums and Cannons*, especially p. 43.

The Half-Child too joins in the chorus of a doomed future: 'I'll be born dead/I'll be born dead.'

The Ants, representing the masses who are exploited by their leaders (they had been mischievously persuaded to come to the trial by Eshuoro) picture their enslaved and exploited state: 'We are the ever legion of the world,/Smitten, for – "the good to come".' (p. 78.) The facile political morality of leaders is given dramatic form in the distorted triplets. They are physical manifestations of the rhetorical distortions which are used to justify political crimes: 'I am the Greater Cause, standing ever ready excusing the crimes of today for tomorrow's mirage.' The satire on human perversity is obvious in passages like these; the significance of these symbols is not obscure.

The Half-Child, it has been suggested earlier, is a symbol for man's future. That this future is doomed is clear in the Half-Child's chorus 'I'll be born dead'. But Soyinka involves him in a further tableau whose significance is less clear. He engages (against his will) in a game of *sesan* with Figure in Red (who turns out to be Eshuoro), and loses. His life is thus forfeited to the bestial Eshuoro. But Eshuoro is not allowed to carry off his prize. Ogun intervenes. We recall here the contrast between the natures of Ogun and Eshuoro and read into his act some sort of salvation for the child. The fate of the Half-Child is for some time in the balance, with Eshuoro and his jester trying to win him to one side, while his mother, Demoke and Ogun all seem to fight on the other side to save the child. These forces are the natural mother (though this is complicated in that this one is dead), the artist representing the noble side of man's nature, and the god of creativity. The peril of the Half-Child is vividly dramatized in the dance in which it is tossed between Eshuoro, the third triplet (posterity) and Eshuoro's jester, while Demoke tries to rescue the child from the obvious peril represented by the knives.[5] It is Ogun, however, who intervenes, rescues the child, and passes him to Demoke. Here the symbolism is so thick that one can only make suggestions for an interpretation.

Demoke having rescued the child stands confused. Although the mother had originally wanted to be relieved of her burden and leave the living child with the living ('I said the living would save me' [p. 26], and 'I thought . . . here was a chance to return the living to the living that I may sleep lighter' [p. 5]), at this point she seems to have changed her mind and wants the child back – she mutely appeals to Demoke (for the child).

[5] This perilous dance, for which Soyinka had to substitute a different tableau in the alternative ending of the play, is done by professional dancers in many parts of West Africa. Geoffrey Gorer describes such a dance in *Africa Dances* (Faber, London, 1935), p. 317.

(p. 82). Demoke apparently cannot in any case be allowed to keep the child because his keeping it would in some way 'reverse the deed that was begun many lives ago'. Therefore 'the Forest will not let you'. (p. 82.) Demoke's act would somehow have broken the cycle. Now this would have been clear had the dilemma been Ogun's – if, for example, he had hesitated between keeping the child under his own protection and hence interfering, or giving the child to Demoke as a representative of the living thus leaving man with his free will. He does not hesitate, however, and hands the child to Demoke. What then is the significance of Demoke's dilemma and his handing the child to the Dead Woman who presumably returns with it to the world of the dead (for ever? Can he be born again?)? At this point even the suggestion that the Half-Child is a symbol for man's future begins to look weak.[6]

Leaving aside intransigent details, the general point seems to be that Forest Head will not intervene; man is returned to his own kind and the exercise of his free will with the risk that he will continue to frustrate his own happiness. The cycle continues as before.

This whole pageant has been laid on for the benefit of the human protagonists. They pass through fire, and the effect on Demoke is traumatic. Although three humans witness the welcome, only two appear afterwards. Adenebi fades out – not surprisingly perhaps because of his insensitive nature. But only the most insensitive can come through the vision unchanged. Demoke suggests that they will never be the same again: 'We three who lived many lives in this one night, have we not done enough? Have we not felt enough for the memory of our remaining lives?' (p. 85.) Certainly Madame Tortoise is not the same. That she survives alive surprises Agboreko: 'I did not think to find her still alive.' She seems regenerated – 'chastened' – having been seared by the same 'lightning' as Demoke.

While there are people capable of undergoing the spiritual experience of total introspection, of piercing 'the encrustations of soul-deadening habit' which is represented by the participation in the welcome ceremony, there is presumably some hope for man's regeneration. Even so, this is not certain. (It is significant that the humans are compelled by Forest Head to face the truth about themselves in this way.) The general picture which emerges from the play is that of man ruthlessly exploiting his natural environment and other men for his own limited, selfish ends; of man so

[6] For a valuable contribution on the significance of Demoke's act, see Nick Wilkinson's 'Demoke's choice in Soyinka's *A Dance of the Forests: Journal of Commonwealth Literature*, 10, 3 (1976), pp. 22–7; reprinted in James Gibbs (ed.), *Critical Perspectives on Wole Soyinka* (Washington, DC: Three Continents Press, 1980).

preoccupied with his material concerns that he neglects matters of the spirit, and grows progressively insensitive. The play suggests the need for an occasional pause for thought – in the case of Nigeria what better time than the occasion of independence and the start of a new cycle? On such occasions instead of a total absorption in the externals of celebration, instead of whitewashing our history and true nature in pageants of splendour, men should face the truth, the whole truth about themselves, and with a mixture of hope and trepidation move into the uncertain future.

A Dance of the Forests has all the ingredients for a spectacular play, but only in the most capable hands. A bad production would be an unmitigated disaster. The set has to suggest the timeless element of the play, particularly in the welcome scene when the stage directions require a setting suggestive of a meeting point of existences. The dark wet atmosphere suggests the 'dark backward and abysm' of time – the scene of the beginnings of amoebal life – while the 'rotting wood' and 'mounds' suggest an apocalyptic scene of death and the end of life. This recreation would require all the ingenuity of the technician:

> *Back-scene lights up gradually to reveal a dark, wet, atmosphere dripping moisture, and soft, moist soil. A palm tree sways at a low angle, broken but still alive. Seemingly lightning-reduced stumps. Rotting wood all over the ground. A mound or two here and there.*

This unearthly scene is necessary to convey the out-of-time atmosphere of the last section of the play. The Mata Kharibu section has to be differently lit again from the here-and-now scenes in the forest.

The costuming too gives opportunity for spectacular designs which should at the same time clearly distinguish the characters one from another and remind the audience of their identities when they appear either in disguise or in different historical periods. It would probably be helpful during Aroni's 'testimony' which introduces the main lines of the play, if the characters appear on the stage in a tableau as they are named. The ironies implicit in Forest Head's exchanges with the human characters would be immediately appreciated by the audience if he has already been introduced and seen as Forest Head disguised as Obaneji during Aroni's 'testimony'. The final tableau with spirits of things (whose distinctive natures would have to be suggested by their costumes), masked humans, a Half-Child, the grotesque triplets, ants, gods, all describing their own movement patterns, would make either a spectacular scene or total confusion. The hazards of staging aptly reflect the hazards of interpreting this grandly complex play.

The Strong Breed

▼▼▼▼▼▼▼▼▼▼▼▼▼▼▼▼▼▼▼▼▼▼▼▼▼▼▼▼▼▼▼

The Strong Breed is an extraordinarily compact play. In spite of its comparative brevity it is one of Soyinka's most significant works in which one of the playwright's constant preoccupations – the need for sacrifice – is dramatized. It is also one of Soyinka's most symbolic plays. (*Camwood on the Leaves*,[1] a radio play, is more obviously symbolic but lacks the subtlety of this play.) It avoids cluttering detail, and thus succeeds in presenting its themes in an archetypal form. Evil, for example, about which the play is so concerned, the evil of the village which has to be expiated is never defined although it hovers over the whole play like a pall. The effect of this avoidance of definition is to give the play a generality of application. Sacrifice too, which Eman represents, is treated symbolically. The 'carrier' obviously in the case of the effigy, but also in the case of Eman-as-carrier is a symbol for the moral force required to save the society.

Eman's sacrifice is modelled on the sacrifice of Christ, whose death is recalled by a number of subtle references. Like Christ, Eman is both teacher and healer. This is economically dramatized before even the first words of the play are spoken. (Soyinka's stage directions are almost always significant, but the opening ones particularly so, for they often have symbolic significance.) When the play opens, '*Sunma is clearing the table of what looks like a modest clinic . . . Another rough table in the room is piled with exercise-books, two or three worn text-books etc.*' (*Five Plays*, p. 237.) The suggestions of this opening tableau are dramatized later in Eman's painful efforts at helping in the rehabilitation of the helpless idiot Ifada, as well as in his kindness to the inscrutable girl who, Judas-like, betrays him. Eman eventually goes on to carry the evil of the village on his own head. The parallel with Christ continues in that Eman works among people who neither understand nor really want him. As Sunma complains, 'You are wasting your life on people who really want you out of their way.' (p. 244.) Other analogies with Christ are Eman's conscious sacrifice of himself for an ungrateful people, his supreme sacrifice taking the form of his being hanged on a sacred tree. Towards the climax of the physical sacrifice, his body flinches, and he needs water. Eman's pathetic appeal to the girl who betrays him parallels Christ's agonized cry 'I thirst'. Eman's death, like

[1] *Camwood on the Leaves* (Eyre Methuen, London, 1973).

Christ's, stuns the people in whose name it had been demanded, and leaves a remarkable impression on some unlikely minds. There is no dramatic parallel to the dying thief, but one of the elders of the village, Oroge, suddenly pauses at a crucial stage of the pursuit of Eman, because he has caught a reflection of something in the victim's face which impresses him: 'He saw something. Why may I not know what it was?' (p. 262.) This influence at his death is also reflected in the inability of the villagers 'to raise a curse' – the traditional curse with which each man is expected to empty his evil on the victim. The analogies with Christ also link Eman with Soyinka's crucified figure in his poem 'The Dreamer' which is examined elsewhere in this book (pp. 130–1). Eman, then, within the play is the saviour.

In consonance with the archetypal nature of the play, the evil against which he works is not treated in detail. It is nevertheless potently symbolized. It is an opposite force to what Eman himself represents. He is sensitive to human need regardless of kinship, while in the tradition of the village, outsiders are fair game. It is easy to see here a symbolic treatment of that ethnic exclusiveness, tribalism, which so bedevils life in modern Africa, but the applications are even wider. Eman represents a responsiveness to human need wherever it arises. He himself is a 'stranger' in a village where the plight of the stranger, particularly on the eve of the New Year, is a fearful one. An early tableau dramatizes this: '*Two villagers, obvious travellers, pass hurriedly in front of the house . . . the man enters first, turns and urges the woman who is just emerging to hurry.*' (p. 237.) The reason for the anxiety of the travellers to escape from the hostile village becomes clear as the play develops. Sunma, an insider who has become disgusted with the village and seeks to escape from it refers to the tribal exclusiveness in one of her appeals to Eman to leave: 'Have you not noticed how tightly we shut out strangers? Even if you lived here for a lifetime, you remain a stranger.' (p. 247.) But the attitude of the village to strangers goes further. A stranger is required to bear the evils of the village, a task none of the villagers has the moral strength to undertake. Their seeming kindness to outsiders like the helpless Ifada is shown to be a mere device for recruiting victims:

> OROGE: No one in his senses would do such a job. Why do you think we give refuge to idiots like him? We don't know where he came from. One morning, he is simply there, just like that. From nowhere at all. You see, there is a purpose in that.
>
> (p. 254.)

Ifada thus becomes a prime candidate for the ordeal of 'carrier'. To Eman this is appalling – 'But why do you pick on a helpless boy? Obviously he is not willing.' (p. 253.) He has been brought up in a different tradition: 'In my home, we believe that a man should be willing.' (p. 253.) There is a confrontation of values here which leads directly to Eman's substitution of himself for Ifada, and his assumption of the role of the willing carrier of the evils of the village, a decision which leads to his martyrdom. Eman's humanity is in contrast to the brutal callousness of the village. He is a moral force without which the village would remain unregenerate in spite of the ritual of an annual sacrifice.

If Eman is the symbol of a human response to need, the inscrutable girl symbolizes the attitudes of the village. She is curiously detached and is totally unaffected by human need. The stage directions make the following requirements of the actress: *'The girl is unsmiling. She possesses in fact, a kind of inscrutability which does not make her hard but is unsettling.'* (p. 240.) Her sickness also isolates her from the rest of the village – a fact she states without much discomposure: 'I am unwell you know . . . Don't you know I play alone? The other children won't come near me. Their mothers would beat them.' (p. 241.) Typically in the play the precise nature of her illness is not stated. It merely isolates her and, in her mother's hope, will disappear, borne away by her carrier with the old year. (p. 241.) It is significant that she does not seek medical help for the illness, and refuses to go near Eman who runs a free clinic. Her sickness seems to be another symbol for archetypal evil. To Sunma, 'She is not a child. She is as evil as the rest of them.' (p. 242.) All her actions confirm her as cold-blooded and selfish, characteristics she shares with the rest of the village.

In the symbolism of the play, her carrier also represents Eman; this effigy is tortured and eventually hanged to represent his fate. Given the child's identification with the village, this use of her carrier is most appropriate, and saves the play from a distracting concern with the details of Eman's agony which could have reduced tragedy to melodrama. The girl of course proves to be a Judas and callously betrays Eman when at the end of the play he asks her for water, and instead of giving it to him she reveals his hiding-place to his pursuers.

Her callousness is manifested particularly in her relations with Ifada whom she merely uses because he is all that is available. Ifada is the play's symbol of need, a need which makes no more impression on the girl than it does on the village she represents. To her Ifada is a despicable object for which, however, because of her isolation she has some need. (This reflects exactly the boy's position in the village as a whole.) The girl's invitation to play comes at the end of a callous inventory:

[after a long, cool survey of Ifada]
You have a head like a spider's egg, and your mouth dribbles like a roof. But there is no one else. Would you like to play?   (p. 242.)

Sunma is a member of the village, but one who moves in the play from consciousness of the evil of the village and a desire to escape from it, to an open renunciation of its evil, a renunciation which totally isolates her from the protection of the village, and thus puts her in line for a path which might, like Eman's, lead to a life of further sacrifice.

Sunma's concern for most of the play is that she and Eman should escape from a village that had come to revolt her. Obviously she has come under his influence and is inclined to his way of life. It is she who is seen clearing away the tools of Eman's trade in the opening tableau. What she lacks is Eman's extraordinary strength which enables him to keep his composure in the face of evil. She has to get away from it:

I wonder if I really sprang from here. I know they are evil and I am not. From the oldest to the smallest child, they are nourished in evil and unwholesomeness in which I have no part.

But you must help me tear myself away from here. (p. 244.)

In her consciousness of evil and her instinctive desire to run away from something she has come to hate, Sunma is a good, humane person, but unlike Eman, an *ordinarily* good, humane person. She lacks the strength of an *exceptionally* good, humane, person such as Eman is. (Eman is after all one of the Strong Breed – an exceptional breed as the play makes clear.) She had in fact run away once before, but had bravely returned to help Eman in his work. (p. 244.) Eman is thus a prop to her weak humanity. Without her strong attachment to him, she would have left the village and its needs for ever. At the opening of the play she is poised once again on a moment of decision: 'Eman, are we going or aren't we? You will leave it till too late.' (p. 237.) And again: 'It is the time for making changes in one's life.' (p. 245.) Eman will not leave and, as the sounds of the departing lorry symbolize, the moment of decision passes, and she stays on with Eman in his battle with evil. She is thus forced to remain and continue to face the evil of the village. Already in her heart she had renounced this evil, but her open renunciation was to come later in the confrontation with her father.

Sunma's attempts at escape are of a piece with her sudden fierce hostility towards Ifada at the beginning of the play. This too is an attempt at escape. She after all had seemed to be as responsive to Ifada's need as Eman who is consequently surprised at her sudden outbursts against the boy. After one of her expressions of disgust – 'horrible insect' – Eman cannot conceal his surprise: 'I don't understand. It is *Ifada* you know. Ifada! the unfortunate one who runs errands for you and doesn't hurt a soul.' (p. 238.) Sunma's frustration at Eman's refusal to leave finds an outlet in the symbol of the need which keeps him tied to the village. Indeed as Eman points out, 'It is almost as if you are forcing yourself to hate him. Why?' (p. 240.) Sunma is trying another break from her responsibility; she is trying to escape into hatred from love – the responsibilities of love make much greater demands than those of hate. Her decision to stay by Eman has committed her to a path the full consequences of which appear later. She reinforces her mental renunciation of the evil of the village with a physical confrontation with her father in which the antipathy of their conflicting attitudes is externally dramatized. Sunma attacks her father savagely, drawing blood. The symbolic struggle is brief but intense:

> [*Jaguna turns just in time to see Sunma fly at him, clawing at his face like a crazed tigress.*]
> SUNMA: Murderer! What are you doing to him. Murderer! Murderer!
> [*Jaguna finds himself struggling really hard to keep off his daughter, he succeeds in pushing her off and striking her so hard on the face that she falls to her knees. He moves on her to hit her again.*]
> OROGE: [*comes between*]: Think what you are doing, Jaguna, she is your daughter.
> JAGUNA: My daughter! Does this one look like my daughter? Let me cripple the harlot for life . . .
> [*Draws his hand across his cheek – it is covered with blood.*]
>   (pp. 262–3.)

This is Sunma's final break with the society. It is true that this open confrontation is stimulated by her personal concern for the fate of Eman who at this point is being pursued as the victim, but it is no less of a conscious break with evil for all that. It is an evil which she had mentally renounced much earlier anyway. Whatever the reasons, her actions had now made her an outsider.

Her position in this regard is dramatized by her new relationship with Ifada. She had tried earlier to reject him, identifying him with the cause of her frustration. Now, after the break with Jaguna, she accepts him as rescuer, comforter and friend. The tableau required by the stage directions after the fight between father and daughter dramatizes the new relationship:

> [. . . *Ifada, who came in with Sunma and had stood apart, horror-stricken, comes shyly forward. He helps Sunma up. They go off, he holding Sunma bent and sobbing.*]   (p. 263.)

Later too they are united by their common feelings at the sight of the hanging effigy which represents the martyred Eman. Their feelings are in contrast to the reactions of the girl who stands 'impassively watching', as detached from any contact with the human situation as she has always been.

The role of Eman has been incidentally demonstrated in the examination of other characters, since he is central to the play. He represents a moral force which transcends social boundaries. His is the broad humanity which the world both needs and rejects at the same time, while individuals and individual societies relentlessly pursue their particular concerns. But Eman is also a man. As a son and a pupil, he has relations with a father and his tutor. As a lover and husband he suffers the agony of losing his wife. He is human enough to prefer a quiet life to a life of self-sacrifice, but eventually an inner urge which he is unable to resist drives him on to accept the burden of sacrifice. He cannot escape this role because he is of the Strong Breed.

Through the concept of the Strong Breed Soyinka makes the point that the quality of personal leadership through suffering is not a common characteristic. It is rare. This is well symbolized in the notion of the carrier. The role carries with it a tremendous moral burden at which strong men flinch. It involves a moral preparedness which is implied in these words of Eman's father as he prepares to carry the evils of his own village:

A man should be at his strongest when he takes the boat, my friend. To be weighed down inside and out is not a wise thing. I hope when the moment comes I shall have found my strength! (p. 259.)

Such is the weight of the burden, that the men of Jaguna's village have to foist the role of an unwilling outsider trapped for the purpose. For them, in the words of Oroge, 'No one in his senses would do such a job.' (p. 254.) Such then is the burden – its weight but not its detail is defined – which Eman assumes on behalf of strangers. The martyr is often a man who in the eyes of the world is out of his mind. His conduct is inexplicable in terms of a selfish rat race in which each man fends for himself. But as Soyinka reiterates in his work, without this type of self-sacrificing man society cannot be saved (even temporarily) from itself.

Eman's path is essentially a lonely one from the start. The main value for him of the traditional period of initiation is the opportunity it gives for individual labour and solitary contemplation. As for the specific ritual 'It is a small thing one can do in the big towns.' (p. 269.) He points out the significance of the period for him to Omae in one of the flashbacks to his earlier life:

This is an important period of my life. Look, These huts, we built
them with our own hands. Every boy built his own. We learn things,
do you understand? And we spend much time just thinking. At least I
do, it is the first time I have had nothing to do except think. Don't
you see, I am becoming a man. For the first time, I understand that I
have a life to fulfil.

And a little later, 'A man must go on his own, go where no one can help
him, and test his strength.' (p. 266.) This is the lonely road of the man of
genius, whose renewing influence society sorely needs.

When Eman discovers the hollowness of his tutor – the latter is one of
Soyinka's many false prophets and leaders – he suddenly leaves the place
of initiation – he has got all he wants out of it – and goes on a lonely
pilgrimage. Once he has made up his mind, nothing can stop him. Omae's
pathetic attempts to hold him back – he actually drags her along as she
clings to him – are paralleled by the fruitlessness of Sunma's attempts to
make him leave her village and its evil. All the essential decisions for Eman
are personal ones made after a lonely internal struggle. In this lies the
uniqueness of this type of character; from it also arises his seeming
callousness to the normal human ties – of love for example. The pilgrim
(another favourite figure for the type – see 'Idanre' for another example)
has to leave all, and follow his chosen life – 'Nothing ties me down'.
(p. 269.)

Eman's sacrifice really ends the play. The possible effects on society
are only faintly suggested. His effect on Sunma is clear; she will never be
the same again after having met and worked with him, but she is an
ordinary individual, without Eman's strength. (His death and her very
isolation might possibly produce the necessary strength.) Oroge's
momentary glimpse of something in Eman's face at the height of the chase
has been noticed earlier. (Will anything come of it?) The most general
effect is seen in the horrified reaction of the villagers at the sight of him
hanging on the tree. In the words of Jaguna himself who is totally
unmoved by the sacrifice, 'One and all they looked up at the man
and words died in their throats.' (p. 275.) They should have poured
their curses on the helpless victim but the sight of their selfless
benefactor hanging dead penetrated to a sensitive vein. They 'fled' their
leaders. That is all the reaction. How far will this experience take them?
How effectively will the already threatened reprisals of Jaguna kill the
incipient reaction? We do not know. It is apparently enough that the
sacrifice has been made and noticed. The silent set tableau on which the
lights fade at the end of the play represents a society still in need of
salvation.

[. . . *Sunma, her last bit of will gone, crumbles against the wall. Some distance away from them, partly hidden, stands the Girl, impassively watching. Ifada hugs the effigy to him, stands above Sunma. The Girl remains where she is, observing . . .*] (p. 275.)

What price salvation?

Soyinka's use of scrambled chronology – a feature of *The Interpreters* – is noteworthy here. The flashback which gives us a glimpse of the past as a fill-in on the present is a favourite device of the playwright. Faintly suggested in *The Swamp-Dwellers* (Makuri's narration of their wedding night's escapade in the marsh) the technique is more elaborately exploited in *The Lion and the Jewel*. In *The Strong Breed* we have the backward flashes into Eman's past, some of which he watches from his position in the present of the play, thus giving an uncanny feeling of a suspension of the dimension of time. This effect is further heightened in the pageant at the end as Eman disappears from the play to his death behind the scenes, symbolically following the path of his father in what must be taken as his mental evocation of his father's last journey as carrier. Soyinka externalizes Eman's thoughts as he must have remembered his earlier attempts to renounce his inherited role, and the words of his father: 'Your own blood will betray you, son, because you cannot hold it back. If you make it do less than this, it will rush to your head and burst it open.' (p. 261.) He has now offered himself as a victim – a role he had declared himself unfitted for – but his body has flinched, and he is now running away from the ordeal. The sight of his father (in his mind, for the father had been long dead) revives his will, and he accepts his role to follow in his father's footsteps (the metaphor is made flesh). 'Wait, father. I am coming with you . . . wait . . . wait for me, father.' (p. 274.) It is the father's turn to flinch, and to try in his paternal concern to divert his son from the path of martyrdom by pointing in the opposite direction. But Eman, with the words just quoted, follows his father to the symbolic river and to the real trap: '[*There is a sound of twigs breaking, of a sudden trembling in the branches. Then silence.*]' (p. 274.) Eman has made the supreme sacrifice.

Soyinka has used a fairly common scapegoat ritual as the vehicle for a tremendous moral statement which once again transcends its setting. One of the playwright's greatest strengths is his ability to manipulate symbols. This is as true of his plays as of his poetry. *The Strong Breed* succeeds in a way that *Camwood on the Leaves* does not. In the radio play both the symbols and what they represent retain their separate entities and operate independently. In *The Strong Breed* there is a complete fusion of object and symbol and a resulting greater suggestiveness.

The Trials of Brother Jero

▼▼▼▼▼▼▼▼▼▼▼▼▼▼▼▼▼▼▼▼▼▼▼▼▼▼▼▼▼▼▼▼▼▼▼▼

The Trials of Brother Jero is a lighthearted satirical comedy based on the activities of the phoney beach prophet, Brother Jeroboam. The satire is there, but it is almost concealed by the predominating humour which depends on a series of undiscovered identities which threaten at any moment to become known and upset the beach prophet's house of cards. As this rickety structure is rocked by one threat after another the comedy of the play is generated.

Brother Jero is a self-confessed rogue who trades on the insecurities of his flock (his 'customers' as he calls them in a moment of candour): 'I know they are dissatisfied because I keep them dissatisfied. Once they are full, they won't come again.' The audience is under no misapprehension about Brother Jero, who describes his approach to his 'trade' from the very beginning of the play. Indeed much of the comedy arises from the discrepancy between what the audience knows Brother Jero to be by his own confession, and the front of holy hermit which he puts on for the benefit of his deluded gulls. The threat of his unmasking sustains the play, and once Chume discovers the true nature of his master, the whole structure threatens to collapse. Soyinka, however, saves the knave in order to make the play's final satirical point.

Chume is the classic victim of the prophet's method. The bane of his life is a wife whose constant scolding and nagging keeps him on the edge of distraction. All the women needs is, according to the desperate husband, 'Just one sound beating . . . But I've got to beat her, Prophet. You must save me from madness.' (*Five Plays*, p. 213.) Brother Jero knows this too, but the release which this beating would bring to Chume's frustrated spirit would deprive the prophet of his most faithful adherent. So he forbids Chume in the name of God to beat his wife. He confides in the audience: 'If I do, he will become contented, and then that's another of my flock gone forever.' The Prophet's grasp of human psychology is sound. But what he does not know is that the woman he is thus protecting is the same dreadful woman who has set up camp outside his house and threatens to keep up the siege until he settles his debt to her. In their double ignorance – Chume of the identity of Amope's debtor, Brother Jero of the relationship between Amope and Chume – lies a potential source of comedy which Soyinka exploits.

Amope's encounter with the unsuspecting prophet is pure comedy; it is the first threat to the prophet's carefully built up image. He escapes from it only because the quarrelsome Amope, instead of maintaining her siege with singlemindedness, picks a side quarrel with a passing fisherwoman during which Brother Jero gratefully escapes. The comedy of the encounter is both visual and verbal. Soyinka is a master of the funny physical situation, and one of his funniest is the discomfiture of the prophet as his careful preparations to climb out of his window and steal away unseen by Amope are shattered by her almost casual [*without looking round*], question: 'Where do you think you're going?' At which, according to the playwright's stage directions [*Brother Jero practically flings himself back into the house*]. (p. 207.) Brother Jero's obvious disadvantage in relation to the entrenched Amope makes him vulnerable so that his attempts to bluff Amope with the prophet façade soon crumble, and the holy man has to change his plea from freedom to do the work of Christ, to an opportunity to get money out of the Post Office Savings Bank. Amope is practised both in repartee and abusive complaint (as poor Chume knows) and she completely demolishes the prophet's façade first with cool repartee then with her indictment:

JERO: [*coughs*] Sister . . . my dear sister in Christ . . .

AMOPE: I hope you slept well, Brother Jero . . .

JERO: Yes, thanks be to God. [*Hems and coughs*] I – er – I hope you have not come to stand in the way of Christ and his work.

AMOPE: If Christ doesn't stand in the way of me and my work.

JERO: Beware of pride, sister. That was a sinful way to talk.

AMOPE: Listen, you bearded debtor. You owe me one pound, eight and nine. You promised you would pay me three months ago but of course you have been too busy doing the work of God. Well, let me tell you that you are not going anywhere until you do a bit of my own work.

JERO: But the money is not in the house. I must get it from the post office before I can pay you.

Only Amope's own inability to miss an opportunity for new quarrels gives the prophet an escape from this tight situation.

Brother Jeroboam's problems with 'the daughters of Eve' are not yet over. He suffers agonies of self-control as the young girl returning from her daily bath in the sea tantalizes the Prophet with her body. When a little later a woman trader runs past chasing the drummer boy, her skirt hitched up for the chase exposing her limbs, the prophet cannot resist this second feminine temptation, and gives chase. From this encounter he returns '*a much altered man, his clothes torn and his face bleeding*'. (p. 220.) The alternation between the devout prophet lashing his flock into holy paroxysms and the woman-chaser – getting for once what he deserves – is good comedy. It is also part of the exposure of the true nature of Jero, but so far only to the audience. Through all his adventures Brother Jero still just manages to mask his unholy activities from his trusting flock but it seems to be only a matter of time before events catch up with him.

The first discovery, however, is his when, taking the opportunity of the prophet's revelation of his own suffering at the hands of 'the Daughters of Discord' Chume pours out once again his sufferings at the hands of his wife, and incidentally reveals her identity to the prophet. Brother Jero is just running into one of his routine injunctions against wife-beating when the penny drops: 'Brother Chume did you say that your wife went to make camp this morning at the house of a . . . of someone who owes her money?' (p. 221.) Brother Jero is unable to resist this obvious chance of vicarious revenge against Amope, and promptly gives Chume permission to beat her. This decision generates more comedy and a further development of the plot, for it leads to Chume's discovery of the connection between Amope and the prophet.

The second encounter between Chume and his wife is in dramatic and comic contrast to their first appearance at the beginning of the play. The comedy here derives from the fact that in the intervening period Chume has become transformed by the prophet's permission, from a tame henpecked husband to a dominating male. First Amope's refusal to recognize the change, then her shock when Chume's unwonted rough handling of her makes the change obvious, produce hilarious comedy. The visual comedy of Chume bundling his wife bodily to the accompaniment of her piercing screams is lively enough. The comic action takes another dramatic turn as Chume in the midst of all this activity makes his discovery. The moment of realization is tantalizingly delayed as he tries to get the screaming woman to answer his questions: 'Did I hear you say Prophet Jeroboam?' . . . Woman, did you say it was the Prophet who owed you money? . . . Is this his house? Does he live here? . . . Is Brother Jeroboam . . .?' Despairing of any answer from the screaming woman Chume turns to a bystander, gets his answer and revelation dawns: 'So . . . so . . . so . . . so . . .'

All would now seem to be set for Chume's confrontation with his master, and a final unmasking, but Soyinka turns away from the obvious ending, and makes an even more telling point. Brother Jero's true nature is no surprise to the audience. He confessed his roguery from the start. An unmasking would have given some physical comedy, but little else. Soyinka introduces a new character, an M.P. who appears just when the prophet needs some prop of influence. Through his help, the prophet can deal with his erstwhile apprentice who has now become troublesome:

> I have already sent for the police. It is a pity about Chume. But he has given me a fright, and no prophet likes to be frightened. With the influence of that nincompoop I should succeed in getting him certified with ease. A year in the lunatic asylum would do him good anyway.
>
> (p. 233.)

The grimness of Chume's fate must not be missed in the general atmosphere of the comedy of the M.P.'s eventual gullibility. That Chume can be treated so unjustly is a telling comment on justice. The plum position which Brother Jero dreams up for the M.P. too has a significance that may be lost in the general comedy; it is 'Minister for War':

> I saw the mustering of men, gathered in the name of peace through strength. And at a desk, in a large gilt room, great men of the land awaited your decision. Emissaries of foreign nations hung on your word, and on the door leading into your office, I read the words, Minister for War.   (p. 230.)

The point is not laid on with a trowel but the passage together with the comment on political influence and justice gives the end of the play and its comic satire a more acid taste. Brother Jero ends the play a more sinister figure than he began. His roguery is now allied to power. He can easily eliminate ordinary mortals like Chume, and, contrary to his deserts (but in keeping with the ways of the perverse world) he survives his day of ordeals and lives to plague his deluded countrymen further. For Brother Jero is a false prophet. His people look pathetically to him for leadership and he replies with deceit. The situation is capable of wider and more sinister applications.

Jero's Metamorphosis

▼▼▼▼▼▼▼▼▼▼▼▼▼▼▼▼▼▼▼▼▼▼▼▼▼▼▼▼▼▼▼▼▼▼▼▼

When Soyinka took up the story of the false prophet again, some nine years later (*Jero's Metamorphosis* was published in 1973),[1] Nigeria was under military rule and had emerged from a costly civil war, the social consequences of which were all too apparent. The Beach, which had given seeming freehold to the rival prophets and their congregations, now provided a more sinister counter-attraction in the Bar Beach Show, the public execution of convicted armed robbers. Prophecy had in a sense been fulfilled, and whether the gullible and ambitious politician in *The Trials* had himself got the job or no, someone had had to function in Nigeria in the office, if not the designation, of Minister for War. Brother Jero, not one to conceal his triumph, reminds Chume, the much misused disciple whose services are once more required – in an even higher capacity – by his master: 'Do you doubt, Brother Chume? Do you doubt my prophecy? Has your sojourn among lunatics made you forget who prophesied war and have we not lived to see it come to pass?' (p. 70.)

The new conditions offer new opportunities for charlatans who can cut their cloth according to the new fashion, and the new fashion is military. To rescue the whole beach Christian movement from utter oblivion, as its 'concessions' are taken over by the tourist facilities to be built with the execution area as its centrepiece, Brother Jero pulls off a coup of his own and emerges triumphant as General Jero, leader of the Church of the Apostolic Salvation Army (CASA). This is the perfect cover for all his new schemes. As he explains to a rather outmanoeuvred Chief Executive Officer of the Tourist Board, 'Our image also conforms at all levels. We are not fanatics. Our symbol is blood. It washes all sins away. *All* sins, Mr Tourist Board.' (pp. 88–9.) The sinister connotation of lines like these, particularly when read with the indictments of *The Man Died* in mind, give the comedy a sombre tinge.

Jero, a professional survivalist, takes the measure of the wind accurately and always points in the right direction – or perhaps, in view of his change of clothing, the chameleon image is more in place because Jero's

[1] *The Jero Plays* (Eyre Methuen, London, 1973). Subsequent page references are to this edition.

methods do not essentially change. The creation of dreams that can be fulfilled only with his aid has always been his chief tactic. So now, going for even higher stakes, the dreams of the military regime must also be fed by sympathetic prophets who will, of course, be suitably rewarded. Brother Jero's account of how he has seeded the ground indicate clearly that his methods have not changed, and the very cynical manner of his flattery of the military rulers carries the burden of the play's comment on the administration of justice, a subject on which Soyinka himself feels strongly:

> JERO: Suppose I tell you, Shadrach, that it has come to the ears of the rulers that a certain new-formed religious body has declared that the Lord is so pleased with their, er . . . spectacular efforts to stamp out robbery, with the speed of the trials, the refusal of the right to appeal, the rejection of silly legal technicalities and the high rate of executions, that all these things are so pleasing to the Lord that he has granted eternal life to their regime? (p. 81.)

Having openly acknowledged the military regime as his pattern, his wheeling and dealing over declarations and definitions of property boundaries, his horse trading with his spiritual colleagues – buying them off with emblems of rank and ruthlessly ruining all who, like Shadrach, fail to come to heel – are a comic representation of the rulers' more serious and more sinister activities off stage. Once in uniform, General Jero is a frightening spectacle as he decrees the start of his regime with his cleansing fire and sword. He is all the more frightening because he is not only a military figure, but one self-reputedly divinely inspired:

> JERO: Just lean on the rotting walls, Ananaias, and the Lord will do the rest. By dawn the entire beach must be cleansed of all pestilential separatist shacks which infest the holy atmosphere of the united apostolate of the Lord. Beginning naturally with Apostate Shadrach's unholy den. The fire and the sword, Ananaias, the fire and the sword. Light up the night of evil with the flames of holiness! Consecrate the grounds for the Bar Beach Spectacular! (pp. 91–2.)

Just in case either the point or the method of the satire has been missed, Soyinka ends with a caricature, complete with accompanying one-liner, as Jero takes down the photograph of the military head of state (secular) and substitutes an even larger one of himself:

CHUME: *blasts the first bar of 'Joshua Fit the Battle of Jericho' in strict*
tempo, then swings elated into a brisk indigenous rhythm to which
the army march-dance out into the night. JERO, *with maximum*
condescension, acknowledges the salute of the army. As the last
man disappears, he takes a last look at the framed photo, takes it
down and places it face towards the wall, takes from a drawer in
the table an even larger photo of himself in his present uniform
and mounts it on the wall. He then seats himself at the table and
pulls towards him a file or two, as if to start work. Looks up
suddenly and on his face is the amiable-charlatan grin.

JERO: After all, it is the fashion these days to be a desk General.
                                                                      (p. 92.)

The Road

▼▼▼▼▼▼▼▼▼▼▼▼▼▼▼▼▼▼▼▼▼▼▼▼▼▼▼▼▼▼▼▼▼

THERE WILL probably always be some question as to the ultimate value of whatever it is Professor finds at the end of his search for the Word in *The Road*.[1] Whatever the estimate of that particular treasure, the play is without doubt a most exciting piece of theatre. *The Road* defies narrow classification; its moods range from the near tragic to the hilariously comic; it contains biting satire as well as religious and mystical speculation; it combines a grim realism with near abstract symbolism. It offers producer and actors an opportunity to blend these different characteristics into a harmonious theatrical event.

For the actors there is a whole range of challenging roles. The combination of rogue, mystic and pundit that is Professor is an obvious starring role, while the versatile mimic Samson should stretch the resources of a comic actor. It is mainly through the mimicry of Samson that the play slips out of the present and extends its range with personalities and scenes from the past as well as the contemporary outside the actual events of the play. He is the main vehicle for the satirical humour, though his role is not confined to him in a play that is never without humour for long in spite of its grim subject – death. The near-hysterical, fast-talking, gun-pulling Nigerian stage cowboy and timber truck driver, Say Tokyo Kid, is a contrast to the slow-moving, sleep-craving, ex-mammy-wagon driver, Kotonu, who carries the psychological weight of his traumatic road accidents like an albatross round his neck. Each one of the other speaking parts – Salubi the frustrated driver with the smelly mouth, the venal hemp-smoking policeman, Particulars Joe, and the politician Chief-in-Town – is a distinctive character. Even Murano who, being dumb, has not a line to speak, is to suggest his mystery by his movements as he limps, always in the shadows with one foot in each world, ministering with palm wine to the needs of Professor and his varied crew. The layabouts alternate as symbols of a purposeless existence and as musicians who provide most of the music that is so intrinsic to the play.

The music too is as varied as the moods and themes which it accompanies. It ranges from the Christian organ music of the neighbouring church through the guitar band of the layabouts to the energetic throbbing

[1] *The Road* (Oxford University Press, London, 1965).

drumming of the drivers' festival. Music is used throughout suggestively and symbolically.

The stage set – a single one for the whole play – is similarly comprehensive. The roadside shack is a perfect set for a play whose characters and themes spring from the hazardous road. The 'AKSIDENT STORE' which occupies one side of it is itself a *bolekaja* (passenger lorry) which with its stock of personal and mechanical relics of numerous road crashes and deaths, is a grimly realistic reminder of the proximity of death to these users of the road. This theme of death on the road is further symbolized by the spider's web with its ever-watchful spider; Murano prods the web several times during the play to call attention to this parallel to the road as a source of sudden death. (The spider itself is also used in a simile of reproof for Kotonu's lethargy.) Death is further suggested by the graveyard which can be seen through the shack, but the graveyard is also a link with the psychic motif which is also part of the play.

Professor's obsessive search for 'the Word' is the principal intellectual feature of the play. His base for this search has shifted from the church which has now disowned him, to the driver's shack which in his more orthodox days he had persecuted. Through the open windows of the shack and the church we have a view of one version of the Word – 'a bronze eagle on whose outstretched wings rests a huge tome'. Soyinka's set thus offers a permanent group of pictorial reminders of the varying themes of the play.

Although the various worlds of the play are blended and interact with each other, it would be convenient to look at them separately. The broad background is the world of the users of the road – drivers, their touts, their passengers and general hangers-on. Through the drivers and their festival, the psychic theme is introduced. These users of the road, as the words of the play underline, are constantly exposed to death: 'The road and the spider lie gloating, then the fly buzzes along like a happy fool.' (p. 34.) In addition to this constant dicing with death, they interact with policemen, forgers of licences, looters, and spare parts salesmen. All of them are linked by the phenomenon of death which is never absent from the scene for long. Kotonu dramatizes this precariousness of the drivers' existence and their rapid turnover by his rhetorical catalogue of departed heroes of the road:

> Where is Zorro who never returned from the North without a basket of guinea-fowl eggs? Where is Akanni the Lizard? I have not seen any other tout who would stand on the lorry's roof and play the samba at sixty miles an hour. Where is Sigidi Ope? Where is Sapele Joe who took on six policemen at the crossing and knocked them all into the river?

SAMSON: Overshot the pontoon, went down with his lorry.   (p. 21.)

Kotonu's chronicle links the excitements of the road with the fact of death. The heroes have gained immortality and passed into legend through death. As Kotonu recites the chronicle there is a combination of glory and tragedy. Soyinka enlarges the drivers' world by giving them a mythology of their own, a mythology arising from the road, and linked with death on the road.

One of the triumphs of the play is its portrayal of the many-faceted nature of death. Side by side with the tragedy and the myth we have grim physical pictures of death at speed and its consequences. This transformation is fascinating to Professor who describes the scene of an accident to Kotonu: 'Come then, I have a new wonder to show you . . . a madness where a motorcar throws itself against a tree – Gbram! and showers of crystal flying on broken souls.' (pp. 10–11.) Professor goes on to paint an even grimmer picture of the scene, which emphasizes the quick onset of physical decay after death in the tropics: 'It is a market of stale meat, noisy with flies and quarrelsome with old women.' (p. 11.) The two pictures, coming so close to each other as they do, complement one another. The souls may be airborne in a shower of crystal, but the bodies rapidly decay. Soyinka portrays the messiness of death and the incongruities it produces, in several passages. Say Tokyo Kid recalls in his racy language the scene of an accident that he had come upon:

> You know, just last week I pass an accident on the road. There was a dead dame and you know what her pretty head was spread with? Yam porrage. See what I mean? A swell dame is gonna die on the road just so the next passenger kin smear her head in yam porrage.
>
> (pp. 27–8.)

Once a crash has taken place it also becomes a source of business. Professor may talk about the psychic aspect of death, but he has always been the brains behind the AKSIDENT STORE. It was he who had invited Sergeant Burma, now dead – his brakes failed going down a hill – to open the store, and he is disappointed at the 'tardiness' of Kotonu (whom he has now appointed to succeed Sergeant Burma) in replenishing the stock by looting crashed vehicles. He reproves Kotonu and his friend Samson when they return empty-handed from the scene of an accident. His first speech to them conceals his real meaning under words like 'revelation' and 'broken words', but his second speech makes his meaning unmistakably clear. (The two speeches also bring out the ambiguity of Professor's nature. How seriously are we to take his constant verbalizing about a mystical Word, and revelations, and quests, when they are immediately coupled with quests for spare parts?)

PROF: And you brought no revelation for me? You found no broken
            words where the bridge swallowed them?

SAMSON: How could we think of such a thing Professor?

PROF: A man must be alert in each event. But the store then?
            Surely you brought new spare parts for the store?

SAMSON: Sir . . .

PROF: You neglect my needs and you neglect the Quest. Even total
            strangers have begun to notice . . . They complained of your
            tardiness in re-opening the shop.

                                                                                    (p. 55.)

This is the business aspect of the road. It is not to be obstructed by the
compassionate aspect of death. Sergeant Burma had been made of sterner
stuff; sentiment never got in the way of business:

> He told me himself how once he was stripping down a crash and
> found that the driver was an old comrade from the front. He took
> him to a mortuary but first he stopped to remove all the tyres.
>
>   (p. 21.)

Some men, like Sergeant Burma, develop (in his case calloused by
his war experiences in Burma) sufficient detachment to reconcile them to
the phenomenon of death. Others like Kotonu cannot develop the
necessary hardness and become psychological victims of the road. He is
finished as a driver, and it appears even as a Manager for the AKSIDENT
STORE.

The play portrays drivers and their touts as professionals, with a fierce
pride in their own special types of vehicle and the special skills which their
particular type of work demands. Indeed Samson who takes pride in his
title of Champion Tout of Motor Parks despises the layabouts for their
lack of professional pride:

> Look at all these touts still sleeping. They have no pride in their job.
> Part-time tout part-time burglar. In any case, they are the pestilence
> of the trade. No professional dignity.   (p. 3.)

Say Tokyo Kid displays his professional pride as he describes the hazards
of wrestling with the spirits of a guy of timber on the back of his truck:

You wanna sit down and feel that dead load trying to take the steering from your hand. You're kidding? There is a hundred spirits in every guy of timber trying to do you down cause you've trapped them in, see? (p. 26.)

Samson recreates Sergeant Burma similarly recounting his skill with large oil tankers. This professionalism is no different from that of a boxer or a surgeon; it is one of the sustaining elements in the drivers' hazardous world.

Apart from their constant duel with death on the roads, drivers have to contend with authority in the form of policemen represented here by Particulars Joe. They have learnt to live with this kind of authority. The policeman has to be bribed, and hoodwinked with forged documents. Soyinka's treatment of the authority of the law is mainly satirical. In the play's first play-within-a-play, Samson and Salubi parody the police force in a piece depicting institutionalized corruption. Salubi's parody of the Lord's prayer – 'Give us this day our daily bribe' – introduces a parody of order by which in strict order of seniority – 'officers first' – the police parade in front of Samson-as-millionaire to receive their bribes. Samson's commendatory comment – 'Now that is what I call a well-disciplined force' is a perfect representation with tough irony of the total inversion of values of a corrupt authority. Particulars Joe as he shares hemp with the political thugs and looks for bribes in unexpected places – 'Money has been left for me in more unlikely places' – merely mirrors the corruption of his superiors. He helps to complete the real world of the drivers and the road, and also functions as a vehicle for satire. Professor too in his role of forger of licences, is another constituent of the drivers' world as well as a vehicle of satire on a corrupt society.

With all the ingredients of the drivers' world as described, *The Road* is rich enough. Soyinka, however, uses this as a backcloth for the 'part psychic, part intellectual grope of Professor towards the essence of death'. It has been shown that death is an ever-present feature of the drivers' world – death as tragedy and death as business. Professor's search is for something more; something which he calls 'the Word' – the prefatory note explains it as 'the essence of death'.

The character of Professor is an enigma. Soyinka probably wants it to remain so, and it is therefore probably vain to look for a psychological unity in him. Most people take him for a madman and he certainly displays a disorientation with his surroundings which is one of the manifestations of madness. Of all Soyinka's characters he is most like those characters who float on the edges of sanity and society in the plays of Samuel Beckett and Harold Pinter (to name just two writers of the Absurd School) though

Soyinka's Professor has a quality of vigour which is absent from the characters of those playwrights.

Although Professor is now outside regular society he is near enough to it. We are constantly reminded of the days when he had been part of regular society. He still spends most of his time literally under the shadow of the church, and his language constantly echoes the liturgy of the church which he has now had to leave. Even his clothes – 'tails and top-hat etc.' – we are told by Samson are the relics of his evensong outfit in those more conventional days. Through mime, Samson gives us a history of Professor's relations with the church which the man himself supplements. Professor's severance from the church had not been voluntary, and thus the implication in some of his speeches of a deliberate abandonment of a false trail to the Word, is to that extent suspect (like most other things about Professor, one is forced to admit). This is the suggestion for example in his explanation to Kotonu of his break with the church. He explains how in those earlier days, and in his enthusiasm for what he thought was 'the Word' he had waged a holy war on the side of the church against drinking shacks: 'Oh the Word is a terrible fire and we burned them by the ear. Only that was not the Word you see, Oh no, it was not . . . And I left the Word hanging in the coloured light of sainted windows.' (pp. 68–9.) This suggests a deliberateness which is contradicted by his later account of how he was thrown out for a highly unorthodox interpretation to his Sunday school pupils of the rainbow, while 'there was the spirit of wine upon me.' (p. 89.) (A drunken Sunday school teacher is hardly likely to have a clear sight of the eternal verities.) There are also nagging reminders of his having pilfered the funds of the church – 'It is, I think, likely that I left the church coffers much depleted . . . but I remember little of this.' (p. 69.) Haughtily though Professor dismisses his fraud, he is still worried by its possible legal consequences. All this (and in spite of his insistence on correct grammar and correct music) does not add up to any inspiring picture of Professor as a devoted or clear-sighted seeker of 'the Word' while he was a member of the church. His severance therefore does not have any claim either to heroism or visionary clear-sightedness.

Professor's previous credentials are thus highly dubious. His present search for 'the Word' is similarly deprived of purity by the conflicting elements in his character. It is possible, because of the corrupt nature of the surrounding society, to forgive him for making part of his living by forging licences and other official documents. Professor, however, is a parasite on the users of the road, charging them exorbitantly for his services to the very limits of their resources. Not only that, but when their backs are turned he even dips into their money-bags. Samson catches him red-handed doing just this, but once caught, he brazenly legitimizes his act:

> [*Samson goes. As he turns his back, Professor tries to extract a coin from the bag but Samson looks back just then. Professor is left with no choice but to carry out his action after a natural hesitation, explaining quite calmly:*]
> For initial expenses you know.

Samson's brave attempt to nail Professor's act for what it is merely produces one of the master's verbal feats of legerdemain, which has the desired effect of reducing poor Samson to confusion:

> SAMSON: With all due respects Professor sir, I don't quite see how that will come under initial expenses.
>
> PROF: We had to get rid of him. Or you can have him spying on us if you like.
>
> SAMSON: But Professor, he was already outside.
>
> PROF: That is why it was necessary to call him in.
> [*Samson scratches his head, puzzles it a bit, gives up.*]   (p. 62.)

Professor's preoccupation with the business side of death has been referred to earlier. If Salubi is to be believed, he is not above causing the occasional accident himself to ginger up the flow of spare parts into the AKSIDENT STORE:

> Tell him the day the police catch him I will come and testify against him. The man is a menace. Pulling up road signs and talking all that mumbo-jumbo.   (p. 32.)

Soyinka quite deliberately gives Professor these unprepossessing aspects to his character, and yet gives him also the role of a seeker of 'the Word', a role in which he fitfully achieves a measure of profundity. He certainly gives the impression of someone who has in his sights something that others cannot see. It is this search that brings in the mystic element of the play, and links the Christian religion with the *egungun* mask through Professor's exploration of both.

In keeping with his elevated role of seeker of 'the Word' Soyinka gives Professor a very impressive speech register redolent with suggestions of the Bible and church liturgy. This register is potentially ironic for it gives

Professor's speech an impressive ring which, however, when put beside other things – his clothes and his conflicting roles – is capable of bathos. There is such a process going on at his first appearance. He enters clutching a road-sign with the word BEND on it, *'in a high state of excitement, muttering to himself'* :

> Almost a miracle . . . dawn provides the greatest miracles but this . . . in this the dawn has exceeded its promise. In the strangest of places . . . God God God but there is a mystery in everything. A new discovery every hour – I am used to that, but that I should be led to where this was hidden, sprouted in secret for heaven knows how long . . . for there was no doubt about it, this word was growing, it was growing from earth until I plucked it . . .   (p. 8.)

There is certainly an impressive prophetical tone here; the words come tumbling out as if from a man possessed; but when this mystery is seen to be identified with a road-sign, much of the profundity which the words by themselves suggest is taken away. This of course is not 'the Word' with a capital 'W', but nevertheless Professor's words endow it with mystery and significance. (All the time too, as has been suggested, his extraordinary attire contributes to the process of deflation.)

There are occasions when bathos is not so obviously suggested, and Professor's voice momentarily becomes less equivocal, but as this is never sustained, he seems constantly teetering between profundity and bathos. The mystic and the proprietor of the AKSIDENT STORE are never far from each other. If the proximity of the two roles makes it difficult to accept him as a true mystic – a single-minded seeker after something profound and important – it also makes it difficult to dismiss him altogether as a charlatan.

His compulsive search for 'the Word' among useless bits of paper is so unpromising as to be a symptom of madness. It is tempting to see Professor – in a play which makes so much use of parody – as a parody of the academic and the learned professional. He is the living image of the absent-minded professor, turning up at the wrong place, and poring intently with the aid of a magnifying glass over pieces of paper which to the uninitiated would appear as useless as the discarded football pools coupons over which Professor so intently pores. This parody there certainly is, but in the very intensity of the search also lurks the suggestion that there just might be something in these unlikely places – out of the mouths of rogues and madmen as it were.

Professor's search is not confined to bits of paper and road accidents, however. Murano has provided him with an unexpected key to the mystery – if only he could use it. Murano has been knocked down by Kotonu's lorry while in a state of possession – in the state of 'transition from the human to the divine essence' (note 'For the Producer') – and Professor happens upon him abandoned by Kotonu and Samson in the back of the lorry. In this *agemo* phase, Murano has one foot in each world; to symbolize this duality, Soyinka gives him a heavy limp:

> When a man has one leg in each world, his legs are never the same. The big toe of Murano's foot – the left one of course – rests on the slumbering chrysalis of the Word. When that crust cracks my friends – you and I, that is the moment we await. (p. 45.)

In trying to make use of Murano in this way Professor is playing with fire; he is in fact trying to use a god, Ogun, for his own purposes. He realizes the danger of this sort of thing, and warns Samson off trying to pierce the mystery of Murano's identity: 'Those who are not equipped for strange sights, fools like you – go mad or blind when their curiosity is pursued. First find the Word . . .' (p. 45.) Professor seems at first to be content to 'await' the moment; not to hasten it. In one sense, his whole search is one of waiting patiently: 'Like you I also wait but you do not hear me complain.' (p. 60.) But it is a most aggravating wait, with his hands so to speak actually on the key (Murano). Finally he can wait no more, and, seeing an opportunity (in Murano's reaction to the mask), he seizes the chance to force the secret out. Both the agony of the wait – for himself as well as for Murano – are conveyed in the words which lead to his desperate decision to 'cheat' in order to understand:

> And waiting, waiting till his tongue be released, [*desperately*] in patience and in confidence, for he is not like you others whose faces are equally blank but share no purpose with the Word. So, surely Murano, crawling out of the darkness, from the last suck of the throat of death, and Murano with the spirit of a god in him, for it came to the same thing, that I held a god captive, that his hands held out the day's communion! And should I not hope, with him, to cheat, to anticipate the final confrontation, learning its nature baring its skulking face, why may I not understand . . .
> [*He stops, looks around him.*]
> So, why don't you ask him you runaway driver, why don't you ask him to try it on, see if it fits . . .
> [*He pulls up Murano, takes him into the store, pulls the canvas behind him.*]
> (pp. 90–1.)

Professor's act here is an attempt to reconstruct the state of possession; to bring the god Ogun into the store, and in some way to find the answer to his riddle. He has lost his patience. He will 'anticipate the final confrontation'. This 'confrontation' leads in a rather indirect way to his death.

Professor still hopes as he approaches the confrontation that his dangerous experiment will reveal the answer without exacting the ultimate price (this is an almost Faustian situation): 'I must hope, even now. I cannot yet believe that death's revelation must be total, or not at all.' (p. 93.)

The danger of the experiment is realized by all in the store. Salubi tries to sneak out, and the frightened band has to be forced by Professor's now overwhelming authority, to play. 'Play you croakers, play.' Events have now been set in train for a climax which is to involve the deaths of Say Tokyo Kid and Professor himself, but in rather unexpected ways.

Made desperate by fear, Say Tokyo Kid interrupts the course of events by smashing the gourd which Professor is carrying. But instead of a contest between Professor and Say Tokyo Kid it is the possessed *egungun* whom Say Tokyo Kid engages. This is an act of sacrilege of which perhaps only the impulsive, trigger-happy Say Tokyo is capable, simply because he is incapable of anticipating the consequences. Professor on the other hand goes into all this with his eyes open. The knife which Salubi slides to Say Tokyo during this fight is thus not meant to be used on Professor but on the *egungun* with whom Say Tokyo Kid is struggling. But Professor tries to intercept it, and is stabbed by Say Tokyo. His death therefore is given the appearance of an accident, and hence seems to lose direct connection with his experiment. Say Tokyo it is who feels the direct wrath of the god. He is humbled for his presumption. As he pulls the knife out of Professor's back presumably to attack the *egungun*, the latter '*appears to come to life suddenly, lifts Say Tokyo in a swift movement up above his head, the knife out and in Say Tokyo's hand, smashes him savagely on the bench. Say Tokyo tries to rise, rolls over into the ground and clutches the train of the mask to him.*' (p. 96.)

Professor's death at the hands of Say Tokyo Kid – instead of at the hands of an outraged god – is unexpected, and seems to underline Soyinka's ambiguous portrayal of both the man and his quest. We are still left wondering about his search, and how much there had been in it. Soyinka does not usually give his characters perorations at the moment of death, but Professor dies with a Jacobean peroration on his lips, the import of which seems to be as ambiguous as everything else about him. It has the sound of a 'moral' without being one. It has the externals of a final revelation without revealing anything.

What for instance are we to make of Professor's parting advice to his survivors in the shack to 'power your hands with the knowledge of death'? How is this to be done? The series of images which follow in expansion of this injunction suggest that it means that somehow Professor's hearers should develop the gift of anticipating the fact of death – of seeing it before it comes. 'In the heat of the afternoon when the sheen raises false forests and a watered haven, let the event first unravel before your eyes.' Mirages, a frequent cause of accidents for hot and tired drivers, have been referred to before in the play. Professor too encountered mirages in his search for 'the Word'. He had called his curious mistake at the beginning of the play a 'mirage' and had counselled his followers to 'Avoid mirages – I had one this morning'. (p. 35.) This final injunction suggests too that the users of the road should be able to see past the mirage to the resulting accident and death – they are apparently unable to prevent it, however. What is the use of such a knack even if it can be developed – this ability to see your own death just before it comes? A quick opportunity for stock-taking or repentance? Professor never talks about this. The other images which represent this ability to see death before it comes, reinforce the first but still do not reveal any profound secret.

The injunction to 'Breathe like the road. Be the road' is expanded as an injunction to develop the treachery of the road. The image of the unsuspected snake is a parallel one to the spider/fly image used earlier in the play:

> Coil yourself in dreams, lay flat in treachery and deceit and at the moment of a trusting step, rear your head and strike the traveller in his confidence, swallow him whole or break him on the earth.

Here Professor does little more than reiterate the treacherous qualities of the road of which no one knows better than users of the road. Why are they to develop this treachery themselves?

I do not believe that the playwright expects anyone to derive eternal wisdom from Professor. If he has at last found 'the Word', he has found it for himself, and he does not communicate it. He is of no more use to his hearers than the dumb Murano. Viewed like this, the suggestion is that each one must find the essence of death for himself – in death. The long trail of Professor has led everyone else nowhere. He has left the enigma behind him. There is an even more sardonic interpretation of the end of the play. What, if after all, there is no Word?[2] The play like its main character remains an enigma.

Through all the meanderings in search of the elusive Word, Soyinka's skill as a playwright remains constant. *The Road* contains a running satirical commentary on chosen aspects of life which sustains the play, whatever we make of the nature of the Word. An exhaustive list of the

[2] See Margaret Laurence, *Long Drums and Cannons* (Macmillan, London, 1968), p. 63.

butts of the play's satire is not necessary. It encompasses the whole of its society, and the picture which emerges of that society is not a flattering one. Through Chief-in-Town and his recruitment of thugs as his bodyguard for political meetings, we have a thrust at the violent political methods which brought disaster and an end to civilian politics in Nigeria for a while. The brief portrait is an ominous warning through comedy of the breakdown of order. Particulars Joe, the representative of the law, because of his total lack of integrity becomes himself a threat to order. Faith in the system he represents is shown to be crumbling, in the drivers who find it less trouble and expense to buy forged licences than to subject themselves to driving tests. The results of this self-licensing process on road safety are all too clear in the incidence of death on the roads. The cycle of corruption and the products of corruption reinforcing corruption is a never-ending one.

Organized religion comes in for its share of the satire. The picture of the church that emerges as we see it through Salubi's mimicry, is a combination of vanity – in the sense of a preoccupation with externals – and corruption. Salubi's comment is an apt condemnation: 'Dat one no to church, na high society.' (p. 15.)

In a situation like this there seems to be no hope from the top of society which is manned by false leaders, preoccupied only with their own vanity and well-being. Again it is through Samson (as millionaire) that we have a satirical glimpse at the methods of self-refreshment and renewal used by the rich and powerful of the society:

Now I want you to take the car – the long one – and drive along the Marina at two o'clock. All the fine fine girls just coming from offices, the young and tender faces fresh from school – give them lift to my house. Old bones like me must put fresh tonic in his blood.

(pp. 7–8.)

It is Samson too who gives us the quick glimpse of the rags to riches story of the messenger who became a Senator via a football pools win: 'A friend of mine – he was a messenger – sent in one of these. He won thirteen thousand. Now he owns half the houses in Apapa and they have made him a Senator. You never know you see.' (p. 66.)

There is a quick side swipe at one of the absurd aspects of war – a topic more fully treated in 'Idanre' and A Dance of the Forests – in Particulars Joe's reminiscence of his and Sergeant Burma's part in the World War when they enjoyed the luxury of killing people who had never done them any harm. His reflection is loaded with unconscious irony: 'It is peaceful to fight a war which one does not understand, to kill human beings who never seduced your wife or poisoned your water.' (pp. 81–2.) Soyinka's neat reduction of war to this level of absurdity is of the same order as the urbane comment of the Court Historian on Mata Kharibu's war in *A Dance of the Forests*; he is similarly oblivious of the ironic implications of his comment: 'I mean this is war as it should be fought . . . over nothing . . . do you not agree?' (*Five Plays*, p. 62.)

Through its satirical thrusts, the play extends its moral range over a wide area far beyond the immediate world of the road. Over the doings of men hover the higher beings whose presences men recognize, with whom they seek contact in life, and to whom they are reunited in death. The Christian God through the church, Ogun through Murano and the drivers' festival, the spirits of timber, as well as the spirits of the graveyard constitute a veritable cloud of witnesses, against whose more absolute standards the deeds of men are measured. With them the universe of the play is complete, embracing all from the dogs slaughtered on the road as 'Ogun's meat' to the unseen presences themselves. *The Road* treats an essentially tragic theme without solemnity; it looks death in the face without losing its humour; it is an extraordinary theatrical achievement.

Kongi's Harvest

▼▼▼▼▼▼▼▼▼▼▼▼▼▼▼▼▼▼▼▼▼▼▼▼▼▼▼▼▼

LIKE MUCH of Soyinka's work, *Kongi's Harvest*[1] is a great deal more subtle than it appears on the surface. It is a perfectly satisfatory play, even if it is taken only as the representation of a clash between a modern dictatorship and the traditional system which it has effectively replaced. It is that, but it is also a great deal more; it is ultimately a representation of the clash between the life-giving forces and death-producing forces. The language of the play constantly links some characters with life and growth, others with death in a way which makes the presentation to Kongi of the head of Segi's father a fitting symbolic climax of this more fundamental struggle.

'Hemlock,' the opening section, is a thematic microcosm of the whole piece. Indeed much of what a thematic analysis of the play eventually yields is summarized in the three images which open the satirical anthem with which it begins:

> The pot that will eat fat
> Its bottom must be scorched
> The squirrel that will long crack nuts
> Its footpad must be sore
> The sweetest wine has flowed down
> The tapper's shattered shins. (p. 1.)

The first two images (they are Yoruba proverbs) contain the idea that every desirable end exacts its price. This applies not only to Kongi's 'self imposed herculean assignment', as Oyin Ogunba suggests,[2] but also to the equally herculean task of trying to unseat him, a task which ends in disaster, thus exacting its price without the satisfaction of achieving the end. This last idea is reiterated in the third image. In mockery of the tapper's efforts – 'his shattered shins' – the sweetest wine has flowed uselessly away.

Even the satirical opening of the play has obliquely (so obliquely that its

---

[1] *Kongi's Harvest*, Three Crowns edn. (O.U.P., London, 1967).

[2] 'The Traditional Content of the Plays of Wole Soyinka', *African Literature Today*, 4 (Heinemann, London, 1970). This is an important article on Soyinka from which, even when I depart from its interpretations, I have benefited.

real significance is realized only through hindsight) presented in imagery a situation of fruitless labour. The jingling anthem goes on further to portray the prevailing political situation. The new regime built on new political theories – the isms of Ismaland – has contemptuously displaced the old:

> To demonstrate the tree of life
> Is sprung from broken peat
> And we the rotted bark, spurned
> When the tree swells its pot
> The mucus that is snorted out
> When Kongi's new race blows   (p. 1.)

The anthem is satirical and ironic. The old regime portrays itself in the words which the 'new race' would use. (Oba Danlola repeats this style of ironical self-mockery frequently in the play.)

The new regime depends for its continuance on its own propaganda; the 'government loud speaker' is thus central to its political machinery. In Ismaland this is a device which pours out propaganda but admits of no reply – even if reply were worth while: 'My ears are sore/But my mouth is *agbanyun*.' (p. 2.) This tyranny of words is later given physical shape in the Reformed Aweri Fraternity (a parody of its traditional predecessor) which in its isolated word-factory, manufactures the words which go into the talking boxes. The satirical anthem silently comments on the value of such words – the very repetition of 'words' throughout the anthem effectively devalues their worth. When the Reformed Aweri appear and are seen in conclave, actually producing the words to order, the devaluation of the coinage becomes complete.

The Superintendent is the first manifestation of the new race in the play. Invested with the insignia of the new era – 'Khaki and brass buttons' – he tyrannizes over the Oba who is now in his power. His action of silencing the royal drums is symbolic of his power conferred on him by the new regime. But his power over the Oba is only physical. This is inconvenient enough (for the Oba), but it is shown to be essentially limited. The Oba has spiritual resources which Kongi does not have, and therefore cannot pass on down to the functionaries of his regime. All the Superintendent's bluster is knocked out of him when the Oba threatens to prostrate before him. The Superintendent is not so remote from his origins as to risk the implied curse of this gesture, and is soon reduced to self-abasement and abject pleading before the physically powerless Oba:

I call you all to witness. Kabiyesi, I am only the fowl droppings that stuck to your slippers when you strutted in the back yard. The child is

nothing, it is only the glory of his forbears that the world sees and
tolerates in him.   (p. 6.)

The father/child relationship which the Superintendent here acknowledges
is the elusive relationship which Kongi does not have with his subjects.
His authority is not similarly rooted in tradition and in the minds of the
governed. (The play suggests that his authority is detached from nature
too. It has no anchor.) It is this lack of a deep-seated base which accounts
for the insecurity and lack of poise, as well as for the brutality of Kongi's
regime. The ambiguity of the Superintendent's plight – he tyrannizes over
the Oba but ultimately fears him – mirrors the ambiguity of the whole of
Kongi's regime. Even in prison, the Oba is still powerful: 'Ogun is still a
god/Even without his navel.' It is in the hope of capturing the Oba's
spiritual authority that Kongi demands that the Oba ceremonially present
the new yam to him in public.

The Hemlock section suggests also that a heavy responsibility accompanies
the Oba's exalted position in the minds of his people. People (like Kongi)
who envy the position and covet it do not realize the depth of this
responsibility. The Oba is a protector of his people to the extent of being
prepared to give his life in protection of their own. In the words of Sarumi,
a junior Oba:

> They complained because
> The first of the new yams
> Melted first in an Oba's mouth
> But the dead will witness
> We drew the poison from the root   (p. 7.)

– drawing the poison from the root – to make eating and living safe for the
governed. This is the ultimate responsibility of rule. This is the *raison
d'être* of rule. Without this kind of attitude to the ruled, the ruler is not
entitled to their deep loyalty and reverence. This idea is fundamental to
Kongi's Harvest. It is because the Oba's regime rests on this basic assumption, that his regime emerges as being morally superior to the physically
more successful regime of Kongi which is based entirely on a shallow
personality cult and a vicious selfishness. Kongi stands condemned because
his is a regime that is self-centred, not people-centred. Ultimately it is a
regime based on death, not on life. Far from drawing out the poison to
give life to the people, Kongi is a dealer out of death.

The Oba is given even deeper spiritual links; his authority crosses the
borders of life. He not only gives life to the already born, but is linked
with the bringing of new life into the world. His links with the unborn are
suggested in Sarumi's words:

Oh yes, we know they say
We wore out looms
With weaving robes for Kings
But I ask, is *popoki*[3]
The stuff to let down
To unformed fingers clutching up
At life? (pp. 8–9.)

Seen in this light the play is rescued from the facile opposition of old versus new. It is an opposition between the humane and the monstrous; between the giver of life and the bringer of death.

Even in this early section of the play, 'Hemlock' portrays Kongi as a monster which should have been scotched before it achieved its full proportions. One parable makes the point:

OGBO AWERI: Observe, when the monster child
Was born, *Opele* taught us to
Abandon him beneath the buttress tree
But the mother said, oh no,
A child is still a child
The mother in us said, a child
Is still the handiwork of Olukori

SARUMI: Soon the head swelled
Too big for pillow
And it swelled too big for mother's back
And soon the mother's head
Was nowhere to be seen
And the child's slight belly
Was strangely distended (p. 10.)

The monster child Kongi to whom this parable is applicable has become by slow degrees and, ironically through the merciful indulgence of his motherland, the smotherer, the destroyer of his country.

'Hemlock' thus sets the scene thematically for the main conflicts of the play and gives no false hope of a comfortable outcome. Even the title, 'Hemlock' with its implication of poison and the death of Socrates[4] indicates tragedy. Only disaster is predicted by the Oba as he dances his slow dignified dance:

[3] Thick, coarse, woven cloth.
[4] The figure of Socrates is invoked again in *Madmen and Specialists*. See p. 108 below.

> Delve with the left foot
> For ill-luck; with the left
> Again for ill-luck; once more
> With the left alone, for disaster
> Is the only certainty we know[5]   (p. 10.)

The thematic microcosm of Hemlock is played out in the two main parts of the play, called simply First Part and Second Part. Soyinka's stage directions require the two sets for 'First Part' to be on stage simultaneously, either being highlighted as it is required. Between these two sets representing 'Kongi's retreat in the mountains' and Segi's night-club, the Organizing Secretary flits to and fro. The two areas of the stage represent opposing forces. Kongi's retreat is gradually revealed as a barren place of forced deprivation. Kongi himself is fasting – a fast which turns out, like his publicized desire for seclusion, to be a mere publicity stunt; for he strikes a number of poses for the benefit of an international press photographer while pretending to be unaware of his presence. Kongi's asceticism is clearly exposed as a mere front. The Reformed Aweri too are kept virtually imprisoned with Kongi on a near-starvation diet – the fifth Aweri continually complains that he is starving – dreaming up an 'image' for themselves and for Kongi, and also manufacturing the words to go with their pasteboard façade. The total effect of the scenes in the retreat is one of barrenness, of a denial of life and truth, and all this, ironically, in preparation for a harvest.

Segi's night-club is by contrast a scene of life. While the Kongi retreat is dimly lit, Segi's night-club is lit with coloured lights. There is music, dancing, and beer. Segi herself, a complex character, but unmistakable for her utter femininity, is an embodiment of the life principle. Daodu too is similarly suggestive of life. He works the land, and hence is close to the source of life. The contrast between the two juxtaposed areas is total. When the Organizing Secretary moves between the two he is spanning a gap in a way which only a cold cynical professional like himself can do; he is negotiating between the forces of life and the forces of death. He can partake of life – he drinks beer at Segi's club – but his profession does not allow him to let up and admit the fullness of life: 'You know, I am very fond of music. Unfortunately I haven't much time for it. Moreover, one would hardly wish to be found in this sort of place.' The fundamental nature of the opposition of the two localities becomes clearer as 'First Part' develops.

[5] Oyin Ogumba sees the whole dirge of *ege* as 'a dance of the death of tradition itself' – 'The Traditional Content of the Plays of Wole Soyinka', *African Literature Today*, 4 (Heinemann Educational Books, London, 1970), p. 9.

First Part opens with the Reformed Aweri in conclave; in the vocabulary of the new regime they are at a 'planning session' – to solve 'the problem of an image for ourselves'. The Reformed Aweri are something of a parody of their predecessors, the traditional Aweri whom they had displaced. The new men are insecure – their very concern for an image is indicative of their insecurity. They lack the style of their predecessors, as First Aweri confesses, and are in obvious disarray. Fifth Aweri demonstrates his weariness with the whole proceeding by ostentatiously going to sleep at intervals. Awake, the Aweri fare little better. Their confusion manifests itself in self-contradictory phrases like 'youthful elders' and 'modern patriarchs'. They are men who have abandoned what they contemptuously call 'proverbs and senile pronouncements' but do not yet understand the pseudo-scientific jargon – 'ideograms and algebraic quantums' – of Kongi's new political philosophy, 'Scientificism'.

The contrast between the Reformed Aweri and the Oba's court – even the rump of it that is left – is reminiscent of the contrast between the assurance of the Bale of Ilujinle in *The Lion and the Jewel* and the confused verbalizing of the school teacher Lakunle. Except when he is play-acting, throwing dust in the eyes of the Organizing Secretary in 'Second Part' – when he adopts a theatrically abusive style – the Oba's speech is dignified, weighted down with proverbs.

The Party Secretary is the focus of the two opposing forces. His job is to persuade the Oba, Daodu's uncle – 'a damned stubborn goat, an obstructive, cantankerous creature and a bloody pain in my neck' – to surrender his power publicly to Kongi and thus (presumably) dethrone himself in the hearts of the people. Kongi hopes that this act would transfer the Oba's spiritual authority to him. It should be recognized that Kongi in his monstrous self-delusion has even greater ambitions than merely displacing the Oba. He wants to replace 'the Spirit of Harvest', the presiding deity himself. As the Secretary explains to the Aweri: 'Kongi desires that the king perform all his customary spiritual functions, only this time, that he performs them to him, our Leader. Kongi must preside as the Spirit of Harvest, in pursuance of the Five-Year-Development Plan.' (p. 20.) Kongi himself declares with manic insistence, emphasizing in successive repetitions 'am' 'Spirit' and 'HAR-VEST', 'I am the Spirit of Harvest'. (pp. 36–7.) That a man whose total personality amounted to a denial of life should so insistently seek to fill the position of giver of life is a measure of Kongi's self-delusion, but more important it is a dramatization of the tragedy which such a reversal of fundamental values brings.

Kongi's regime is a regime of repression. The Reformed Aweri are the instruments of intellectual and spiritual repression, while the mallet-swinging carpenters (their Captain is also superintendent of the Detention

Camp), are the instruments of physical repression. As Kongi euphemistic-
ally puts it:

> They [the Carpenters Brigade] complement my sleepy Aweris here.
> These ones look after my intellectual needs, the Brigade take care of
> the occasional physical requirements.   (p. 36.)

That all Kongi's machinery of suppression goes little deeper than the
flesh is shown by the occasional bomb-throwing which rocks his regime.
This is the only kind of harvest over which Kongi is qualified to preside –
a harvest of death. The bomb-throwers of course have to be hanged, while
the Reformed Aweri on Kongi's orders have to counter the effects of the
bomb-throwing by organizing slogans around the key-word 'Harmony'. It
seems unlikely that even Kongi really places much faith in the effects of
such words. Regimes like his are doomed to go on multiplying villainies.
The Reformed Aweri, no less than the lower orders of the society, are
pathetic victims of a regime of death. Their reaction as the Organizing
Secretary announces the sentence on the bomb-throwers, dramatizes their
plight. The word 'hanged' in the passage stuns even these hardened cynics
into silence, but only momentarily until one of them can translate the
brutality of 'hanged' into the meaningless jargon of the new politics – 'An
exercise in scientific exorcism'. Thus translated, the horror is covered with
a façade of words and they can approve the action. The section with the
stage directions reads:

> SECRETARY: And the key-word, Kongi insists must be – Harmony. We
> need that to counter the effect of the recent bomb-throwing.
> Which is one of the reasons why the culprits of that outrage
> will be hanged tomorrow.
> [A nervous silence. They look at one another, stare at their feet]
>
> FOURTH: An exercise in scientific exorcism – I approve.
> [Followed by murmurs and head-nodding of agreement by the majority.]

Thus men in a trapped situation, to keep their sanity – at least for a time
– play tricks with words and lives. It is most effective that in the playwright's
arrangement this scene of mute condonation of death should be broken by
'loud chords on guitar' which announce the shift to Segi's night-club on
the other side of the stage to which the Organizing Secretary now ferries
himself.

Segi's night-club has been characterized as a contrasting scene of light
and life to Kongi's retreat. It, and its habitués, deserve a closer look. In a

general way, the night-club represents the rest of the society. When the Organizing Secretary comes into it for the first time, accompanied by 'The Right and Left Ears of State', the reactions which the playwright requires are variously representative of differing characters and political persuasions. They are not all of one kind:

> *A few night-lifers pick up their drinks and go in, there are one or two aggressive departures, some stay on defiantly, others obsequiously try to attract attention and say a humble greeting.* (pp. 13–14.)

They represent the various reactions to a repressive regime; cowardly (frightened) retreat, surly disavowal, aggressive confrontation, obsequious coat-tailing. Presumably the faint hearts never come back, and the club becomes something of a centre of opposition to Kongi's regime. The Left and Right Ears are in fact soon whisked away as political hostages.

Segi and Daodu are the focal points of this opposition to Kongi's regime. Segi is another of Soyinka's extraordinary women (Madame Tortoise/Rola in *A Dance of the Forests*, Simi in *The Interpreters* and Iriyise in *Season of Anomy* are other manifestations). Her attraction for men is certain and total. Even the Organizing Secretary is not unaffected. He is half fascinated, half frightened by her:

> Does that woman have to keep looking at me like that?
> · · ·
> I just wish she'd . . . what do they sing about her? What are they saying?

Segi is an embodiment of sex and hence potentially at least, of the creative principle. However, hers is no easy relationship. She turns men mad. Those who dislike and distrust her, call her dangerous and worse. The Organizing Secretary calls her 'witch', and Oba Danlola calls her 'A right cannibal of the female species'. (p. 51.) (It is interesting that the Oba subsequently recognizes her, howbeit grudgingly, as an ally.) Segi is heady wine as her praise singers declare:

> The being of Segi
> Swirls the night
> In potions round my head
>
> But my complains
> Will pass
>
> It is only
> A madman ranting

> When the lady
> Turns her eyes,
>
> Fathomless on those
> I summoned as my go-between.

Once tasted, the effect is permanent:

> But Segi
> You are the stubborn strand
> Of meat, lodged
> Between my teeth
>
> I picked and picked
> I found it was a silken thread
> Wound deep down my throat
> And makes me sing

Her inscrutability totally discomposes the Organizing Secretary. This inscrutability indeed pervades the whole club, making it a milieu in which the cool Secretary cannot concentrate: 'This place bothers me.' (p. 31.) Apart from their brief encounter when he first asked to see Daodu and finds him dancing with her, the lady herself speaks only once to the Secretary, on the last of his visits to the club; he had shied away from earlier contact when Daodu suggested it and even here the encounter is a frightening and fatiguing one for him: '[*Secretary stares at her, experiencing fear . . .*]' (p. 42.) and (at the end of a very brief exchange) '[*sits down, dog-tired*]'. Elaborate care is taken to build Segi up as a creature with hidden depths and great resources.

She has been a lover of Kongi, not just a lover, but one who had once believed in him and his cause, and had been prepared to devote her resources to his work: 'Kongi *was* a great man, and I loved him.' (p. 45.) The tense is significant. Now she is a woman who has lost her faith: 'If I could again believe . . .' (p. 44.) Her faith is now to be put on Daodu. In spite of her poise and her apparent imperturbability, Segi is human and has feelings. She is a daughter (whose father is in detention and is later killed) and she knows moments of fear. She seems to be an element which all human institutions need – devotion to life. She has abjured the cause of death symbolized by Kongi and now clings to a new hope in Daodu.

Daodu too is a complex character. He is a prince, being son to the junior Oba Sarumi, and heir to Danlola's throne – a throne which Kongi's regime makes little more than an empty chair, except for its hidden spiritual resources. Daodu is thus linked with the spirit of the people. He is also linked to the earth, being a successful farmer. But he has also partaken of the influences out of which the new regime of Kongi derives its being. He has been abroad: 'Lately returned from everywhere and still/Trying to find his feet.' (p. 54.) He may be still trying to find his feet but he has not broken his traditional links. After his wide experiences, he has gone back to the earth and to his traditional role. In this lies his potential strength. He has retained the links with humanity and with the source of life, while opening himself to other influences.

One of the characteristics of Kongi is his a-sexuality. It is another symbol of his denial of life. Daodu by contrast is shown in a sexual role. Segi, who is the symbol of sex and hence of reproduction and growth, invites Daodu to an almost symbolic acceptance of his sexual role on the eve of the harvest which is also to be the occasion for the challenge to Kongi's regime. Daodu at first resists this role, pleading business in preparation for the morrow. The exchanges are couched in growth and harvest symbols:

SEGI: Come through the gates tonight. Now, I want you in me, my Spirit of Harvest.

DAODU: Don't tempt me so hard. I am swollen like prize yam under earth, but all harvest must await its season.

SEGI: There is no season for seeds bursting.

DAODU: My eyes of kernals, I have much preparation to make.

SEGI: I must rejoice, and you with me. I am opened tonight. I am soil from the final rains.   (p. 44.)

Daodu eventually accepts the invitation, but not before a very significant choice of love and life made at the insistence of Segi.

As Segi and her women drape the symbolic harvest robe about him – he is to represent the Spirit of Harvest – Segi, suddenly dramatizing the paramountcy of this role, kneels in front of him: '[*She comes round, surveys him. Suddenly she kneels and clings to the hem of his robes.*[6] *The other women kneel too.*]' Segi exclaims 'My prince . . . my prince.' This reverential tableau confronts Daodu with his role of opposition to Kongi. He pleads to be allowed to play it out through hatred; to match Kongi at his barren game. (Does this mean a straightforward armed revolution? or a regime

---

[6] Once again a biblical tableau is evoked – that of the sick woman touching the hem of Christ's garment.

which outmatches Kongi's in brutality?) But Segi urges him to play it out
the other way through life and love:

SEGI: My prince . . . my prince.

DAODU: Let me preach hatred, Segi. If I preached hatred I could match
            his barren marathon, hour for hour, torrent for torrent . . .

SEGI: Preach life, Daodu, only life . . .

DAODU: Imprecations then, curses on all inventors of agonies, on all
            Messiahs of pain and false burdens . . .

SEGI: Only life is worth preaching my prince.

DAODU   [*with mounting passion*]:
            On all who fashion chains, on farmers of terror, on builders
            of walls, on all who guard against the night but breed dark-
            ness by day, on all whose feet are heavy and yet stand upon
            the world . . .

SEGI: Life . . . life . . .

DAODU: On all who see, not with the eyes of the dead, but with eyes of
            Death . . .

SEGI: Life then. It needs a sermon on life . . . love . . .

DAODU   [*with violent anger*]:
            Love? Love? You who gave love, how were you requited?

SEGI: [*rises*]
            My eyes were open to what I did. Kongi *was* a great man, and
            I loved him.

DAODU: What will I say then? What can one say on life against the
            batteries and the microphones and the insistence of one inde-
            fatigable madman? What is there strong enough about just
            living and loving? What?

SEGI: It will be enough that you erect a pulpit against him, even for
            one moment.

DAODU   [*resignedly*]:
         I hate to be a mere antithesis to your Messiah of pain.

                                                                (pp. 45–6.)

For a moment Daodu is transformed by his symbolic robe. His imprecations against the Kongis of this world are those of a representative voice. He speaks for the forces of life against the forces of death. To realize this then he cannot be another Kongi, overthrowing his regime by a bloodier. He has to overcome him by being what he in his resigned acceptance calls a mere antithesis, but an antithesis he must be. This throws some light on the rather undramatic nature of the morrow's gesture. It is to turn out to be just that; a gesture – 'a pulpit against him, even for one moment'. The efficacy of this type of gesture against the regime of 'an indefatigable madman', can almost be predicted. However resignedly, Daodu accepts his role, and in symbolic celebration, the invitation of Segi. He thus unites with his counterpart in the cycle of life and growth. He is ready for his role of the morrow.

In contrast to this scene, 'First Part' ends with a quick look at Kongi, the Messiah of Pain, and he is seen in a fit of uncontrollable anger – it ends in an epileptic fit – as he decrees death. Because one of his prisoners has escaped, he withdraws his amnesty – it is only a word after all. His epileptic fit leaves him struggling for breath and life, and hence a living symbol of his regime of death.

First Part then has deployed the forces, with Daodu taking the foreground as the protagonist of life. But his uncle, Oba Danlola is still Oba, and now that he has been released to present the new yam to Kongi, resumes the foreground.

Oba Danlola goes through an elaborate piece of play-acting in order to deceive the Organizing Secretary into thinking that he is preparing to make the formal presentation of the new yam to Kongi – an act he has no intention at this point of carrying out. Soyinka uses poetic registers subtly here. He gives the Oba his characteristic dignified imagic style when he is speaking his real thoughts, and a fruity, scatological, abusive style when he is play-acting. His explanation of his deceptive preparations illustrate his two styles. In the first section of the passage he uses his natural style; in the second, he speaks in his newly adopted theatrical role of an enthusiastic supporter of Kongi, badly let down by his inept servants:

> When the dog hides a bone does he not
> Throw up sand? A little dust in the eye
> Of His Immortality will not deceive
> His clever Organizing Secretary. We need to

Bury him with shovelfuls.
[*Re-enter Dende*]
You horse-manure! Is this a trip
To gather mangoes for the hawker's tray?
Tell me, did I ask for a basket fit
To support your father's goitre?   (pp. 48–9.)

Even the Organizing Secretary is taken in. That the Oba has to play this
role is itself a sign of the times. The wily old man is playing the new
regime's word game upon which the opening 'anthem' had been such a
telling comment. He could be as good at the game as anyone else. He
defends himself against Daodu's accusation (which would have been
damning in other circumstances).

You should, my son, when you deal in politics
Pay sharp attention to the word. I agreed
Only that I would prepare myself
For the grand ceremony, not
That I would go. Hence this bee hum fit
For the world's ruling heads jammed
In annual congress.   (p. 50.)

There is a seeming conflict in this section of the play between the aims
of the Oba and those of his heir. Daodu is seen in the strange role of acting
for the Organizing Secretary in persuading his uncle to attend the festival
and perform as Kongi wishes. Indeed the opposition between the two
leads to a dramatic climax when Daodu seizes the Oba's ceremonial whisk
and bursts the royal lead drum with it. This appears to be the final act of
disloyalty; even the Superintendent in 'Hemlock' had only seized the wrist
of the drummer. He had not silenced the drum finally:

That prison
Superintendent merely lay his hands
On my lead drummer, and stopped
The singing, but you our son and heir
You've seen to the song itself.   (p. 60.)

Daodu's silencing of the song itself is a significant symbol of the end of
effective chieftaincy of the Oba's sort in the face of the competition offered
by modern political regimes. There is no suggestion, however, that the
particular manifestation of modern political power in Kongi's regime will
survive either. Some form of government which combines the moral

authority and humanity of the Oba's regime with the efficiency of modern regimes (the Daodu/Segi combination) seems to be indicated as the hope of stability. So although his personal loyalty to the Oba is not really in dispute, Daodu's act performed 'with sudden decision' is significant for the future of the society. It is an open acknowledgement of the fact that a different road lies ahead – a fact which the Oba's continued role-playing had tended to mask.

The Oba has now become part of Daodu's plan of the day – 'a vital part'. It is significant that what finally persuades the Oba to take part in the plan is the revelation to him of the true identity of Segi towards whom he had been so hostile:

> DAODU   [*desperately*]: The woman you warned me about, Segi, the
>   witch of the night-clubs as you labelled her, is the daughter
>   of this man who has escaped. And she wants the Harvest to
>   go on as we all planned, as much as I.
>   [*Danlola turns slowly round*]
>
> DANLOLA: Is this the truth about that woman?
>
> DAODU: The truth
>
> DANLOLA   [*hesitates and a far-seeing look comes into his eyes*]:
>   There was always something more, I knew
>   To that strange woman beyond
>   Her power to turn grown men to infants.   (p. 63.)

It is Segi, ironically, now recognized as an ally, whose participation reconciles the Oba to a plan, the details of which he does not even know.

All is now set for the climax (which in Soyinka's typical style turns out to be a deliberate anti-climax). The preliminaries to the arrival of Kongi confirm the earlier suggestions of the nature of his regime. The music of penny whistles in contrast to the royal drums demonstrates its shallowness for one thing. Its repressive nature is symbolized by the heavy mallets of the carpenters who will defend the 'creed of Kongism' relentlessly: 'And heads too slow to learn it/Will feel our mallets' weight.' That the regime's primary concern is with the surface of things rather than with essentials is illustrated by the dreadful plight of the speech-writing Aweri who suddenly discovers that the four-and-a-half-hour-long speech he had written for Kongi is too short because the neighbouring President has just spoken for seven hours. The concern with triviality that this implies is not only characteristic of the festival but of the whole of Kongi's regime.

The entrance of Segi and her women with their sarcastic songs and defiant gestures help to set the scene for a confrontation which is to be signalled by Daodu's speech, especially when Segi's women 'form a ring around Daodu with their pestles' – at which even the Organizing Secretary retreats to a safe distance. But the expected dramatic confrontation does not come.

Daodu's speech is wasted on Kongi who does not hear it, and at the crucial point when the dethronement (possibly assassination) of Kongi should have taken place, the sound of gunfire heralds the death of Segi's father who, it transpires, was to have done the crucial act. The plot obviously fails and Kongi goes on to make a triumphant speech as Daodu ruefully comments: 'There should have been no speech. We failed again.' (p. 81.) The gift which throws Kongi off-balance in his moment of triumph is a hastily thought-up gesture by Segi to take the place of the failed *coup*. In the middle of what is described as 'a real feast, a genuine Harvest orgy of food and drink' (p. 81.), Segi returns with a covered dish which is taken to be the festival yam, but *'In it, The head of an old man, Segi's father'*.[7] Thus in the middle of the feast of life being celebrated by his subjects, the tyrant is given a harvest dish more in keeping with his denial of life. This is a dramatization of the opposed values of Kongi and his people – death against life. He obviously takes the meaning of this curse on his regime – 'Kongi's mouth wide open in speechless terror'. (p. 84.) It is not that he is afraid of the sight of physical death – by now he must be inured to it – but he sees the eventual futility of his terror staring back at him through the dead man's eyes.

Daodu's more dramatic revolution fails, and in this Soyinka is consistent with his avoidance of grand dramatic endings in which evil is put down and a brand-new regime of good succeeds. But the point has been made. Daodu (with the help of Segi) has led an assertion of life against the death principle that Kongi represents. Although it is unsuccessful, the mere assertion keeps hope alive that this principle is still there, and can reassert itself, and in due course might prevail. For the time being Kongi's barren Scientificism (the very clumsiness of the name is satirical) prevails, but even in the midst of his barren cult, his people can momentarily assert life in a *real* harvest feast. Food, feasting, and sexual fulfilment in Soyinka's work are usually symbolic of life. In his poem 'Civilian and Soldier', the civilian throws life in the face of the soldier in the form of 'meat and bread, a gourd of wine/A bunch of breasts'.

Daodu too represents the kind of force through which the society can be saved. He has been shown to have the spiritual sanctions necessary to establish continuity with the now outdated regime of Oba Danlola and carry over its spiritual authority into the modern age – an age for which he is also equipped. There is no certainty at the end of the play of the precise

[7] The head of St John on a platter is a biblical parallel.

fate of Daodu and Segi. The Oba himself seems to abandon flight and 'starts briskly back in the opposite direction', that is, back into Ismaland, and since the symbolic 'iron grating descends and hits the ground with a loud, final clang', his end both as an effective personal and traditional force can be said to have been symbolically represented. The grating represents the general 'clamp-down' which the Organizing Secretary predicts (p. 80) and from which he flees. But whether Sarumi and his volunteers succeed in getting Daodu and Segi away is not clear. The presumption is that they do not. The text suggests that Daodu does not want to leave. Danlola describes the role of the party which has gone after him and Segi:

> If he's not already
> In Kongi's hands, they'll abduct him
> Forcibly and parcel him across the border.
> And that woman of his. (pp. 88–9.)

Daodu seems to be determined to stay and face the consequences of his action or continue his opposition within the country. The odds are against him whatever his intentions, but the odds are always loaded against the true saviour of his society in Soyinka's work. He frequently has to make a sacrifice of himself in order to save the society. So whether Daodu falls into Kongi's hands and is killed or whether he is able to hold out in his farm settlement (hardly likely) his role would be fulfilled. He has released a spirit in the land. To the cynical Organizing Secretary who cannot understand the meaning of sacrifice, Segi and Daodu are mad – 'Roadside lunatics'. But they have definitely released a potential force which has infected even the old Oba, and made him momentarily one in spirit with the revolution: 'The strange thing is I think/Myself I drank from the stream of madness/For a little while.'

There is an interesting parallel to Daodu's refusal to leave, with a situation in Soyinka's radio play *The Detainee*.[8] Konu, the detainee, is visited in prison by Zimole who has up to now protected Konu's children because of his position in the repressive regime. But even his position is now threatened and he can no longer protect his friend's children. He can, however, send them out of the country where they will be safe from tyranny. But this offer Konu resolutely refuses:

If the worst happens, they should be here. Let them know what fear is, so they can choose to fight it or live with it. I want them all to have that choice. Don't take them out of the country, Zimole.

[8] Broadcast B.B.C. African Service, September 1965, otherwise unpublished.

This helps to explain the anti-climax with which *Kongi's Harvest* ends. The struggle merely continues; it is this continuity, however feeble, which holds out any hope for particular situations and societies, and, eventually for mankind.

The film version of this play,[9] with Ossie Davies as narrator and Soyinka himself as Kongi, has a very different ending. Instead of a failed coup and the presentation of the head of the old man to Kongi, there is a successful overthrow of the dictator, and a shot of the new leader mouthing the same formulas as the overthrown Kongi. This successful coup bludgeons in the moral that the more things change, the more they remain the same. The effect on the screen is cruder than the more suggestive stage ending and indeed characterizes the general quality of the film. Daodu, who now really has no significance – a new leader of the opposition turned dictator having been trumped up for the film – also loses the subtlety of his portrayal in the play as the prince of hope, and he emerges as a rather unmotivated violator of shrines.

[9] Callpenny Films.

Madmen and Specialists

▼▼▼▼▼▼▼▼▼▼▼▼▼▼▼▼▼▼▼▼▼▼▼▼▼▼▼▼▼▼▼▼

Madmen and Specialists[1] was first produced in Waterford, Connecticut, U.S.A., in the Summer of 1970, and it shows significant developments in Soyinka's technique; developments which at least by the benefit of hindsight could be seen as arising logically from his earlier work.

For this play he has abandoned the traditional concern with plot, and the portrayal of fixed characters. There is very little story as such; rather, there is a situation from which the play radiates into wider situations. This is not in itself entirely strange for Soyinka. Even in *The Lion and the Jewel* which seems to be a long way off in technique from *Madmen and Specialists*, the author had resorted to deepening and widening the scope of the play through flashbacks into earlier events. He used this fluid approach increasingly in later plays, particularly in *The Strong Breed* and *The Road*. But in all those earlier plays the changes in time had been fairly clearly signalled so that there was discernible a controlling framework from which these flashbacks departed and to which they returned. In *Madmen* the whole structure is far more fluid, and there is a continual fading back and forth so that time and place become almost abstract.

The references to time make it necessary to invoke the idea of the two clocks so often used in interpretations of *Othello*. One set of references point to a lapse of only a number of hours between the surreptitious incarceration of the Old Man in the surgery and his shooting by Bero after his one and only meal. Aafa refers very clearly to 'Last night when we got him into that underground place . . .'. (p. 231.) All the other events of the play can be fitted chronologically into the rest of this one day. The Earth Mothers wake Si Bero from sleep at the next fall of night. Within this time frame, however, there are references to the passing of larger units of time. The Mendicants, for example, seem to have been in the neighbourhood for a long enough while to note changes in its patterns of life. 'The lane is deserted. Nobody comes and goes any more.' (p. 219.) Even more

---

[1] The play, which was unpublished when the first edition of this book was written, has since appeared in *Wole Soyinka Collected Plays*, vol. II (O.U.P., London, 1974). This version shows some variations from the mimeographed version kindly made available by Mr Soyinka for the first edition. Page references to the play are to the edition referred to in this note.

significantly, the Earth Mothers have by the end of the play given Bero every chance but have had to abandon him as irredeemable. 'Have I not sat with the knowledge of abuse these many days and kept the eyes of my mind open?' (p. 274.) Between the time of Bero's return and the burning of the herbs, they say 'We waited as long as we could' and 'Time has run out.' (p. 274.) These latter references point to long notional stretches of time within the narrower scale.

There is a similar abstraction of character. The villagers in *The Lion and the Jewel* are firmly delineated and have a fixed social entity from which they consciously, and with fair warning to the audience, elect to take part in a play within the play. Similarly some characters in the control framework of *A Dance of the Forests* double as characters in the Court of Mata Kharibu which is essentially a flashback. No such boundaries and signals are given in *Madmen*. The characters are fluid and change back and forth continually, requiring constant attention and interpretation from audience or reader. They start in fact by being nearly abstract characters whose names and appearance invite detachment rather than identification on the part of reader or audience.

Although in some parts of the play Africa is faintly recalled, this is Soyinka's most unlocalized play, the scenes being performed in a vague 'down here' with constant references to 'out there' from which fearful deeds are reported. The names of the characters strike no obviously associative chords – Goyi, Aafa, Bero, Iya Mate, Iya Agba[2] and Si Bero – while others bear representative labels rather than names – Blind Man, Cripple, Priest, The Old Man. This tendency towards abstraction and anonymity invests the play with a strangeness and effects a distancing of what goes on on the stage. Soyinka here closely approaches Brecht's alienation effect, and the atmosphere achieved by the practitioners of Theatre of the Absurd. He has, however, arrived here in his own time and in his own way, in a logical development of ideas and techniques which had been hinted at in earlier plays.

Not the least of the uses of this style of writing is its insulation from too particular references to times, places and persons, a not undesirable advantage to writers in 'sensitive' societies. It does have the additional advantage of making the play even more universally applicable. It would need hardly any adaptation to fit into any particular society.

One way in which the play seems to differ from the plays of, say Beckett and other practitioners of Theatre of the Absurd, is that though insulated from everyday reality, with *Madmen and Specialists* the connection with this reality is fairly readily made. With reasonable attention, the seemingly disjointed and illogical dialogue reveals a tough strand of its own internal

[2] *Iya* is Yoruba for Mother.

logic running through, and although words seem to be batted about as meaningless counters, this itself is thematically significant; it is a representation of the verbiage which in real life is a mere smoke screen for the actions of the rulers of our increasingly authoritarian societies in many parts of the world.

There are many themes in *Madmen* but it seems that the central enveloping theme is the erosion of humanity in a well-organized, tightly controlled authoritarian society. The very appearance of the Mendicants portrays men as victims – as sufferers. These men, disabled or deformed, are victims of an undefined 'blast' – some sort of explosion – which had taken place 'out there'. This has reduced them to beggars who put on a macabre act – exaggerating their disabilities – to catch the pennies of passers-by. But they also function ambiguously in the more active role of spies and secret agents of Bero the 'Specialist' who is the symbol of the authority 'out there'. (The Mendicants have other roles – particularly as a kind of chorus.)

When the play opens, these Mendicants are engaged in a macabre game of dice, the stakes for which are parts of their already disabled bodies. Goyi who has gambled away all his limbs and has become 'just a rubber ball' as a result, insists on playing on, offering to use his mouth to throw the dice. The picture is of men eagerly, even greedily, enhancing their further ruin. As the Blind Man fatalistically puts it 'Sooner or later we all eat sand.' (p. 218.) This opening tableau can thus be taken as a miniature representation of man in his world, or in the cryptic words of the play, 'The Creatures in the timeless parade'; man in a pantomime of perpetual self-destructive folly. Man is both sufferer and activator of his own suffering. The Mendicants have similarly ambiguous roles throughout the play.

Si Bero, who is next introduced, industriously collects herbs for her 'Specialist' brother who is absent 'out there'. Her whole life is wrapped up in her herb collection which is obviously a symbolic occupation; it keeps her anchored to her humanity. In her words to her brother 'I like to keep close to earth'. Her devotion to earth (p. 234) and humanity has brought her into an alliance with the mysterious old women ('Earth Mothers') Iya Agba and Iya Mate. These pointers to Si Bero's significance in the play are enough to contrast her with the thing that her brother has now become 'out there'.

Once, Bero's life too had been devoted to medicine; he had been similarly tied to 'earth' and humanity. He has now exchanged this humane existence for its very opposite. When his sister ceremonially pours a libation of palm wine in front of the doorstep on his return, he makes a chilling reference to the less humane preoccupations of his new world 'out there': 'We've wetted your good earth with something more potent than that you know.' (p. 234.) His sister recoils from the implications of his sinister hint with horror: 'Not you. Neither you nor father. You had nothing to do with it.' But it becomes increasingly clear that Bero is now committed to quite opposite principles from his sister. Human blood rather than palm wine is now his customary offering to the earth. For his sister, this is an abomination. This is the central polarity of the play; the humane on the one hand, represented by Si Bero and the Earth Mothers, and the inhumane represented by Bero and the world 'out there', an inhumanity conveniently symbolized by the eating of human flesh.

Bero, whose return is the central event of the play, is revealed as the jailer of his own father now imprisoned in his own house. The Old Man has fallen ideologically foul of the regime in which his son is a powerful figure. The father's crime is manifold with two or three aspects being prominent. He, apparently in irony, gave the regime the name of its philosophy – 'As' – which the adherents adopted before they really understood what it or the Old Man meant. One of the son's tasks now is to torture his father into revealing the real meaning of 'As'. The Old Man seems to have got the new men to face the full logic of their own inhumane actions; he tricked them into eating human flesh, on the ironic principle that all intelligent animals killed for food, and that these inhumane rulers might as well save on meat by eating their victims – a grim piece of logic typical of the play. The Old Man thus made the new men face the full inhumanity of their regime which they were otherwise too apt to cover in a smoke screen of words.

The Old Man is also fleetingly but very significantly pictured as Socrates. His son obliquely suggests suicide to him by dropping some poison berries over the Old Man's head with these words: 'If you ever get tired and feel you need a nightcap like a certain ancient Greek you were so fond of quoting, just sink a handful of them in water.' (p. 262.) The Old Man has, like Socrates in the eyes of his accusers, been corrupting the youth by teaching them to think. (The youth are conveniently represented by the Mendicants in another of their multiple roles.) In a speech to Si Bero, Bero puts the case against their Father thus:

> Father's assignment was to help the wounded readjust to the pieces and remnants of their bodies. Physically. Teach them to make baskets if they still had fingers. To use their mouths to ply needles if they had none, or use it to sing if their vocal cords had not been shot away. Teach them to amuse themselves, make something of themselves. Instead he began to teach them to think, think THINK! Can you picture a more treacherous thing than to place a working mind in a mangled body?   (p. 242.)

Bero himself emerges as a cold-blooded technocrat totally devoid of humanity. His one remaining link with his human condition – and hence with any obligation to being humane – is his father. While the Old Man remains living, Bero cannot forget that he also is human. The Old Man therefore has to die in order to sever Bero's visible bond with humanity. The Old Man puts the point to Bero: 'I am the last proof of the human in you. The last shadow. Shadows are tough things to be rid of. How does one prove he was never born of man? Of course you could kill me . . .' (p. 253.) The logic of the Old Man's reasoning is demonstrated when at the end of the play Bero shoots him. This is a further step in the son's attempt to dehumanize himself. Since he is a symbol of the technocratic regime 'out there' this dehumanization is characteristic of the whole regime. (Bero's growing alienation from the humane is also seen in his renunciation of his earlier humane profession, his lack of sympathy with his sister, and his driving out of the Earth Mothers.)

Bero is dressed in military uniform, carries a swagger stick and a gun, both of which he does not hesitate to use. These and other hints suggest that he represents a military regime, a suggestion compatible with the totalitarian nature of life 'out there'. These military suggestions should not unnecessarily limit the applicability of the play; it is relevant to all kinds of regimes military or otherwise which are based on inhumanity and repression. There is also something comprehensive in the slogan which the Old Man devised for the new political philosophy that suggests the permanence, and hence the constant recurrence in human history, of human perversity: 'As was, is, and shall ever be'. (Especially with the cannibalistic overtones in this play, this is very reminiscent of the Warrior's prediction in *A Dance of the Forests*: 'Unborn generations will be cannibals and eat each other as we have done.' Bero and his associates are manipulators of this 'timeless parade' of the negative aspects of the human personality.

Pessimistic though the play seems to be, there is always a suggestion of the eventual futility of regimes like Bero's. They are certainly grimly successful for a time and pile up against themselves a horrible toll of victims. But even at the height of their success they display a knowledge of their own precariousness. This is why they have to go on torturing and killing. This is why they have to have spies. This is why Bero has to torture out of his father information of the real meaning of 'As'. The forces of life which such regimes violate have a way of presenting a silent continuing threat. Bero and his crew live in constant dread of this. This is what the Old Man points to when he defies Bero to do his worst: 'I recreate my tentacles so, cut away.' (p. 262.) In spite of Bero's bluster he knows that this is true. What little hope there is in the ability of humanity to triumph is admittedly buried under the physical realities of the repressive regime which is for the time being all too successful, and the play cannot be called really optimistic. The hope is too faint, but it is there.

As has been suggested there is little dramatic action in the play. All the action lies in the words, which are very suggestive. It is the words, continually fading away into new meanings, elusive, slippery which keep the play alive. The very slipperiness of words is significant. It is one of the themes of the play – the total unreliability of manifestos, promises, laws, indeed all that society is supposed to be based on. In this slippery world even breaches of faith can become manifestos. A good illustration of this is the incident in which Bero forces his father to accept a cigarette when the Old Man preferred his pipe. Bero starts with an assertion: 'I promised you the best of everything and this will prove to you what I mean.' The 'proof' turns out to be a refusal of the man's wish for his pipe. The Old Man (in the published version),[3] using the style of the new regime – for which he was partly responsible anyway – launches into a justification of this violation of a promise, exalting it in fact into the level of doctrine. Soyinka's handling of this speech in the two versions of the play is illuminating. In the mimeographed version used for the first production, the corresponding version of the speech had been given to Bero and had thus functioned simply as an example of the cynical lack of good faith of the regime. By attributing an amended version – with additions like 'Shall I teach you what to say?' and 'Are you cramming it up for the next victim?' – to the Old Man, Soyinka also underlines his portrayal of the Old Man in the ambiguous role of tongue-in-cheek political adviser to the regime, particularly since in this new version the speech ends with a reference to the crucial occasion when the Old Man had tricked the junta into eating human flesh:

OLD MAN: . . . Shall I teach you what to say? Choice! Particularity! What redundant self-deceptive notions! More? More? Insistence on a floppy old coat, a rickety old chair, a moth-eaten hat which no certified lunatic would ever consider wearing, a car which breaks down twenty times in twenty minutes, an old idea riddled with the pellets of incidence. Enough? More? Are you cramming it up fast for the next victim? A perfect waterproof coat is rejected for a patched-up heirloom that gives the silly wearer rheumatism. Is this an argument for freedom of choice? Is it sensible to cling so desperately to bits of the bitter end of a run-down personality? To the creak in an old chair, the crack in a cup, a crock of

[3] In the earlier mimeographed version this speech had been given to Bero. See p. 94 of the first edition of this book.

an old servant, the crick in the bottleneck of a man's declining
years . . . [*Pause. His voice changes.*] But it did come to the
test and I asked you all, what is one meat from another?
Oh, your faces then, your faces . . .   (p. 252.)

The same technique of demonstrating the devaluation of words into
mere sounds is seen in this exchange between father and son:

BERO: They were provided a Creed but they talked heresy. Same
           as you.

OLD MAN: Creed? Heresy? Bread, Pleurisy and what next? Will you
           try and speak some intelligible language?

Sometimes the echoes lead us, through association, from innocuous to
sinister suggestions which help to give the play its insidious undertone
of terror. In this next example the dialogue moves from the innocuous
suggestions of 'lamps' to grim suggestions of torture and death through
electrocution:

OLD MAN: A lamp has its uses.

AAAFA: So, electricity.

GOYI: Bleeah! Election promises.

CRIPPLE: What we want is individual manifestos.

AAAFA: Manifestos for every freak? General Electric!

OLD MAN: Electrocutes. Electric chair. Electrodes on the nerve centres
           – your favourite pastime I believe? . . .

This seemingly disconnected dialogue is seen to be full of suggestion;
broken election promises feature cheek by jowl with political torture. This
technique of free association makes the range of suggestion of which the
play is capable almost boundless.

At the end Bero shoots his father, who is just on the point of operating
on the Cripple (the latter's question still unasked) to find out what makes a
heretic tick. The Old Man seems suddenly to have become possessed with
the need to 'practise' on the questioning cripple. He hands Bero an excuse
(if one were needed) to kill him a justification for what has now become a
necessity.

Bero cannot now hope for an answer to his question about the significance of 'As' – 'Why As?' All he is left with is the tyranny that he has collaborated in setting up, without any guiding philosophy or justification. He can thus only look forward to perpetuating the regime of death.

He lives on; so does Si Bero, representing two opposed principles. Both are, in the idiom of the Earth Mothers, to be tried by fire. Life has got to continue from whatever survives among the ashes. We are left with a picture of a great deal of good destroyed, of an episode ended in waste, but with the possibilities of another start, another attempt to remix the old ingredients with what survives from the fire. The pattern of the recurring cycles of human history, as portrayed so graphically in *A Dance of the Forests*, is once again set before us. In the earlier play the traditional apparatus of gods and spirits provided the enveloping metaphor. Here, the imagery of civil strife, military tyranny, provide the vehicle for another look at man as the victim of his own nature. To emphasize this, once again, the characters fade back and forth into different, sometimes conflicting, roles, sometimes the victims, sometimes the perpetrators of cruelty, so that in the end we are left with the impression of a general taint of which no one is really free. It becomes hard, either from their speech or from their attire, to tell madmen apart from specialists.

A note on
The Bacchae of Euripides

▼▼▼▼▼▼▼▼▼▼▼▼▼▼▼▼▼▼▼▼▼▼▼▼▼▼▼▼▼▼▼

SOYINKA'S ADAPTATION of Euripides' *Bacchae* was commissioned by the British National Theatre, but he must have been prompted to undertake the task by inclination as well. In his introduction to the published version[1] he quotes from his own essay 'The Fourth Stage' a passage which makes it clear that certain similarities between Dionysos and the Yoruba god Ogun drew him to look at the functioning of a god in another mythological tradition who also had more than a hint of waywardness in his nature. The helpless bewilderment of the people of Thebes as they ponder the 'justice' of Dionysos is similar to that of the people of Ire when their protector turns upon them.[2] Then men are forced, even at the risk of blasphemy, to pass adverse judgements on gods. 'Oh, this is a heartless/ Deity, bitter, unnatural in his revenge,'[3] declares the Old Slave of Dionysos, and Kadmos, straining to achieve balance concludes: 'Dionysos is just. But he is not fair!' Ogun in 'Idanre' attracts to himself, from his own people, such epithets as: 'Lust-blind god, gore-drunk Hunter/Monster deity.'[4] A mythological play – that is, safely distanced both by time and civilization – whose climax was the dismemberment of her own son by a mother while possessed, would have presented an opportunity to deal more objectively, and on a purely symbolic level, with the theme of internecine strife which Soyinka had looked at rather more nakedly in writings like *The Man Died*, *Season of Anomy* and *A Shuttle in the Crypt*. In her distorted vision, Agave bears the severed head of her son back to the city in triumph, even, ironically, looking for her son to participate in the glory of her conquest. Only gradually does the full horror of her unnatural deed send her into an almost wordless acceptance of a fate she cannot understand. To Kadmos' anguished question 'Why us?' she replies simply, 'Why not?'. In this tortured, roundabout way she has accepted a

[1] *The Bacchae of Euripides* (London, Eyre Methuen, 1973).
[2] 'Idanre', especially 'The Battle'.
[3] *The Bacchae of Euripides*, pp. 86–7.
[4] *Idanre and other Poems* (London, Methuen, 1967), p. 75.

sacrificial role which at the beginning of the play was the lot of unwilling slaves.

Possibly an even more important attraction of the play for Soyinka was the opportunity it gave him to look once again, in this removed context, at the theme of government and its attendant themes of justice and freedom. Here the portrayal of the militaristic Pentheus is crucial. His regime is a tyranny based on the unwilling labour of slaves. The first view of his kingdom in the opening set shows a road 'lined by the bodies of crucified slaves'. He himself is aptly characterized as a man of chains. His tyrannical nature is evidently the result of a refusal to come to terms with the whole of his nature. In the metaphor of the myth, he has shut out the element controlled by Dionysos. This he never accepts. Instead he allows himself to spy on the rites of the god's devotees and is torn to pieces by them, under the leadership of his own mother Agave, who at this point is blinded to his identity, being possessed by the god. This picture of intra-family and intra-civic violence is what seems so relevant in countries far removed from the home of the original myth. The revolutionary principle which Dionysos represents is blind, violent, and self-destructive. 'Just', perhaps, but certainly not 'fair'. Its costs, even when conditions (as in Thebes) make it inevitable, are terrible.

The adaptation of such a well-known classic is restricting – though Soyinka stretches the time span to include a mime of Christ's miracle of turning water into wine – and he himself has reservations about his original, in particular the ending.[5] What seems least satisfactory is the shifting moral centre of the play. Although the ideal of 'balance' between the two principles of earth and ether is extolled, no character, neither Tiresias nor Kadmos, is strong enough to demonstrate it, and even Dionysos himself cuts a rather uninspiring figure. Although he is credited with being the source of self-knowledge, his devotees lose their vision and act under the most terrible illusions. He is also nominally the god of freedom, but he does not provide the rallying vision for the slaves, so that they never develop into any significant force. The Dionysiac direction seems to be towards anarchy rather than reform, which is unlikely to come from mere excitement and hallucinated agitation. In a similar way, Soyinka's play is attractively written, with a number of imaginative details and exciting opportunities for directorial brilliance, but it does not achieve an overall unity, nor does it define or indicate a coherent moral position.

[5] *The Bacchae of Euripides*, p. xi.

Death and the
King's Horseman

▼▼▼▼▼▼▼▼▼▼▼▼▼▼▼▼▼▼▼▼▼▼▼▼▼▼▼▼▼▼

THE CONSCIOUSNESS of an overwhelming public responsibility and a total commitment to it even when this involves death had been the theme of an earlier Soyinka play, *The Strong Breed*. There are analogies between the call of blood in that play and the fatal call of duty in *Death and the King's Horseman*.[1] When Eman in the earlier play seeks to evade the call of his destiny, his father predicts: 'Your own blood will betray you, son, because you cannot hold it back. If you make it do less than this, it will rush to your head and burst it open.'[2] In spite of the call of blood, the play goes on to show how, when confronted with the ultimate sacrifice, the human will is apt to flinch, and that the act of self sacrifice is no mere mechanical ritual. In *Death and the King's Horseman* the Elesin Oba's destiny, his 'blood', has similarly destined him for the ultimate sacrifice: 'It is not he who calls himself Elesin Oba, it is his blood that says it. As it called out to his father before him and will to his son after him. . . .' (p. 35.) The play examines the Elesin's response when the actual call for which his whole life has been a preparation, and on which the future of his people depend, sounds in his ears.

His response, the play makes clear, has cosmic significance. The Praise Singer, himself a custodian of values, is fully aware of the consequences of a failure to maintain the integrity of a civilization at a crucial point in history: 'There is only one home to the life of a river-mussel; there is only one home to the life of a tortoise; there is only one shell to the soul of man; there is only one world to the spirit of our race. If that world leaves its course and smashes on boulders of the great void, whose world will give us shelter?' (p. 11.) The responsibility for keeping the world on course rests on the Elesin; and there are ominous signs of a wavering of his will in the face of the enormous task.

A demand for richer cloths first stuns the market women under their leader Iyaloja, and their relief that this trivial request is all that has seemed

---

[1] *Death and the King's Horseman* (Eyre Methuen, London, 1975).
[2] See above, pp. 60–7.

to threaten a cosmic disaster is tinged with embarrassment. Iyaloja, as 'Mother of the market', has a representative role, and, like the Praise Singer, speaks for the people and for tradition.[3] She voices the anxiety of the whole community when the Elesin's demands grow and he asks for the hand of a young girl – who is betrothed to Iyaloja's own son. Nothing must be withheld from one who has such a great mission, however, and the request is granted. But after such demands – in themselves unworthy at this time – a failure to live up to the expected level of honour would be little short of pollution, and the anxious reminders of his role are never far from Iyaloja's thoughts. 'The living must eat and drink. When the moment comes, don't turn the food to rodents' droppings in their mouth.' (p. 22.) By the end of the first section of the play the Elesin's involvement with things of this world and his evident irritation at being reminded of his coming death have sown doubts about the firmness of his will.

This first section also introduces us to the heart of a culture. Its privileges and its responsibilities are understood by all, so that they are accepted, faced or shirked knowingly. What the portrait of the District Officer and his wife, Simon and Jane Pilkings, dancing the tango dressed in the captured regalia of an *egungun* masque presents to us is a trifling travesty of that same culture, which shocks even the converted Christian Sergeant Amusa. The Pilkings' act is *prima facie* one of desecration, but it is even more significant as a demonstration of their essential irrelevance, and that of the imperium the husband represents in the spiritual environment. There is irony, however, in the fact that through no special virtue, he represents great physical power. Pilkings is portrayed as a nervous, unimaginative, totally ungifted administrator. Soyinka is at pains to emphasize in a prefatory author's note that the District Officer is not the victim of a cruel dilemma. His lengthy pauses for thought are only to resolve such weighty problems as to what extent his actions are likely to disturb the sleep of His Visiting Highness. When the level of thought and action, coupled as it is with military power, is put beside the gravity of the trauma facing the people of Oyo, the cruel irony of the portrayal becomes glaring. To Pilkings the Elesin's sacrifice is a meaningless suicide which it is his duty to prevent. Pilkings's intervention does not start the weakening of the Elesin's will and is ignored by Iyaloja as a major factor in the Elesin's failure. For her, Pilkings is a 'child' and she addresses him persistently as such. She is, by contrast, unrelenting in her censure of the Elesin – fittingly so because of her representative position of 'Mother of

[3] In his essay 'Mediation in Soyinka: The Case of the King's Horseman, James Gibbs (ed.), *Critical Perspectives on Wole Soyinka*, (Three Continents Press, Washington, D.C., 1980), Dan Izevbaye discusses, with interesting references, the representative role of markets in Yoruba society.

the market' and also as the one who has been called to sacrifice her son's betrothed bride to the Elesin's untimely surge of lust. He has ignored her warning and has not only blurred his own vision but also, by fathering a child in those circumstances, has threatened even the unborn. She is as unsparing of her contempt as she was generous and accommodating when she thought the Elesin deserved indulgence:

> You have betrayed us. We fed your sweetness such as we hoped awaited you on the other side. But you said No, I must eat the world's left-overs. We said you were the hunter who brought the quarry down; to you belonged the vital portions of the game. No, you said, I am the hunter's dog and I shall eat the entrails of the game and the faeces of the hunter. We said you were the hunter returning home in triumph, a slain buffalo pressing down on his neck; you said wait, I first must turn up this cricket hole with my toes.   (p. 68.)

In the face of her unrelenting prosecution of him, the Elesin asks not for pity but for understanding – 'Even I need to understand' – and in this attempt to understand he suggests the nature and extent of Pilkings' role. The Elesin might have overcome even the late pull of the flesh ('even that, even if it overwhelmed one with a thousandfold temptations to linger awhile, a man could overcome it'); but the unexpected appearance of 'an alien hand' encouraged the belief that this was indeed the hand of the gods, a blasphemous thought which finally eroded the lingering vestiges of will and duty: 'I had committed this blasphemy of thought – that there might be the hand of the gods in a stranger's intervention.' (p. 69.)

Iyaloja brushes this and all other explanations aside. The reasons for the Elesin's failure are relevant to his personal peace of mind, but by now more than this is involved. The Elesin has betrayed history; he has pushed the world from its moorings. The son has now had to assume the role of his father and become – before his time – the bearer of the traditional responsibility of accompanying the dead king on his journey.

This loss of honour and the sacrifice of his son make up the Elesin's real tragedy. His suicide – Pilkings' judicial term would now be applicable – is now merely a matter of personal relief, mercifully executed with speed. The tragedy is that of a man faced with responsibilities which tax his human powers to their limit and collapsing under the weight. Does this also represent the erosion of a people's will?

The 'Mother of the market' has not flinched. True, both the old plantain and its young sapling are dead, but in his final day, the Elesin has left a seed. The young bride ceremonially seals the eyes of her dead husband and prepares to face the future under the guidance of Iyaloja: 'Now forget the dead. Forget even the living. Turn your mind only to the unborn.' (p. 76.) In this third part of the Yoruba cosmology, with all its uncertainty, lies the hope of the community. There is also some indication of the strength of the community in the voluntary return of Olunde to assume his traditional responsibility on the death of his father, but even more in his readiness to take his father's place in death when the latter's will crumbles. In this willing acceptance of his role, and in the promise latent in the unborn child, lie the society's hope of regeneration and of continuity.

Opera Wonyosi

▼▼▼▼▼▼▼▼▼▼▼▼▼▼▼▼▼▼▼▼▼▼▼▼▼▼▼▼▼▼▼▼▼▼▼

OPERA WONYOSI was written and performed in 1977 just before President Bokassa's crowning manifestation of *hubris*, his imperial coronation. Soyinka used him as a coat-hanger for a combined swipe at that dictator's excesses and the extremes of religious, political and economic corruption in Nigeria. It is a direct, deliberately coarse, popular entertainment as its literary progenitors, Gay's *Beggar's Opera* and Brecht's *Threepenny Opera* had been. According to Soyinka himself, the piece appealed to all classes when it was staged at the University of Ife:

> Any serious student of the sociology of theatre who witnessed *Opera Wonyosi*, and the reactions of the audiences would not dare deny the social impact of that experience on a truly wide spectrum of the audience, across all class divisions – from the 'lace' madams to Oduduwa Hall kitchen-hands; from the Military Governor to the victim (or victim acquaintance) of his soldiers' code of anti-civilian conduct; from the university don to the parks attendant.... (Foreword, p. iv.)

In *Kongi's Harvest*, Soyinka had handled the theme of dictatorship and its consequent ills, but the handling there was largely generalised by the use of metaphor, so that while the playwright started it with one dictator in mind, Kongi reminded audiences and readers of quite others. By contrast, Folksy Boksy is directly referred to in *Opera Wonyosi*, and for good measure he is compared with his East African counterpart, Amin, in their grotesque posturings – both of them would have been wholly comic, had not their follies been so murderous in their consequences. From Bokassa's own mouth their childish fondness for dressing up and their casual coldblooded disregard for the sanctity of human life are ridiculed as Bokassa routinely consigns an offending subject to the tender mercies of Amin:

> BOKY: Cut out his tongue and send that silenced item to my friend Idi Amin, with my compliments. No. Stop. Send Amin the entire wretch and add that his tongue is not to be trusted. He'll know what to do. . . . But he's (Amin) also an ape. You know, he apes. He apes me. I appear in a uniform – an official uniform

understand – Amin sees me, and straightway he orders a
duplicate, complete with medals, plus a few more he's dreamt
up. I earned my medals fair and square – in action. And then to
make it worse he carries his own much better. Got the size for
it you know. I didn't like that photo of him and me together. It
was my medals weighing me down on one side, but he didn't
feel his own at all. Of course mine are pure gold – trust him to
resort to a trick like gold-plated aluminium. No class. (p. 25.)

Just as direct as the references to Bokassa and Amin are those to particular
events. Soyinka himself provides a gloss on the Marble village Igbeti which
is referred to in the *Opera*:

A village in western Nigeria whose rich marble resources have become
the monopoly of a private group. Several mysterious deaths have
overtaken the champions of public rights to the marble. (This deposit
has since been taken over by the Civilian government in Oyo State:
1979)   (Textual Notes, p. 85.)

Equally direct are references to Udoji, the Kano Rampage of soldiers, Tai
Solarin's gift of a rotting corpse to the Lagos City Council, the burning
down of the Kalakuta Republic,[1] Bokassa's massacre of school children
over uniforms, the wedding of Gowon, the Bar Beach Show and many
more glances at topical matters that would have been gleefully appreciated
by the audience.

Wonyosi is opera, and popular, low-life opera at that. The published text,
1981, thus gives only an indication of its effectiveness as a performance.
The book and lyrics were written for direct, brutal, multi-class appeal and
give a satirical picture of the foetid decadence of a corrupt society. One
lyric would illustrate both the matter and the manner of this opera as it
represents the plight of ordinary people at a time when their country was
booming with oil wealth:

Have you seen those workers daily jostling
To catch a bus to beat the factory deadline?
And the pregnant mother wedged with elbows
Barely dodging those haphazard blows
You'll claim the boss is also on the breadline
The 'go-slow' has wrecked his daily hustling

[1] The popular Band Leader, Fela Anikulapo-Kuti (formerly Ransome-Kuti) cousin
of Wole Soyinka, had his compound burnt and ravaged by soldiers and the inmates
severely beaten up, apparently with impunity.

Well, a whole day in an air-conditioned car
Is sweeter than one hour in over-heated air.

CHORUS: Explain the smugness on the face of the chauffeur?
He knows that at the bus stop life is even rougher.

Have you been to the hospital lately
And seen despair on faces in the line
Insolence from clerks lolling on the table
A waiting-room that smells worse than a stable
You'll say the rich are also laid supine
Diseases fell them though their life is stately
Well the rich can telephone for private cure
While for an aspirin the poor must long endure

CHORUS: Explain the joy-on-the-face of the Medical Apprentice?
The Medical Council has voted for Private Practice.

Did you go to the cathedral the other Sunday
And hear the bishop on the theme of pain?
Suffering is sent to make a fellow great
Fighting with rats for gari in a garret.
Bullshit! Let riches fall on me like rain
And keep your starving greatness any day.
A life of ease is what a rich man knows
Glory is cold when the wind of hunger blows

CHORUS: Explain the beggar's rapture hustling by the mosque
He's chewing fleshy nuts while the prisoner gets the husk.
(pp. 62–3.)

In the directness of its appeal to the ordinary Nigerian, the *Opera* has a
great deal in common with Wole Soyinka's popular long playing record,
Unlimited Liability Company (1983), the agit-prop pieces, *Priority Projects*
(1983) and *Requiem for a Futurologist* (1983).

Although the action of *Wonyosi* is set in Bangui, thus making the
references to Bokassa relevant, the characters are Nigerian expatriates,
hired or tolerated for the convenience of the neighbouring dictator, the
expatriates being past masters in the art of manipulating and surviving in
corruption. As in *Requiem for a Futurologist*, appearance is everything to
the characters in *Wonyosi*. Significantly, wonyosi itself is described as a
particularly expensive, glamourously vulgar kind of dress material:

POLY:[2] ... the one and only – Wonyosi. The only fashion in the right
      circles. This one costs some five hundred dollars a yard.
      When you wear this at home it's a sign that you've arrived.
                                                                          (p. 38.)

The beggars are not what they seem. They are carefully costumed to fit
their assumed deformities and fictitious histories. One of them is even a
professor enjoying a sabbatical from his university and public service jobs,
enriching his pocket (while no doubt resting his intellect) with a spell of
professional begging. He is illustrative of the grotesques with which
Soyinka makes his satirical thrusts. Equally illusory is Lucy's pregnancy
which suddenly disintegrates into a heap of padding. Corruption embraces
all. The profits of illicit activities are shared throughout the society. Polly
catalogues the persons who have to be cut into the Marble deal:

POLY: ... Five hundred went to Commissioner Brown. Five hundred
        went to a mistress of Emperor Boky, another five hundred was
        bought in the name of one of his latest bastards. Five hundred
        went to the Director of Prisons and the final thousand were
        personally handed to the Deputy Chief Justice of the Empire
        for re-distribution if and as how he thinks fit.   (p. 40.)

In Bangui all government is at the whim of the ridiculous but sinister
Bokassa. The name Folksy Boksy is meant to indicate the 'charm' that so
often was cited in defence or in condonation of the crimes of some of these
evil figures. In Nigeria, government is conspiracy; a secret society
consisting of the top few – the Cartel in *Season of Anomy* – for the
exploitation of the mass of the people. *Wonyosi* thus repeats in a popular
capsule a recurring theme in Soyinka's work.

Wonyosi bubbles into the Bar Beach style execution scene in which the
whole society –mothers with their young children, dying patients in wheel
chairs – all jostle for good seats to see Macheath shot with the maximum of
blood:

PATIENT: ... before they shoot them, they should drain their blood
          and put it in a blood-bank. Then upright lawabiding citizens
          like me can gain something at least from their worthless
          existence.

          Correction! I wasn't thinking. If they drained their blood in
          advance then there'll be no blood spattering around when

---

[2] It is curious that in his transformation of Brecht's *Threepenny Opera*, Soyinka let
the names of Macheath and Polly survive without Nigerianisation.

the bullets land would there? (p. 78.)

Those who point out the dehumanising potential of this kind of justice are called 'bleeding-heart *cynics* and *liberals*'. In this particular instance, however all the bustle of expectation is defeated. The capricious Emperor declares an amnesty and Macheath lives to cheat and kill again:

> DEE-JAY: 'We, Our Serene Highness, newly reincarnated, and crowned Emperor Charlemagne Desiree Boky the First, Lion of Bangui, Tiger of the Tropics, Elect of God, First among Kings and Emperors, the Pulsing Nugget of Life, and Radiating Sun of Africa hereby pronounce, in honour of our coronation on this day, a general Amnesty for all common criminals. . . .' (p. 82)

Wonyosi shares features with other works, serious as well as comic. Its fierce exposure of corruption in government which has its reverberations throughout the whole society, is general in Soyinka's work. The resulting deformity of society is given physical representation in the deformed beggars in both *Madmen and Specialists* and *Wonyosi*. The theme of 'the appearance is the reality', the lack of integrity in a corrupt society is represented by the quick changes of clothes and personality in *Wonyosi* and *Requiem for a Futurologist*.

The satire is topical, naked and direct enough to require little further comment. Soyinka adds to the value of the published text by providing an uncharacteristic almost Shavian foreword which not only gives a general defence of satirical (even sick) comedy, but a particular defence of *Wonyosi* from criticisms which remark on the work's lack of a 'solid class perspective'. He asserts the comic writer's role:

> Those of us who see no reason to present a utopian counter to the preponderant obscenities that daily assail our lives and, whose temporary relief is often one of 'sick humour', will continue to press this line of confrontation by accurate and negative reflection, in the confidence that sooner or later, society will recognize itself in the projection and, with or without the benefit of 'scientific' explications, be moved to act in its own overall self-interest. (Foreword, p. iv.)*

In this assertion he links up with the tradition of comedy stretching from Aristophanes through Ben Jonson and Molière to Soyinka himself. If society does not hear, it is not because the playwright is silent.

* My numbering.

Requiem for a Futurologist

▼▼▼▼▼▼▼▼▼▼▼▼▼▼▼▼▼▼▼▼▼▼▼▼▼▼▼▼▼▼▼▼▼▼

IN A SOCIETY floundering in a sea of unformed values, where having lost its spiritual roots, the acquisition of wealth and its conspicuous consumption are taken as the ideal, appearance becomes everything. A man is what he seems, for as long as he can keep up the pretence in the eyes of a gullible public. Costuming, the glib line of sales promotion, and the theatrical props to maintain the facade are all-important. Only the surface matters. Thus in *Opera Wonyosi*, 1977, Chief Anikura's wardrobe of costumes to go with the assumed personae of his beggar troupe was as essential as are those of the quick change artists, Alaba/Dr Semuwe/Eleazar Hosannah, in *Requiem* (if he was not the man in the Egungun mask as well, then he ought to be!).

Requiem for a Futurologist brings old themes up to date. *Jero's Metamorphosis* had updated the charlatan prophet of the trials. Now in the person of the Rev Dr Godspeak Igbehodan the phenomenon is brought further forward into the booming oil-rich setting which offers even more opportunities for vulgar ostentation in life-and-death-styles. Tycoons are now buried in coffins shaped like their cadillacs, or television sets, aerials projecting throught the orifices of the marble angels adorning their tombs, the aerials hopefully picking up their favourite programmes via satellite; *Dallas* has become the universal soap, a reminder that the play may be set in Nigeria, but as the initial stage directions indicate, could be in most places. Nigeria is only one manifestation of a universal cult of materialism.

The central situation too is familiar; a prophet's protégé is out to out-manouvre and supersede his master, only this time, the instrument is the simple one of a suitably phrased obituary notice following on a plausible prediction of the master's death. Once the public has accepted the truth of the prediction of Eleazar Hosannah, his master Godspeak Igbehodan is doomed. He is locked in a farcical situation, in which the more he protests that, contrary to the false prediction, he is alive, the more he is 'accused' of being dead, but refusing to lie still and be buried. Even Dr Godspeak's reality is in question. He himself, under the professional ministrations of the physician/psychiatrist, Dr Semuwe, is made to admit the possibility that he may after all, and contrary to all his own convictions, be dead. Under Dr Semuwe's relentless examination, Dr Godspeak is stripped of all his external props and is revealed in his true state as 'dead' – as he really is, spiritually, for all his sales talk:

GODSPEAK: [*Desperately*] They mean it. They insist on it. Semuwe, they accuse me of being dead.

SEMUWE: [*Unmoved*] Oh. And you?

GODSPEAK: [*Lying down*] And I what, doctor?

SEMUWE: You say they accuse you of being dead. How do you plead?

GODSPEAK: Doctor, don't make a joke of it please

SEMUWE: A joke? I don't find it funny. Is what you say true? After all it is a very serious charge you've made.

GODSPEAK: Doctor, you don't think I would lie about such a thing do you? You saw the mob with your own eyes. They have been keeping wake around my house for the past....

SEMUWE: That isn't what I meant. Is it true *what* they are saying?

GODSPEAK: But doctor, how can you ask me such a thing, even in jest? You can see me with your own eyes. You are this very moment examining my condition. I mean the fact that you can ask me at all....

SEMUWE: So?

GODSPEAK: So? [*Sits up sharply*] So? Is that all you can say?

SEMUWE: You haven't answered my question.

GODSPEAK: Oh I'm lost! Now I know I am lost!

SEMUWE: No you're not. And even if you are, it doesn't answer my question.

GODSPEAK: [*Groaning*] I am lost. I am done for. Finished.

SEMUWE: Good. We are making progress. I told you I have my methods.... (p. 27.)

GODSPEAK: [*Collapsing flat on his face*] Oh God, I'm dead.

DOCTOR: [*Sighs*] You said it not me.   (p. 28.)

Yet in his heyday, immaculately tailored and costumed, armed with the
jargon of futurology, he had been pursued by the media, his every vague
prediction latched upon by a public almost anxious to be deceived. 'Never
tell the public they've been had. They much prefer to remain fooled.'
(p. 48.)

The multiple irony of the stripping down of Dr Godspeak is that it is
done by Dr Semuwe, who is no other than Eleazar Hosannah in disguise
and who in turn as Alaba is yet another manifestation. Thus even when Dr
Semuwe in the authority figure of a psychiatrist reveals truths about the
nature of the society, they are suspect because he himself is a fraud – even
the personality that he adopts of Dr Semuwe is that of a man long dead.
Nothing is firm; everything in sight turns out to be something else.

Although Dr Godspeak uses a slick pseudo-scientific astrological jargon
and passes himself off as a Christian priest, yet when he wishes to bind
Alaba with an oath he does not employ the *Bible*, but makes him bite
Ogun's cutlass. So perhaps it is in the old spiritual values that we can find
solid rock? Can the society be after all firmly based in tradition in spite of
all the surface trumpery? But when the sacred Egúngún appears, the
ancestral spirit of prophecy and the old repository of moral sanctions, this
also turns out to be only another false substitute for the real thing, a
desecration dreamt up by Eleazar Hosannah to fool the public. Once more
solid rock turns out to be sinking sand.

Where then is hope when Godspeak is replaced by Hosannah? The
people only remove their trust from one charlatan to repose it in another,
cleverer than his master. As with priests and prophets, so with politicians,
civil and military. The satire is all pervasive. The immediacy of *Requiem
for a Futurologist* to Nigeria dominated by religious, commercial and
political opportunism is obvious. Soyinka prefaces the published version of
the play with excerpts from Nigerian newspapers which read like excerpts
from one of his own farces, but are apparently straight:

On the Fuji scene with directions of my crystal ball, Alhaji Kollington
Ayinla will continue to dominate the scene. He will this year introduce
new dance styles and instruments. We have it on the stars of the super
conscience plane by cosmic intelligence that the appearance of seven
commets [*sic*] on the significator adjacent to the planet venus such
Musician can dominate the scene for the next seven years.

(*Sunday Times* 9 January 1983)

I can observe the occultation of the planet, Venus whose appearance in the 5th House of Jupiter appears as difficult planet. I foresee lazyness laxity and truancy in the rank and file of workers generally both in the private and public sectors.

An unprecedented wave of Industrial uprising is visible throughout the first nine months of this year. This is due to the position of the planetary ruler of workers, Neptune, retrograding into Sagitarius.

(Sunday Times 30 January 1983)

I foresee three gigantic edifices contesting for power on the political arena, this melee is seen to precipatate a state of tension that may markedly upset the integrity and the stability of the Second Republic. On my crystal ball it seems to what can be described like a Chinese fighting called CHAL-CAL-COOL – 'Riding the Horse backwards.'

(Sunday Times 9 January 1983) (p. vi.)

The play merely dramatises and reduces to further absurdity everyday reality. Those absurdities are however put into wider context by excerpts from Swift portraying similar absurdities in other times and other places. Nostradamus is claimed as only a later incarnation of an Indian futurologist of an earlier era. Folly is universal!

A shorter version of this play *Die Still Dr. Rev. Godspeak* was broadcast by the BBC World Service with the rich middle section missing, more spectacular visual effects ommitted, and a different ending. In this truncated version (still a very funny farce) Dr Godspeak ends by jumping off the ledge outside his house to the death which having been predicted for him, had meant his effective demise as the darling of the media and the coiner of money through his spiritual fraud. In the stage version of which the published version is the text, Dr Godspeak is spared this spectacular suicide and is lured into a formal laying out by his clever assistant now costumed to succeed him – after a live burial? He can only look forward at best to a life of obscurity, his particular bubble having been finally burst. The shorter version (meant for sound radio) misses a good deal of the comedy and the layers of irony and satire. The multiple role of Hosannah for instance, which illustrates the utter unreliability of the evidence of eyes and ears is lost. In the stage version this mixture, this conflict of roles reaches a climax when in the person of Dr Semuwe, the psychiatrist, Dr Godspeak is induced to rise from his couch and re-enact a scene in which in front of television cameras he and his assistant Hosannah had faked a spontaneous prediction (which was to be his undoing) but in which, departing from the rehearsed script, Hosannah had predicted his master's death! The audience is thus treated to a flashback – filling out the background in a way that the sound version does not – but also giving a multi-dimensional image. Dr Godspeak was re-enacting the scene with Semuwe (Hosannah) the very man who had in fact participated in it originally. The more spectacular visual effects are also missed. The descent of the Television cameraman and his disappearance back into the flies with his zoom lens (armed with misinformation) illustrates the length to which the media were prepared to go in pursuit of a trivial story. Less spectacular but perhaps more valuable as an economical source of satire is the coffin designed for Dr Gospeak, appropriately, considering his concern with heavenly bodies, in the shape of a comet. From it emanates a few relevant comments on death-styles. Nana Okoromfo Dopevi 'formerly of Kumasi, Ghana. Currently domiciled among you, one of the flotsam and jetsam of our Great Economic Dispersal' briskly advertises his other lines to the interested crowd:

M.C.:   The last wishes of the dead are sacred – rich or poor, we oblige. Any shape and form, you'll find me ready. Luxury yachts, private jets, that streamlined first class railway coach you have envied overseas. The Mercedes 600 that flashes by you daily. That elusive Cadillac. . . . Only last week a sleek tycoon entered his last slumber in a giant television set. The sides were black afara, the screen was tinted glass. Each knob was gleaming brass. The aerials were authentic, nickel plated, guaranteed not to rust in a thousand years, retractable. Before the grave was filled, we pulled them out to the fullest length – go to St Peter's cemetery, you'll find those aerials sticking out in either ear beamed, we trust, on his favorite programme transmitted through the satellites.

2ND
WOMAN: And what was that?

M.C.:   Dallas. He was an oil tycoon.   (p.30.)

The comic wheel comes full circle when Dr Godspeak is persuaded that he can outwit his disloyal disciple by turning his own murder weapon, the prediction and an obituary notice against him. But his fellow conspiritor is – alas for him – the disloyal disciple himself.

This play gives full rein to Soyinka's comic genius as well as his gift for barbed social satire. The reduction of Dr Godspeak and the complementary rise of Hosannah are the two axes on which the play moves leaving the society, unfortunately not a step nearer salvation, but the audience probably more aware.

Part 4
Poetry

Idanre and other Poems
Introduction

▼▼▼▼▼▼▼▼▼▼▼▼▼▼▼▼▼▼▼▼▼▼▼▼▼▼▼▼▼▼▼▼▼▼

THE FIRST separate collection of the poems of Wole Soyinka was published in 1967 by Methuen under the title *Idanre and Other Poems*. His poems had previously appeared in small clusters or singly in journals and anthologies including *Encounter, Ibadan, Black Orpheus*, Langston Hughes' *African Treasury*, Francess Ademola's *Reflections*, Moore and Beier's *Modern Poetry From Africa*. He has featured since in other anthologies including Donatus Nwoga's annotated anthology *West African Verse* (1968). In 1969 Rex Collings Ltd. issued in a broadsheet *Poems From Prison*.

Since Soyinka himself selected the poems for the collection *Idanre and Other Poems* the selection gives a valuable clue to the poet's view of his own poems. Excluded from the collection are the light satirical poems 'Telephone Conversation' and the twin poems 'Two in London' which – particularly the former – had hugged the foreground of attention and established Soyinka almost exclusively in many minds as a writer of light satirical verse. The exclusion of these poems from his own collection gently directs attention to the much greater part of his poetry which is of quite another mood. On balance he is not essentially a humorist – although even his graver poems are startlingly witty and sometimes grimly humorous – and his exclusion of his brilliant but on a general assessment uncharacteristic 'Telephone Conversation' was a shrewd authorial indication. It is well therefore to look at Soyinka's early poetry using *Idanre and Other Poems* as the essential corpus.

Soyinka emerges from this collection as a serious poet concerned with the grave issues which face him as a man in first of all his own country Nigeria, but eventually as a man living in the twentieth century. Because Soyinka objectifies the particular stimuli which give rise to the poems by using representative images, the poems have an independent existence from those stimuli, and stand as art irrespective of them. It is therefore not necessary to pry too closely into biographical or historical events even when, as is often the case, the poems are expressions of intense personal feelings arising out of actual experiences. Often the poet saves the critic a good deal of trouble by announcing the historical or other background of the poem in the title – 'Massacre, October '66', 'To My First White Hairs' etc. His titles not only place many poems in this way, but often supply important keys to their meaning.

An appreciation of Soyinka's poetry depends primarily on a sensitive realization of the significance of a well-organized system of images within each poem, and a willingness to follow wherever the images lead. Very few writers in any age or tradition are better able to use words more suggestively than Soyinka. In his ability to fuse a whole wealth of meaning into the small compass of a poem he reminds one of the best of the English metaphysical poets, particularly Donne and Marvell and, although he is not usually grouped with them, of Shakespeare.

Although Soyinka is essentially neither a descriptive nor a narrative poet, he is particularly sensitive to landscape; not landscape in a pictorial sense, but as an informing environment which supplies the essential images which ultimately *are* the poems. As an introduction to the generalizations inevitable in a work of this kind a particular demonstration of Soyinka's method will be given through a close examination of one of his poems, 'Massacre, October '66'.

The title points directly to a particular historical event. The poet gives the further information 'Written in Tegel', which is a suburb of Berlin. The poem's images, even without this information, announce through 'willows' the cold lake, 'dying leaves' and 'falling acorns' that the setting is autumn or in a northerly climate. But the information 'Written in Tegel' is useful, and helps to suggest a richer meaning for the last stanza of the poem than might have been easy to arrive at without it.

The northern landscape as has been suggested provides the system of images for the poem which starts innocuously with a location of the poet and a suggestion of his mood, the mood being expressed through the same image of the lake which helps to locate the poem:

> Through stained-glass
> Fragments on the lake I sought to reach
> A mind at silt-bed

The poet is not only looking into a lake, he is looking into his own mind which is plunged in despair, and therefore is, in the image of the lake, 'at silt-bed'. This fusion of different objects or ideas through a single image is characteristic of Soyinka's work and is the main source of his compactness.

The second stanza continues the dual process – the physical description which at the same time suggests other meanings. That the poet's mind as well as his eye is engaged, is suggested by his picture of the dying leaves which, defying the gardener's attempts to sweep them into orderly piles,

> flew in seasoned scrolls
> lettering the wind.

The dried curled autumnal ('seasoned') leaves suggest scrolls on which words are written which therefore inform the wind with wisdom – 'lettering the wind'.

In what seems therefore to be a physical description we have intimations of deeper meanings. The autumnal landscape also provides the acorns which the poet infuses with grave and sinister signficance. As he treads on them,

> each shell's detonation
> Aped the skull's uniqueness.

Shells are of course primarily the covering of the acorns, but along with 'detonation' the word suggests more sinister shells, and all of a sudden the physical treading on shells suggests the crunch of human skulls, the violation of human life which is what the poem is all about. The shape and the sound of the acorns underfoot have been economically turned to graver purpose.

The acorns are exploited further; they are the favoured food of hogs and they fall in such numbers that they remind the poet of heads which were being as wantonly cropped in his own country which he has left temporarily. This attempt to match acorns with heads and to compare their massive fall to the killings in his own country is the 'sharper reckoning' in the first line of the fourth stanza:

> Came sharper reckoning –
> This favoured food of hogs cannot number higl.
> As heads still harshly crop to whirlwinds
> I have briefly fled.

The linking of human heads with the favoured food of hogs deftly suggests the devaluation of human life which is implied in the wanton killings. (Hogs are particularly despised in the area where the killings take place, an idea exploited more fully in stanza 8.) The image of an untimely harvest also underlines the wantonness and the waste of the killings. (The harvest image, as will be seen, is one of Soyinka's most frequently used images.) The harvest being premature – the result of 'whirlwinds' – spells famine; a period of barrenness and deprivation, in the future.

The mind boggles at all this and seeks refuge from the contemplation of this terrible waste of life; it takes temporary refuge in the externals of the autumn landscape. But as more acorns fall his mind goes back to the terrible events (in stanza 7). The victims of the slaughter have been rendered as silent as the acorns, but they once laughed; they had been human, and in being human – in being able to laugh at the same things as those who killed them – not strangers. The idea which is expressed tentatively here (stanza 7) –

> They are not strangers all

is stated even more finally in stanza 8

> not strangers any.

(It is almost redundant to state here that those who were massacred were 'strangers' to the area in which the killings took place.)

The grim irony of the fact that the killings took place in an area dominated by Islam, an area whose commonest greeting involved 'peace', and which shunned 'unholy' acts like the eating of pork, is the burden of stanza 8.

The last stanza has the surface look of an apology for using an alien landscape as the basis of a poem about his own country, but the landscape offers a particularly apt message. This 'alien' land – Tegel (one now sees the value of this piece of information) is an area in Berlin, a city which under Hitler had seen the flourishing of a racial myth revolting for its exclusiveness. The borrowing of this landscape has special signficance in the context of a slaughtering of 'strangers' – those who do not belong:

> I borrow seasons of an alien land
> In brotherhood of ill, pride of race around me
> Strewn in sunlit shards. I borrow alien lands
> To stay the season of the mind.

The poet is in fact surrounded by the ruins (shards) of the Herrenvolk myth, in the name of which millions had been slaughtered for not belonging. The poet's own land becomes linked 'in brotherhood of ill' with the alien land. (There is a suggestion of the poet's own pride being also in ruins about him.) The selection of an 'alien' set of images, the distancing of the events which this provides, saves the mind from collapsing under the strain of the actual events.

I suggest that not just here, but everywhere in his poetry, Soyinka's use of images provides him with the means of distancing the primary object, event, or experience which gives rise to the poem, and enables him to produce a work of art instead of a chronicle of events. 'Massacre, October '66' is by this means far more than a historical record. It is a network of images sensitively arranged to suggest the essence of the massacre and its terrible human consequences. It is a moral presentation of a historical fact.

The poems in *Idanre and Other Poems* are grouped under general thematic headings, and apart from this one poem which is taken out of its place, it is convenient to follow these groupings in an examination of the poems.

Of the Road

▼▼▼▼▼▼▼▼▼▼▼▼▼▼▼▼▼▼▼▼▼▼▼▼▼▼▼▼▼▼▼▼▼▼

THE FIRST group is headed 'Of the Road'. All of the poems are vaguely connected by the fact that they are based on experiences obtained while travelling (by road or air) or events which – like the death of Segun Awolowo in a car crash – took place on the road. The poems are not all of the same mood. The opening poem 'Dawn' celebrates the dawn as it is seen by someone who has been driving through the night. Although a number of physical objects appear in the poem, it is not primarily a photographic description. It seems to attempt to capture the essence, the spirit of the dawn – a time of day which often in Soyinka's poetry represents hope. (In 'Death in the Dawn' this hope becomes ironical in that dawn provides the setting for death.)

As the dawn breaks, the tall palm tree is the first object that becomes visible. First its spiky fronds 'piercing' the air. The palm is endowed with a conscious pride in its position. It appears almost like an athlete glorying in his achievement.

> As one who bore the pollen highest.

> The red fruit of the palm become

> Blood drops in the air . . .

Some of Soyinka's images vaguely suggest a human figure gaily, even coquettishly, attired:

> above
> The even belt of tassels, above
> Coarse leaf teasing on the waist . . .

The entry of the sun is also portrayed in terms suggestive of human action. It comes like a Tarquin, first stealing in – representing the gradualness of the first approach of dawn – then, erupting into action:

> The lone intruder, tearing wide
> The chaste hide of the sky

A rape indeed which is echoed by the disarray implied in:

> Night-spread in tatters . . .

(Tarquin's rape of Lucrece is strongly suggested here.) The last stanza delicately suggests the worship with which dawn is greeted. Not only do the words 'celebration' and 'rites' suggest this, but the blood-red kernels of the palm become an apt sacrificial offering to a god who is himself 'aflame'. In the end we have somthing like the character of the dawn (rather than a photographic picture of it) through images which suggest not only how the dawn comes, but what it means.

It is on this ironic counterpane that the central event of the next poem, 'Death in the Dawn', takes place. Dawn is represented as a time of hope, but hope tinged with fear. Men rise from their beds, quench their lamps, take up their burdens, and make for the markets through the early morning mist; uncertain mortals peer into the future through folk augury, and hope that through propitiation of the gods they might avoid disaster. Underneath all this, the road, like a beast of prey lies in wait. All this is evoked through a series of interlocking images:

> This soft kindling, soft receding breeds
> Racing joys and apprehensions for
> A naked day, burdened hulks retract,
> Stoop to the mist in faceless throng
> To wake the silent markets – swift, mute
> Processions on grey byways . . .

Neither the accidental killing of the cock (imaged as a vain sacrifice – 'futile rite') nor the prayers of a fond mother:

> . . . Child
> May you never walk
> When the road waits, famished

are of any avail, however. The crash takes place and, as he does in other places in his work, Soyinka captures the terrible and sudden transformation from life to death which takes place in a car crash. Here the dominant element is one of surprise as man (not just *a* man) becomes trapped in his own invention:

> . . . Brother,
> Silenced in the startled hug of
> Your invention – is this mocked grimace
> This closed contortion – I?

Soyinka succeeds in generalizing the particular through his use of images. The placing of 'Death in the Dawn' after 'Dawn' which is a celebration of the promise of dawn, is not without a touch of irony. Within the second poem itself there is a suggestion of fatalism; a suggestion that man's fate is independent of his attempts to propitiate the gods. The die seems to be cast in spite of prayers and propitiation.

Dawn (the time of day) connects 'Around us, dawning' with the poems which have gone before; it also is connected by the theme of travelling, though this time the travelling is not by road but by plane. Soyinka manages to convey the ambiguous nature of the plane itself; it is a creation – it was 'fashioned' – but once created it takes on a being of its own; it becomes a proud, majestic, beast of prey:

> This beast was fashioned well; it prowls
> The rare selective heights
> And spurns companionship with bird.

The irony goes further, for even the creator, man himself, becomes the victim of his own creation. He yields his will to the machine:

> Passive martyrs bound to a will of rotors.

Indeed 'martyrs' introduces a sequence of accompanying images which further indicate how close the plane in its pride is to its fall (and its contents with it – the 'martyrs'). It takes only 'an alien mote' in the machine to bring the whole thing down:

> . . . when
> Death makes a swift descent.

This proud machine in its vulnerability becomes 'a carbuncle' and the mountain peaks potential 'lances' to prick it open. Thus man in his machine is poised between triumph and disaster. The plane is further cut down to size as its false dawns pale into insignificance with the coming of the true dawn. In the darkness the plane had with its trails produced

> a linear flare of dawns
> the incandescent
> Onrush.

This false dawn which the plane produces is nothing to the 'power' of the sun when it 'explodes' in the last stanza. The last stanza itself works on two levels, a further meaning being suggested by 'dessication' which glances at the burnt-out remains of a crash, reinforced by 'explodes' even though in the primary meaning it is the sun that explodes; in the context it is difficult not to apply the explosion to the vulnerable aeroplane as well.

'Luo Plains' yields its meaning less readily than some of the other poems but is a no less suggestive a poem ultimately. Some of the suggestions which can be derived from the images may perhaps not have been intended by the poet. The setting, as the title announces, is Kenya, and thus the landscape of the poem is made up of objects from that area: egrets, lakes, the animal at the water hole, spears, cowherds, the cactus, and the eagle. However these are used not just as an evocation of a physical landscape. The dawn, for example, which is central to the meaning of the poem is a more significant event than the start of a new twenty-four-hour day. It is the beginning of a new era, something as significant as the coming of independence. This central event is treated in the third section of the poem:

> That dawn
> Her eyes were tipped with sunset spears
> Seasons' quills upon her parchment, yet
> The hidden lake of her
>
> Forgives!

A physical dawn, and a physical lake had been introduced in the preceding section, but here the dawn is more momentous. It is a dawn which had been preceded by fighting – 'Sunset spears'. The sharpness of 'spears' is echoed in 'quills' although primarily they are the pens with which the momentous document 'the parchment' is signed. (The parchment seems to confirm the idea of independence.) The event which is confirmed by the signing of the parchment has been achieved through fighting, but in spite of this, the country forgives her foes. The isolation of 'Forgives!' and the use of the mark of exclamation suggest the massiveness of what is to be forgiven as well as (or is this reading too much?) a certain incredulity that such massive forgiveness is even possible. The last section reinforces the idea of the enormity of what has to be forgiven with images like 'red sunset spears' and 'reeds of poison'. All these are thoughts which are inspired by a mind dwelling on a landscape (during an aeroplane flight) which suggests deeper thoughts. The process by which this poem comes about is quite similar to which produced 'Massacre' which has been treated earlier.

'In Memory of Segun Awolowo' which ends this section arises from the death in a car crash of a friend of the poet. The personal nature of the loss is indicated by the use of 'my' in 'this fresh plunder/Of my youth'. The untimely death of the victim is imaged as an untimely harvest (a favourite Soyinka image):

> For him who fell among reapers
> Who forestall the harvest.

The familiar figure of the anthropomorphic road bent on plunder reappears but this time the road is already glutted (and hence did not need this particular victim) so he 'retched' on his latest victim. The drama of death itself is captured in the opening lines of the poem:

> For him who was
> Lifted on tar sprays
> And gravel rains
>
> In metallic timbres
> Harder than milestone heart.

The end of the poem attributes crashes of this kind to the whims of Ogun; attempts to seek other causes – blaming shifting earth – are vain. The suggestion seems to be that we really cannot explain why a young man is suddenly selected to die in his prime in this way. It is the whim of the god. The figure Ogun, the embodiment of both the creative and the destructive essence, occupies a prominent place in Soyinka's artistic and critical writing.[1] That the god is also prone to caprice is evident in his devastation of his own people of Ire in the poem 'Idanre'. Ogun is also the god of the road by whose caprice men die in car crashes. This resolution of this particular poem is neither satisfactory not comforting because there can be no explaining away the waste involved in such a tragedy.

[1] See in particular 'And After the Narcissist', *African Forum* and 'The Fourth Stage' in D. W. Jefferson (ed.), *The Morality of Art* (Routledge and Kegan Paul, London, 1965).

Lone Figure

▼▼▼▼▼▼▼▼▼▼▼▼▼▼▼▼▼▼▼▼▼▼▼▼▼▼▼▼▼▼

'THE DREAMER' introduces a figure which frequently appears in Soyinka's work, namely, the lonely inspired man in society who sees what others cannot see, and who, because he does not fit comfortably into the society's pattern, is martyred. Eman in *The Strong Breed* particularly exemplifies this figure – he too is martyred, high on a tree. The soldier Mulieru in *A Dance of the Forests* is another such martyr to the society he tries to save, as is Sekoni, the engineer in *The Interpreters*. In the poem 'Idanre', while all men await the promise of the harvest and the blessing of the god in passive hope, only the poet dares to make the perilous pilgrimage to watch the god in his agony. Although 'For Fajuyi' is not included in the section 'Lone Figure' he too earns death (and later glory) by walking the lonely path by which society, in spite of itself, could possibly be saved:

> What goals for pilgrim feet
> But to a dearth of wills
> To hills and terraces of gods
> Echoes for voices, shadows for the lonely feat.

'The Dreamer' deliberately evokes memories of Christ's crucifixion. Indeed if the dreamer is not Christ himself he is a Christ-figure. His crucifixion as one of three, his crown of thorns, the nails on his flesh, myrrh (one of the presents of the wise men) as well as his words – not just the 'words' on the cross but all his preaching – are all evoked in the first stanza:

> Higher than trees a cryptic crown
> Lord of the rebel three
> Thorns lay on a sleep of down
> And myrrh; a mesh
> of nails, of flesh
> And words that flowered free

The influence of the martyred man is pictured in the images of growth; the seed falls to the earth and dies but then germinates and grows, spreading its influence over the seas. This happens to the martyr here in the last stanza, which also economically defines the nature of his influence with words suggestive of Christian church organization and ritual – 'see', 'thrones' and 'incense'. Incense on the sea at the end also suggests the great spread of the religion:

> The burden bowed the boughs to earth
> A girdle for the see
> And bitter pods gave voices birth
> A ring of stones
> And throes and thrones
> And incense on the sea.

This poem is the first of the few in the collection in which Soyinka employs rhyme (abaccb) as well as alliteration and other echoic poetic techniques. All these make the poem one of his most deliberately musical. The last three lines are particularly so with 'And' separating stones, throes, thrones, slowing up a line which through the repeated closed 'O' sound seems to suggest the inexorable spread of influence which the lexical meaning of the words implies.

In addition to his interest in the more obviously prophetic or visionary type of lone figure, Soyinka in several works shows a concern with another type – the physical or mental deviants and others who tend to be left out of the main stream of society. Sometimes they are even the unexpected vehicles of revelation. Lazarus, the Albino prophet, Usaye, the myopic albino girl and Noah, the reformed thief, all represent the type in *The Interpreters*. The blind beggar in *The Swamp Dwellers* and Ifada, the idiot boy in *The Strong Breed* were early forerunners, while the mute, giant, trusty prisoner in *Season of Anomy* continues the line. The hunchback of Dugbe in the poem of the same name is a lonely madman who plies his lonely 'in-sealed' way in the teeming market, detached from his surroundings.

What happens in the poem and to the hunchback does not become clear until (as with a number of Soyinka's poems) we see the significance of subtle changes in the tense. The poem opens, and goes on for five sections, in the past tense. 'I wondered' . . . 'The devil came'. After the advent of the devil the tense changes to the present:

> . . . the world
> Spins on his spine, in still illusion.

This is in fact the historic present. It describes the gruesome death of the man who had

By day, stooped at public drains
Intense at bath or washing cotton holes,

and whose night paths had been a mystery. In spite of his death, however,
the hunchback walks on, visiting his old haunts in Dugbe in his ghostly
nudity:

At night he prowls, a cask
Of silence; on his lone matrix
Pigeon eggs of light dance in and out
Of dark, and he walks in motley.

The imagery of the poem, without which in fact it remains a puzzle, is
worth close attention. The presentation of the hunchback in the three
opening sections is straightforward enough. His clothes, more holes than
cloth are 'cotton holes'. His own twisted mal-formed figure – twisted body
on crooked legs – is suggested in

An ant's blown load upon
A child's entangled scrawl.

The dramatic moment seems to occur with the arrival of the devil 'one
sane night/On parole from hell'. This was when the hunchback's transfiguration took place. In an earlier reading I suggested tentatively that the
transfiguration was from life to death. But it would be more interesting to
take this as the moment when the hunchback passed from sanity to
madness. His madness is seen as a transfiguration into a higher state of
being. His calm detachment, seen against our mundane preoccupations,
represented by the mad bustle of Dugbe market – 'Song or terror, taxi
turns/And sale fuss of the mad', 'ugliness and beauty' – raise the question,
with typical Soyinka irony, of who is really mad. On this reading it would
be a living lunatic whose insulation from our 'mad' world provides from
his vantage point of truth a critical point of observation of our world. His
is ironically the superior position, for he is

. . . in truth immune
From song or terror, taxi turns
And sale fuss of the mad, beyond
Ugliness or beauty, whom thought-sealing
Solemnly transfigures . . .

Who is 'mad'; the hunchback or us? What happened when 'The devil came' is crucial to an interpretation, and to me the images in the crucial stanzas are confusing. There is enough wit apparent in the poem as a whole, however, to make one return to it again and again for a way through its apparent obscurity in parts. Sometimes Soyinka has the fascination of an intellectual crossword puzzle.

'The Last Lamp' is a poem in which the original object has been totally transformed into new images. As is not unusual, the poem starts with a physical image; a delicate image of a weak light in the surrounding darkness:

> A pale
> Incision in the skin of night.

The image of 'incision' is sustained by 'bled' which suggests ebbing life, and reinforces the idea of the precarious state of the light. In the context of this image of bleeding to death, 'dye' (surely a pun) and 'shroud' fall into place, underlining the imminent death of the flickering light, and gently introducing the human object for which the light seems to be a symbol. This is confirmed by 'her' in the second stanza. All the associations here are of an old and frail woman – she is described through her shadow which now gathers close about her and is:

> A lying depth

– a phrase which already points to the length of the old woman laid out as a corpse. The phrase 'generations' patient stoop' suggests both the great age of the woman as well as her figure, bent with age, as she goes in and out (the doorways are also crooked) and as she patiently waits out her time in spite of her troubles ('peace denied'). The tense changes in the second line of the last stanza:

> She was a vespers' valediction, lit
> Within deserted ribs

suggesting that the light has now gone out. She has come to the end of her long day, but she *was* the valediction which suggests that not only she, but an era died with her.

'Easter' produces yet another lone figure; the man who distils the wisdom of the surrounding world, but who has to do this in isolation. The poem is organized around the idea of the distillation of perfume from frangipane flowers. It starts with the evocation of a scene in which, in the stillness of a particular evening – 'This' – the poet smells the perfume of

the frangipanes. The evocation of the scene and thoughts arising from it
continues for four stanzas with other objects from the surrounding environment brought in. The central image (and with it the main thread of the
poem) returns with the frangipanes in the fourth stanza. These flowers are
weak and fall easy victims to the wind:

> These pink frangipanes of Easter crop
> Eager to the wind . . .

yet they are vital ingredients with which to counteract the deep-seated
decay of earth. For this purpose they have to be gathered and distilled.
But the odds against this halting or counteracting of the earth's decay
being successfully accomplished, are very heavy indeed. There is only
'ONE' bough, and there are millions waiting for the balm – the whole earth
is rotten . . .

> One bough to slake the millions? Decay
> Caulks earth's centre; spurned we pluck
> Bleached petals for the dreamer's lair.

The business of redemption has to be undertaken by the 'spurned', solitary
'dreamer' in his 'lair' – away from the mass of men. (I am inclined to treat
this particular 'we' as a majestic 'we'. It is essentially singular. 'Dreamer's'
is singular too, and in the next stanza, the pronoun becomes 'I'.) The
dreamer then, armed with the petals he has saved, proceeds to his lair for
the distillation:

> Borne passive on this gift, wound-splashes
> From wind scavenger, sap fragrance for
> A heady brew, I rode my winged ass and raged –

Once again the change of tense from present to past introduces a note of
historicity:

> I rode my winged ass and raged.

This is the poet in his state of possession, but the source of the imagery –
Christ's triumphal entry into Jerusalem on Palm Sunday is unmistakable.
It confirms faint references to the Passion – too weak to lead to confident
assertions by themselves – 'palm' and 'crown' in stanza 4. Thus we have a
recurrence of the Christ-figure – the martyr to his own society – the man
who is spurned but who nevertheless has the perfume with which to halt

the decay of the society which rejects him. This is the heart of the poem. The emphasis is on the Passion, on the agony of isolation, not on the glorious resurrection which the title 'Easter' would lead one to expect. The Easter lies in the fact that the solitary does collect some frangipanes, does distil some perfume and does rage. His words, like the words of the dreamer in the opening poem of this section, might yet bear fruit, but in the uncertainty of human affairs, only *might*. At the end of the poem the children – like the indifferent society – unconcernedly continue their wonted activities:

> As children wove frond yellow from the palm
> Plucked at the core, within the spadix heart.

Of Birth and Death

▼▼▼▼▼▼▼▼▼▼▼▼▼▼▼▼▼▼▼▼▼▼▼▼▼▼▼▼▼▼▼▼▼▼

THE SECTION 'Of Birth and Death' is delicately graduated. It starts with 'Koko Oloro' a children's propitiation chant, playful in rhythm and tone, which by its very artlessness conveys the helplessness of man. The section continues through poems arising from the birth and death of children to one of the first reminders of old age, 'To My First White Hairs', and ends with 'Post Mortem', which pictures the dead man on a slab unknowingly yielding the secrets of life to the investigating fingers of the pathologist.

'Dedication' invokes a blessing on the newly born infant in language which is based on that used by elders in ceremonies like that of *komoja* when the child is formally recognized as having been born and is introduced to the world. From its proverbial opening to the fossilled sands at the end, the poem proliferates with images from the surrounding environment, all made to yield significance in particular wishes for the child. The gecko falls from the perilous height of the hut's rafters to the hardness of the dung floor beneath, so (runs the implication) in the inevitable falls the child is bound to encounter she will similarly receive no hurt:

> Earth will not share the rafter's envy: dung floors
> Break, not the gecko's slight skin, but its fall.

The yam, the springs, the baobab, the earth, all combine in a wish for life – secure, continuing, productive. Like 'peat', a symbol of unhurried development and long life, the child is to grow free under the benevolent influences of nature – rain, the sun's shadow and the night's protection. Nor is the child to grow into a spineless butt. Symbolic items like pepper, palm wine, and the various preparations used in the child's toilet combine to invoke a full, healthy, productive life, all leading to the final wish that the child's life may leave a permanent influence:

> . . . Yield man-tides like the sea
> And ebbing, leave a meaning on the fossilled sands.

The light, heady atmosphere of buoyant hope in 'Dedication' is chilled by the hopeless grief and lamentation of the mother of a still-born child in 'A

Cry in the Night' – another ironical sequence. The posture of grief – the mother beating her head on the floor – provides the opening:

> As who would break
> Earth, grief
> In savage pounding, moulds
> Her forehead where she kneels.

In an uncharacteristic use of the pathetic fallacy the poet isolates the mother from any source of comfort as even the stars desert her:

> No stars caress her keening
> The sky recedes from pain

(Soyinka has reached in 'keening' for an unusual Irish word. A 'keen' is an Irish funeral song accompanied with wailing; hence to keen is to wail or lament bitterly for the dead.) Apart from the very apt 'keening', the selection of 'caress' here is extremely sensitive; it suggests the warm comfort of which the mother is here deprived, and thus dramatizes her loneliness which is further underlined at the end of the poem. It is the mother herself who buries her child 'in haste'. Her physical pain, as well as her mental anguish, are fully evoked:

> Such tender stalk is earthed
> In haste. A stricken snake, she drags
> Across the gulf, re-enters to the retch
> Of grieving wombs. Night harshly folds her
> Broken as her afterbirth.

The image of earthing the stalk here ironically echoes the earthing of the living yam tuber in 'Dedication'. This earthing is a mocking of that earlier hope. The mother in her state of pain and physical exhaustion – 'Broken' – becomes a wounded snake whose slow painful progress is highlighted by 'drags' while the pain makes the journey seem endless – 'gulf'. The bleeding which is inevitable in birth but which is accepted in a joyful birth is now mere revolting waste expressed by 'retch'. Once again Soyinka's extraordinary ability in selecting the apt word to produce the appropriate set of suggestions has made art of an almost intolerable human situation.

'A First Deathday' has a similar inspiration – the death of a child, this time on her first birthday – but it is of a different tone altogether. Here the grief has been got over and there is an attempt to distil some meaning from the event:

> Grief has long receded, yet the wonder
> Stays.

The third stanza contains the attempt to rationalize the experience and is the burden of the poem:

> Knowledge as this is growth's diffusion
> Thins, till shrouds are torn from swaddlings.
> She was not one more veil, dark across
> The Secret; Folasade ran bridal to the Spouse
> Wise to fore-planning – bear witness, Time
> To my young will, in this last breath
> Of mockery.

At the end of 'In Memory of Segun Awolowo', Soyinka had attempted a similar rationalizing of the experience attributing the death to the whim of Ogun. That attempt seems almost cursory in the face of this more elaborate one. Here it is suggested that at birth we bring with us a certain knowledge which 'thins' as we remain in this world – 'in growth's diffusion'. (This as the basis of the rationalization reminds one of Wordsworth's 'trailing clouds of glory'.) By living, Folasade would thus have dissipated this knowledge; but by assuming her shroud almost as soon as she sheds her swaddlings, she preserved this knowledge intact. In her case there was no 'veil' across the 'Secret' (which life would have provided). Hers was a wise deliberate act – 'fore-planning' and 'will' emphasize this. The deliberateness of the child's act, her conscious will is seen (in a different mood) also in 'Abiku'. Folasade's was also a joyful act as she 'ran bridal to the Spouse'. In her joy at meeting her spouse, the incidental 'mockery' of the hopes of her parents (hopes beautifully elaborated in 'Dedication') is inconsequential. The Spouse (capital 'S') is the creator to whom the child returns and who seems also to be an embodiment of knowledge. The poem rests on the idea of the continuum of life from pre-existence through life on earth to a continuing existence after death.

The idea of a purer form of being – called knowledge – which is dissipated by life and growth on earth, recurs in 'For the Piper Daughters' where, in contrast to the purity, innocence, and openness of childhood, age is characterized by a false appearance, deceit, and lies. The children are enjoined therefore not to grow old in this way, but to retain the qualities of their childhood:

> . . . I would you,
> Thus, never never old.

The poem turns on this contrast between the purity of childhood and the guilt of age. Not only is there a contrast portrayed for example in the open-handed 'largesse' of childhood contrasted with the miserly 'slits' of age, but age actually poses a threat to youth which must be resisted. The children have to be armed against the lascivious wiles of the false priest and (like the child in 'Dedication' using her pepper) must take extreme action against him. The double-edged image of the rose is exploited here:

> The rose, you know, is thorned. And if
> The cozening priest would slay you, panting
> How your cheeks are rudded like the . . . !
> Riddle him with lethal pips!

The opposition is total; the priest's intentions are murderous – 'slay'. The children's protection must also be total; the pips of the rose must become deadly – 'lethal'. Fortunately every good beautiful creation comes with its protection (and its price):

> To the date
>   A stone
> The linnet
>   Height
> Pearls
>   Depth and the clam

The rose is similarly 'thorned' and its pips potentially lethal. The wish for a free, healthy fruitful life under the influence of nature for the children is similar to that of 'Dedication'.

The death of a child portrayed as a positive act of its will has been noticed in 'A First Deathday'. The Abiku child, who comes to plague its mother with a temporary stay only to return to its mischievous kind in the other world soon after, is a figure in Yoruba belief. In 'Abiku' Soyinka emphasizes the callous wilfulness of such a child who haughtily scorns the pleas, the sacrifices, the ritual scarrings and all other efforts calculated to 'earth' her; make her stay:

> Yams do not sprout in amulets
> To earth Abiku's limbs.

(The earthed yam image has been noticed before in 'Dedication' and ironically in 'A Cry in The Night'.) The continuity of the Abiku cycle as well as its terrible linking of birth and death is suggested (as do 'shrouds' and 'swaddlings' in the different context of 'A First Deathday') by the juxtaposition of 'mounds' (graves) and 'yolk' (the source of life):

> In silence of webs, Abiku moans, shaping
> Mounds from the yolk.

'To My First White Hairs' is a fairly light-hearted greeting of the first signs of age; light-hearted but still not averting the eyes from the direction to which they point – decrepitude and death. There is a progression in the suggestions of the images of the last line and a half of the poem:

> . . . Knit me webs of winter sagehood,
> nightcap, and the fungoid sequins of a crown.

The 'three white hairs' of stanza three give way to the prospect of 'winter sagehood' – winter suggesting the total whiteness through the image of snow, but sagehood introducing the idea of the wisdom that comes with it. 'Nightcap' takes the idea further into debility and death, while 'crown' (even though somewhat deflated by 'fungoid') looks hopefully beyond life towards higher things.

This easily leads on to 'Post Mortem' which also has a half-mocking approach to a grim subject. Soyinka deliberately cuts man down to size with this picture of the body on the slab. Man is reduced in the opening lines to the status of beer, being only another possible item in the stock of a refrigerator. The process of deflation is more explicit in:

> his mouth was cotton filled, his man-pike
> shrunk to sub-soil grub
>
> his head was hollowed and his brain
> on scales . . .

It is to this unprepossessing object that man has shrunk, and yet (glory be!) even this object has some use; it may yet, ironically, teach through the investigating fingers of the pathologist

> . . . how not to die.

The wit of the poet was never more apparent. Soyinka's wit is just as evident in his treatment of this rather grim subject as it was in the lighter and earlier 'Telephone Conversation'.

For Women

▼▼▼▼▼▼▼▼▼▼▼▼▼▼▼▼▼▼▼▼▼▼▼▼▼▼▼▼▼▼▼▼▼

THE POEMS in this section are linked by the fact that a woman is part of the stimulation for each one, but the section contains poems of varying moods. It is another series of variations on a theme. The first two poems 'Song: Deserted Markets' and 'Psalm' are as different as two poems can be; they are in fact opposites. The image of the seed or grain as the source of growth is the dominating image in both poems. In the first, the seed is to be frustrated; it is not to be allowed to grow; therefore it is deprived of moisture:

> My soul shall be dry
> In an ebony grain
> Keep it from sprouting
> In a stranger's pain.

Thus the seed is not tended; it is gobbled up – greedily devoured – hence destroyed by the white bird:

> A white bird she comes
> And gobbles the grain

Consequently there is no harvest:

> And the dew leaves no mark
> Where my head has lain.

The fate of the seed in 'Psalm' is more fortunate; it has been tended, and has reached a happy harvest. All the images suggest fullness, mature growth, and harvest:

> the seeds have ripened fast my love
> and the milk is straining at the pods.

The straining pods – the full breasts of the delivering mother – are in contrast to the

Moon-breasts of pain

of the 'stranger' of 'Song: Deserted Markets'. Moon reinforces the racial
identification of white in 'white bird' in contrast to 'ebony'. 'Stranger' is
used in both poems, but in 'Song:' it typifies an alien spirit with whom
there is minimal spiritual contact, while 'stranger' in 'Psalm' – 'the stranger
life' – means new life, referring to the child which is the harvest of the
grain. The harvest is triumphantly celebrated at the end of the poem as a
manifestation of the mystery of the continuing cycle of life:

> . . . and a mystery
>
> of pulses and the stranger life
> comes to harvest and release
> the germ and life exegesis
> inspiration of your genesis.

The encounter in 'Song' is a dry, commercial, unproductive one whose
negative nature is shown up when compared with the fruitfulness of 'Psalm'.

'Her Joy is Wild' also looks forward to birth:

> This is the last-born; give me
> A joyful womb to bind:

but the emphasis is on the ecstatic, joyous abandon of the woman in the
sexual act itself. Unlike the restraint of the central event in 'Song' there is
to be no withholding or frustration of the seed; no lingering at the edge of
the experience. The invitation is to total involvement with the kernel – the
heart of the fruit, not the rind:

> Your strong teeth will weaken
> If you nibble the rind.

The wild joy is dramatized by the 'skeins of hair' plucked unconsciously
by the woman at the height of her joyous delirium. The man's willing
response expresses the total mutuality of the act –

> . . . and I denied her
> Nothing, maimed on her vision of the blind.

These three poems then form a three-part variation on the theme of sex and
its fulfilment (or the absence of it). The restrains of 'Song' are prompted
by racial overtones – the 'ebony grain' and the 'white bird' – which

contribute to an absence of the full mutuality (there is a positive suggestion of pain) and produces a very different kind of experience from that of the other two poems.

'Black Singer' conveys the reaction of the poet to the song of a black female singer. One way into the heart of the poem is through an examination of the images in the second stanza:

> A votive vase, her throat
> Poured many souls as one; how dark
> The wine became the night.

The singer's throat is a 'votive vase' – a sacrificial vessel – out of which 'poured' her song (the wine) which is not only her song, but also a representative cry, since what was poured out was also 'many souls as one'. The selection of 'souls' introduces the idea of the depths of man's being. Thus the singer's song springs out of and expresses the deep feelings of a whole host of people for whom she speaks through her song. The darkness of the 'Song' (wine) expresses the background of suffering of the souls for whom the singer speaks. It evokes the whole history of suffering of the Negro people. This is confirmed by the suggestions in stanzas four and five of:

> . . . Dark, lady
> Dark in token of the deeper wounds

> Full again of promises
> Of the deep and silent wounds
> Of cruel phases of the darksome wine.

The darkness of the lady's complexion merges with the darkness of her song and with the darkness of the night:

> . . . how dark
> The wine became the night.

The singer is no opera prima donna but a 'soul' singer; a natural:

> Fleshed from out disjointed, out from
> The sidewalk hurt of sirens . . .

As the lonely envoy of her race, the darkness, the whole history of suffering of her race, comes pouring out as a sacrificial offering out of the 'votive vase' that is her throat.

'Bringer of Peace' presents the qualities of a woman whose tactful influence has a steadying effect on the person who speaks in the poem. The imagery of the poem has to be followed with some care. The woman's influence, symbolized by light rain, does not act in total opposition to the fire; its influence is more subtle. By questioning out, testing his rage (rather than by opposing it with equal force) she acts as a touchstone – tests the quality of his rage:

> You come as light rain, not to quench
> But question out the pride of fire.

This tact is again portrayed in the last stanza as

> This cunning sift of mild aggression . . .

In the second stanza she is again characterized through the action of light rain, as a soothing influence. The effect of 'deft' to qualify intrusions is to show the woman though gentle, to be adroit; deliberate in her gentleness. Thus her gentle rain produces a 'hiss'. A hiss is a sound of anger, but it is also a sign of the loss of heat in fire, hence a sign of cooling (of the poet's rage). Both meanings are relevant here. Even in the act of raging (in reaction to the gentle rain) the rage is stilled.

The third stanza reveals the man's rage as a protection – 'that hold the beast at bay' – with which he represses the instinctive reaction which is to 'howl' when he is hurt. The man's rage then is consciously built up, as 'accomplishments' suggests. The rage is also a cover for the frustrations of his spiritual imprisonment:

> Yet fires that hold the beast at bay
> Inclose, with all accomplishments of rage
> The inborn howl, proud lacerations
> Futile vaults at high bounds of the pit.

This is the rage which the 'bringer of peace' prods, identifies, evaluates, and stills subtly, even imperceptibly:

> This cunning sift of mild aggression, then
> Is your rain, a tacit lie of stillness
> A smile to test the python's throes, a touch
> To bring the bowstring's nerve to rest.

'To One, In Labour' yokes the process of gestation to the social organization of ants. Thus stated, the yoking might sound far-fetched and over-ingenious. Indeed on early readings the ideas seem to be uneasily yoked together. The opening of the poem – the first two stanzas and the first line of the third – present the analogical image which is to be applied in the second half. It presents the industry of the ants in building, and in ministering to the queen ant. The most important detail in this presentation of the social organization of the ants is contained in the lines:

> . . . some to labour some to yield
> A queen her labour.

It is the function of some of the ants to make the queen ant pregnant. Elementary biological knowledge supplies the information which is employed a little later in stanza three that male ants die after mating. These are the 'dead lovers' and 'master masons' who having done their work, have now departed. The ant-hill now forms the poet's symbol for the process of gestation in which only one sperm is required to fertilize a single ovum for the process of gestation to start. The superfluous sperm are also 'dead lovers' and 'departed . . . master masons':

> . . . And I think
> Gestation is a Queen insealed
> In the cathedral heart, dead lovers round
> Her nave of life$^{1/3}$

'Cathedral heart' and the related architectural term 'nave' echo the building (and labouring) image first introduced through the industry of the ant 'architects'. In 'master masons', 'mud spires', 'colonnades', 'shrines' and 'catacombs' the architectural image reverberates throughout the poem.

The process of gestation then resolves itself eventually into a union of two entities – 'Desolate/Wonder of you and me'. The sperm and the ovum are microscopic echoes of the human 'you and me' who start the process. Once the seed is sown the process takes place – 'insealed/In the cathedral heart' – in the womb, now a 'shrine of pain' (it was once a shrine of love and pleasure). As the 'lethal arc' – the pregnant womb – contracts, and the secretions flow, the process of labour begins. The poem has moved full cycle from the 'regurgitations' of the ants to the secretions of the one in labour – an ingenious exercise of the poet's wit, demonstrated by his extremely sharp eye for analogies.

The seed which comes to fruition in 'In Paths of Rain' is sown during one highly charged explosive moment in a compulsive instinctive act, when the deep drives take control, and conscious attempts to strangle the seed give way. The seeds assert themselves with an independent will of their own at this charged moment . . .

> . . . and strangled seeds
>
> Unleashed, exult . . .

These are the seeds of life which in the opening lines of the poem 'In Paths
of Rain' write lives on moments:

> In paths of rain, in rock grooves, may
> These rare instants of wild fox-fires
> Write on moments, lives.

(Here as elsewhere syntactical analysis helps to reveal the meaning of
complex passages: 'These rare . . . fox-fires' is the subject of 'write', and
'lives' is the object. 'On moments' is adverbial. In stanza 3 'strangled
seeds' is the subject of 'exult'. In stanza 5 'still-traps' is a verb to which
'sable oil' is subject, and 'A straining thunderhead', object.) Even this
early stanza suggests the momentary nature of the essential process which
is vividly symbolized in succeeding stanzas. But the momentary act is
produced in a social context and thus breeds a train of consequences of an
entirely different nature from the act itself. The act is instinctive; marriage
is social. The act may be begun and ended in total mutuality; the vistas are
clean:

> . . . Clean vistas –
> Flecked mica after rain, plankton in antimony
> Off rain-washed shores.

But the end of the poem suggests that the mutuality of the instinctive act
may produce quite other results in the larger context of the society. The
suggestions of this section are very compactly presented – the earlier part
of the poem is more expansive; the structure itself is suggestive. Everything is bright, the poem suggests:

> Till the chronicle of severance,
> Gold spelling, lantern sanctuaries around
> Birth-point, and chapter . . .
>
> Ground skins of the unshelled
>   hand over hand of fire
> A kernel's freak communion
>   windpools in the ash of palm.

The 'severance' in contrast to the mutuality implied in the earlier stanzas takes place in an atmosphere suggestive of church and ritual: 'lantern sanctuaries' and 'chapter'. In this context 'gold spelling' would suggest a book with gold lettering – e.g. the prayer book. 'Birth-point' suggests an advanced stage of pregnancy. Altogether the suggestion is of a marriage required by society because of a pregnancy. The two 'unshelled' – i.e. ungloved – hands are here in a 'freak communion' in contrast to the more natural communion portrayed earlier. The glitter of 'mica after rain' the fruitful suggestions of 'plankton in antimony'; have become a more barren:

> wind-pools in the ash of palm.

This union in fact has, ironically, become 'the chronicle of severance'. The poem separates the instinctive physical act from the social rigidities which often complicate it. It is an important variation on the theme of this section.

The occurrence of 'By Little Loving' in the section 'for women' tends to inhibit a liberal interpretation of the poem. In my reading 'loving' suggests something more general than feelings for an individual; it suggests rather a total commitment to life. The poem seems to suggest a period ('once' i.e. not any more) in the subject's life when, by holding back from a full commitment to life, he sought to avoid the agony which total commitment can bring. In the first stanza this idea is focused on love – he withdraws from a total commitment to love – but the other stanzas put this into perspective since the withdrawal is from other aspects of life as well.

The first stanza represents the subject's attempt to insulate himself from love, love being equated with the life-giving forces. The imagery suggests a retreat into a dead unproductive state. This is clear in the following passage:

> . . . a bank of bleached
> Shells kept floods at bay – once
> By little wisdom, sought the welcome drought.

The qualifier 'bleached' suggests dryness which is later reinforced by 'drought'. 'Shells' in the context suggests the mere outside covering of the organism (which presumably is now dead the shells being now used as a barricade). So that the total state portrayed is a dead unproductive barrenness. The retreat into this state is from the irrigating 'floods' which had they not been barred – kept at bay – would have brought life. In the subject's perverse state, this drought was welcome; the choice of death for life was deliberate. That he recovered from this perverse state (which is further elaborated in most of the poem) is suggested briefly in the last stanza when the forces of life assert themselves from within, instinctively:

> They kept vigil long, the winds and the stilled
> Night rage, and the tread of waters proved a lie
> Bursting from within . . .

The details of the poet's flight are portrayed in different images. What seems to have been a retreat from the liberal use of his imagination seems to be suggested in:

> . . . I kept
> My feet from flowered paths. I bared
> The night of stealth, watched thwarted
> Winds beat cycles, deafened as a crypt.

By refusing to see what was going on around him he found a false comfort at the still centre 'off the ruptured wheel/Of blood'. The cosiness of his position at the centre of the wheel gave him the illusion that he had discovered permanent truth through this retreat – 'by little yearning'. ('Little' here has the force of a negative.) He had had enough of the agony of involvement:

> Of pulses, stretch of flesh hunger hourly howled.

He found a temporary refuge in a naïve position, refusing to reason himself into a personal position. He had accepted 'hate' for example in this way. He had in fact, in the suggestions of the last stanza, been on the path of eternal death (without benefit of the phoenix's powers of self-reincarnation), but mercifully the instincts he had tried to suppress asserted themselves, and he was spiritually redeemed.

For me, then, the poem has meanings far larger and more significant than its place in this section would seem to suggest. A denial of love in the restricted sense of personal feelings for a person would have been only one symptom of what was in fact a state near to spiritual death; a total denial of his real self, and a mock existence in a false comfort.

Grey Seasons

▼▼

IN SO FAR as 'I think it Rains' pictures a state in which rain, instead of liberating, restricts and imprisons, it has something thematically in common with 'By Little Loving' in the previous section. 'Rain', as has been hinted earlier, in Soyinka's symbolism represents a life-giving force. When it comes it should dissipate the forces of death. This is what is asserted in the first stanza as the true function of rain. The tense of 'rains' – the present of custom or habit – is crucial here, and makes the first stanza a statement of a general truth, in contrast to the past tense 'saw' in the second stanza which gives that stanza a particular historicity. The first describes what rain *does* or ought to do while the second describes what it *did* (or failed to do) on a particular occasion:

> I think it rains
> That tongues may loosen from the parch
> Uncleave roof-tops of the mouth, hang
> Heavy with knowledge.
>
> I saw it raise
> The sudden cloud, from ashes. Settling
> They joined in a ring of grey; within,
> The circling spirit.

Contrary to expectations, instead of liberating, the ashes reacting abnormally to the rain have imprisoned the human spirit which circles helpless within the restraining circle. The 'closures of the mind' in stanza three, then, are (surprisingly) the results of rain which, as needs to be reiterated, is normally liberating. It has brought negation. In the fourth stanza, it 'beats' on wings (hence restricting flight) and suppresses desires.

In stanza five there seems to be a separation of the poet from others which is signalled by 'my' in contrast to the plurals 'us' and 'our' earlier. The rain has had a quite different effect on him. The raindrops which look soft but really are quite powerful have eroded his top soil and exposed the 'crouching rocks' beneath:

> Rain-reeds, practised in
> The grace of yielding, yet unbending
> From afar, this your conjugation with my earth
> Bares crouching rocks.

'Crouching' has the suggestion of ready to pounce. The effect of rain on the poet is therefore liberating. It releases latent energies in him.

One needs, for total satisfaction from this poem, a correlative for 'rain'. Freedom in a general way, or independence, more particularly, would seem to serve the purpose. This freedom, instead of liberating the mind brings an odd closing which in some ways parallels the denial of life that is the subject of 'By Little Loving'.

The image of a restricting circle – 'a ring of grey' – within which the spirit is enclosed, central to 'I think it Rains', is more explicit in 'Prisoner' where the subject is also in a mental prison:

> . . . And time conquest
> Bound him helpless to each grey essence.

By the end of the poem, the 'walls' are set and the prisoner is 'closed' in sadness. The accumulations of grey which set into the prison walls are not sudden formulations. They form and harden imperceptibly from the grey wisps and the 'threads' and catch the subject unawares when the 'sudden seizure' of the last stanza occurs.

A change in tense in the middle of the poem is once again significant. The present tenses of the first two stanzas 'Curl', 'breed', 'begin' convey general truths. The change to a measure of particularity comes in the third stanza. The general truth seems to be that the prisons of thought and position in which men find themselves are not sudden outgrowths, just as, the imagery suggests, heads do not suddenly turn grey. The single threads 'compulsive of the hour' presage the 'wise grey temples' of later years. Intimations of the later positions come even in the wild years of youth, well before the febrile years.

The images in the third stanza, suggest wild youth; particularly nimbleness and agility over wild territory:

> – even amidst the
> Crag and gorge, the leap and night tremors.

Even here, 'intimations came', but the potsherd stayed; preserved a wholeness. (It is stricken in the next stanza.)

The end of the fourth stanza introduces the dramatic event at the end of which there are changes. The alienation between erstwhile companions is evident

> For that far companion,
> Made sudden stranger when the wind slacked
> And the centre fell, grief.

(The 'threnody' – song of lamentation – had been heard in the middle of the storm.) The 'potsherd' which had 'stayed' up to now, 'lay disconsolate'. 'He' (the far companion – far because alienated) suddenly found himself in a position of alienation. But the 'intimations' had been there all along; they did not come with the storm which only revealed what had always been latent. Time had now conquered. The walls had set; the wisps had become grey temples; the prisoner is now truly encircled. All the earlier suggestions unite to form the final prison in the last stanza:

> . . . He knew only
> Sudden seizure. And time conquest
> Bound him helpless to each grey essence.
> Nothing remained if pains and longings
> Once, once set the walls; sadness
> Closed him, rootless, lacking cause.

It is worth mentioning that in one version the poem[1] ends with the line

> Bound him helpless to each grey essence.

The poet prefers the longer version in his own collection, but the poem is essentially complete in the shorter version. The prisoner is already bound to the grey essences; he is a prisoner. The additional three lines of the longer version reinforce the idea of a walled prison, but in addition suggest a possible definition of the grey essences by the phrase 'pains and longings'. If these 'pains and longings' are identified with the individual wisps and threads earlier, then they suggest something like the individual's own struggles and ambitions, his daily struggle to reconcile personal goals and possibilities. These are the hourly threads which eventually build the grey temples. (The pun on temples – edifices and heads – should not be missed.) My personal preference is for the shorter version without the particular suggestions of 'pains and longings'.

[1]This is the version in Francess Ademola's *Reflections* (African Universities Press, Lagos, 1962) and in the first edition of G. Moore and U. Beier, *Modern Poems from Africa* (Penguin, Harmondsworth, 1963).

If this poem had been written after the Nigerian Civil War, it would have been easy to see in the 'Sandstorm' the war which suddenly revealed erstwhile friends in opposed attitudes on either side of the cause. But it appeared long before – in Francess Ademola's *Reflections*, 1962 – and is thus saved from this narrower interpretation. The possibility of such an interpretation, however, is a good illustration of one of the paramount qualities of Soyinka's poetry. Because it is couched in images, and is thus removed from particular incidents – because the poetry is not essentially 'narrative' – it achieves a generality of application which transcends the particular local application. This is one reason why his poems are likely to survive any incidents from which they might have sprung. It is also this characteristic that makes Soyinka far more than a local poet, either in space or time.

The theme of 'Season' is summarized by its epigrammatic opening: 'Rust is ripeness'. By juxtaposing 'rust', a symbol of age and decay, with 'ripeness' – maturity and full growth – Soyinka suggests the cycle by which growth leads to death and a new beginning of the cycle.

The poem employs the present and the past tenses to convey subtle shifts of emphasis. The present tense of 'Rust is Ripeness', etc., indicates general truths. The section 'And we loved', etc., refers to a particular past time, i.e. youth. With 'now' in the second section of the poem we come to the present state of 'we' namely the evening of life when

> . . . we
> Awaiting rust on tassels, draw
> Long shadows from the dusk . . .

The rhythm of birth, growth, and decay – 'Laden stalks/Ride the germ's decay' – is also suggested in the passing of afternoon (which is the time setting for the 'spliced phrases . . . rasps in the wind, etc.') into the evening implicit in the 'now' passage. Soyinka tends to see human history, both individual and collective in terms of cycles. Thus even rust can be promising for it points to the decay of the germ, which brings new life. The poem therefore ends in hope, a hope couched in irony:

> . . . Laden stalks
> Ride the germ's decay – we await
> The promise of the rust.

'Night' is one of the few Soyinka poems in which the physical image remains at the centre of the poem rather than an applied situation which arises from it. It is an evocation of the effect of night on the poet, with a call at the end for deliverance from 'night children' which haunt the earth.

'Fado Singer' is a tribute to a performer in the genre. (Fado is a type of popular Portuguese song and dance with a guitar accompaniment.) The poem is a record of the poet's reaction to the sadness of the song. The singer had captured the grief of the gods as in a net spun from the strings of her instrument:

> Your net is spun of sitar strings
> To hold the griefs of gods . . .

The same strings later intensify in the imagery and become sutures (surgical stitches). The image of pain which is implied in 'sutures', a pain which is the effect of the song, runs through the whole poem. By the end of the poem, the poet longs for relief from the grief induced by the song.

October '66

▼▼▼▼▼▼▼▼▼▼▼▼▼▼▼▼▼▼▼▼▼▼▼▼▼▼▼▼▼▼▼▼

EXACT DATES when things happened are not as important to a study of Soyinka's poetry as they would be in a study of the work of a chronicle poet. This is true even when one is considering poems springing from actual events such as those falling under the general title 'October '66'. This date points roughly to its central event, the killings of 'strangers' in northern Nigeria which took place during September and October 1966. (The first killings were reported on September 29.) By October '66 Lt. Colonel Francis Adekule Fajuyi, Military Governor of the Western Region of Nigeria, had been seized and killed. He and General Ironsi were abducted on July 29. Even a poem as pointedly dated as 'Ikeja, Friday Four O'Clock' does not depend on the precise date on which a particular truck-load of soldiers was seen, since the poem is really about the waste and negation of life that war (not just the Nigerian war) brings.

All the poems spring from experiences during the troubled period from about October 1966 to the months leading to the Civil War. These were obviously traumatic events for the poet – he was to spend most of the war in detention – and the miracle is that he can write about them with the artistic detachment which these poems display. Together with 'Poems from Prison', written while he was actually in detention, they are an excellent demonstration of Soyinka's ability to distance the immediate object or event through imagery. This ability enables him to portray dreadful and devastating events as well as intimately personal ones without prosiness or sentimentality. The poem 'For Fajuyi', for example is a self-contained whole which yields its meaning without any knowledge of who Fajuyi was. (This knowledge of course gives a further bonus.) Like *A Dance of the Forests*, a grim warning of how easily man could destroy himself and transform his potential for life into negative channels, these poems gaze with horror at man, the victim of his own power, substituting death for life.

'Ikeja, Friday Four O'Clock' is as particular as a title can be, pinpointing as it does both place and time. The poem is obviously inspired by a truck-load of soldiers bound for battle action. However, interest does not lie in their particularity but in the waste of life that they represent –

They were but gourds for earth to drink therefrom.

The perversity by which the contents of the gourds are uselessly spilt when they should have been put to better use, is echoed throughout the poem. The sacrifice was unnecessary; the gods did not ask for it; the altars (hence the priests) were false:

> Unbidden offering on the lie of altars.

The familiar images of the bad harvest ('crop of wrath') and the perverted feast reappear. The resulting revulsion is signalled by 'retch' in

> No feast but the eternal retch of human surfeit.

The echo of the injunction in Christ's miracle of the feeding of the five thousand as recorded in the Gospel of St John – 'Gather up the fragments that remain, that nothing be lost' – dramatizes the irony. The needs of the country require that 'nought be wasted' yet the wine is being poured into the ground, and human lives are being devoured and retched in a degrading orgy of waste. The life-giving 'loaves' of the miracle (of the loaves and fishes) have been travestied by 'loaves of lead'.

In all this the soldiers appear as worthless sacrificial victims, so close to their sacrifice that they are even now 'a mirage of breath and form'. These particular soldiers are Nigerian (except for the title, however, the poem does not stress this) but they represent the sacrifices of false priests to false gods in numerous wars all over the world, all over history. Relieved of its particular title the poem becomes a universal picture of the waste that is war. The substitution of death for life, 'loaves of lead' for loaves of bread, is a constant preoccupation in Soyinka's work.

The image of the bad harvest reappears in 'Harvest of Hate'. (The death of Segun Awolowo is also portrayed as an untimely harvest – he is a victim of 'reapers who forestall the harvest'.) Here the harvest is equally untimely and on a more massive scale. The songs of harvest, the joys of harvest, the whole hope and promise of harvest have been frustrated:

> There has been such a crop in time of growing
> Such tuneless noises when we longed for sighs
> Alone of petals, for muted swell of wine-buds
> In August rains, and singing in green spaces.

The waste is itemized in earlier stanzas; its massiveness is signalled by the untimely death of the sun, and a spoiling of the fruits of the harvest:

> So now the sun moves to die at mid-morning
> And laughter wilts on the lips of wine
> The fronds of palm are savaged to a bristle
> And rashes break on kernelled oil

There is a grim reminder that this 'forfeit of old abductions' is to be paid in human lives; the lives of a new generation:

> The child dares flames his fathers lit
> And in the briefness of too bright flares
> Shrivels a heritage of blighted futures.

The image of destruction by fire which runs throughout portrays both the physical painfulness of the process and the totality of the waste.

In 'Massacre, October '66'[1] the poet uses the imagery of the environment in which he finds himself at the time of the massacres – 'seasons of an alien land'. This not only has a therapeutic value for him – the distancing stays his mind from collapsing under the enormity of the event – but it has a similar value for the reader too. The alien images of autumn provide an artistic machinery through which the uninvolved reader can be brought to the heart of the experience. The use of the surrounding landscape is an illustration of Soyinka's ability to start from where he is, and express his meaning by the means immediately available to him. He always harnesses the environment to his purpose. Tegel (a residential section of Berlin) in Autumn is made to do service as the environment through which the horror of the October massacres in the poet's own country are portrayed. There is an astonishingly intelligent fusion of the falling and fallen acorns with the more gruesome image of heads being cropped and crushed at home:

> I trod on acorns; each shell's detonation
> Aped the skull's uniqueness.

The transformation of the acorns is effected through the pun on 'shells' – the protective covering of acorns and cannon shells – which leads naturally to 'detonation' of both types of shells which are then fused with the human skulls in the next line. The mind of the poet in the depths of depression had been similarly fused with the very bottom of the lake in the opening stanza. He had been looking both into the lake and into his own depressed mind:

> . . . I sought to reach
> A mind at silt-bed

[1] A complementary analysis of this poem appears earlier, pp. 122–4.

It is through such yoking of the objects of the surrounding landscape with what was happening at home that Soyinka makes his point. The acorns also provide the vehicle through which he expresses the devaluation of human life which the massacre implies. Acorns are plentiful and cheap:

> The oak rains a hundred more

and are

> This favoured food of hogs . . .

There is an implied cheapening of human heads which are being equally indiscriminately harvested in his own country:

> As heads still harshly crop to whirlwinds
> I have briefly fled.

The hog idea is to be given even more ironical significance in the penultimate stanza when Soyinka uses it to dramatize the irony of the fact that the massacres took place in a land whose everyday greeting involved the idea of peace and where in observance of religious teaching the eating of pork was taboo. The juxtaposition of the observance of such teachings with the 'desecration' of human life provides an eloquent comment:

> Whose desecration mocks the word
> Of peace – *salaam aleikun* – not strangers any
> Brain of thousands pressed asleep to pig fodder –
> Shun pork the unholy – cries the priest.

The immediate environment is made to yield one more vital significance in the last stanza which is much more than an apology for using an alien environment to portray Nigerian events. The environment could not have been more apt in one sense. Not only acorns lie around him in this alien land, but:

> . . . pride of race around me
> Strewn in sunlit shards.

We recall that this was the home of the Herrenvolk theory which because of its exclusiveness led to the massacre of millions. The parallel is instructive. Perhaps this too helps to stay the mind – It had happened before, and man had survived.

War as a travesty of life is implicit in 'Civilian and Soldier' where the civilian is on the side of life and the soldier on the side of death. The soldier is a victim of his situation and training. His finger itches instinctively for the trigger on which all his training is focused. His instinctive reactions are towards inflicting death. This is his 'plight'. The sudden appearance of a civilian in his area therefore sets in train this mechanical reaction which brings the civilian within an eyelash of death. The irony is that behind the seeming certainty of the soldier's outward reactions is fear and uncertainty. The poet sees the 'plight' of the solider:

> . . . and when
> You brought the gun to bear on me, and death
> Twitched me gently in the eye, your plight
> And all of you came clear to me.

(Apart from anything else, the poise of these lines, particularly the clause 'and death/Twitched me gently in the eye' illustrate Soyinka's control.) The soldier is engaged in his trade of death and has nothing to offer but bullets. The civilian's revenge therefore (when the opportunity is favourable) is to bombard the soldier with life-giving items:

> . . . No hesitation then
> But I shall shoot you clean and fair
> With meat and bread, a gourd of wine
> A bunch of breasts from either arm . . .

The poem is more than an indictment of a single soldier; it is a confrontation between the processes of life and death. The soldier's position is all the more pathetic because he too is caught in spite of himself. His is a 'plight' of being involved in death, a 'plight' brought about by forces much larger than himself. The larger questions which determine peace or war are all beyond him. His answer to the question at the end of the poem would no doubt have been 'no':

> . . . do you friend, even now, know
> What it is all about?

The tribute 'For Fajuyi' arises from the fact that Fajuyi tried to find out what it was all about. He was a soldier, but he was also that recurrent figure in Soyinka's work – the lonely seeker; the man who sacrifices himself for the good of his society; whose 'lonely feat' must be offered for the redemption of his society. 'The Dreamer', the lonely poet in 'Idanre', Eman in *The Swamp-Dwellers* all trod the lone path Fajuyi trod:

> . . . What goals for pilgrim feet
> But to a dearth of wills
> To hills and terraces of gods
> Echoes for voices, shadows for the lonely feat.

The irony here, as elsewhere where these lonely figures appear, is that while they fall, 'Weeds triumph'.

In all the terrible events which gave rise to these poems, the poet retained an objectivity both as an artist and a Nigerian. He was able to see above 'us' and 'them'. For many people – and again this is implicit in a number of poems – only the superficialities were visible and their joys as well as their sorrows were strictly partisan. Only the few – the lonely pilgrims – have the imagination to suffer with 'enemy' as well as 'friend'; to see into the essence of things, and recognize essential humanity. In 'Malediction' Soyinka rains terrible curses on one who rejoiced, no doubt at one of the disasters to 'them' rather than to 'us':

> Unsexed, your lips
> have framed a life curse
> shouting joy where all
> the human world
> shared in grief's humility.

For this denial of life she is cursed to a life in which death appears where most she looks for life, and laughter, when sorrow is more appropriate to her condition. Her bier is thus to be impiously hooted to its grave by her inebriated children, even as she has laughed in an hour of human tragedy:

> that their throats laugh Amen
> on your bier, and carousing hooves
> raise dust to desecrated dust – Amen.

Idanre

▼▼▼▼▼▼▼▼▼▼▼▼▼▼▼▼▼▼▼▼▼▼▼▼▼▼▼▼▼▼

FOR HIS long poem 'Idanre', written in 1965 and published in 1967 while the poet was in detention,[1] the Yoruba mythological background, with Ogun as the featured deity, provides the metaphorical framework for the presentation of ideas which have appeared in one form or another throughout Soyinka's work. An equally familiar human figure, the lonely seeker, appears in the person of the poet who, while the rest of the community waits in passive piety and hope for the blessings of the harvest, dares to undertake a lonely and hazardous journey into Ogun's lair, to witness the god's pre-harvest agony:

> I walked upon a deserted night before
> The gathering of Harvest, companion at a god's
> Pre-banquet . . .

It is to those only who dare to gaze alone on the naked truth that the hills 'yield their secrets'. 'Idanre' is a record both of the poet's pilgrimage and of the secrets which it yields.

This framework allows the poet to introduce many of his favourite themes – the waste of war, the consequences of free will, the celebration of individuality, death on the roads, man's potential as well as his proneness to self-destruction, the nature of the god Ogun – all themes which reappear elsewhere, but which in 'Idanre' are given a new form and unity.

Section I of the poem, 'deluge', sets the scene at the start of the pilgrimage. The storm which precedes the walk is described in terms which evoke the presences of the gods behind it; Sango the god of lightning and electricity – 'the axe-handed one' – and Ogun, the god of iron whose metallic cables bear Sango's electricity to earth:

> He catches Sango in his three-fingered hand
> And runs him down to earth . . .

And more specifically later:

[1] In *The Man Died*, p. 115, Soyinka describes the moment when he saw a printed copy of the volume *Idanre and Other Poems* while he was a prisoner in Kaduna.

> One speeds his captive bolts on filaments
> Spun of another's forge . . .

The storm is now over, and only the occasional flashes of lightning making patterns with the clouds, and the dripping leaves carry evidence of its fierceness. But terrible though the storm may be it is also the promise of harvest. The harvest image, as will be seen later, is central to 'Idanre'.[2] Men as well as the land welcome this rain without question (only the poet dares further into 'secrets hidden from him'):

> And no one speaks of secrets in this land
> Only, that the skin be bared to welcome rain
> And earth prepare, that seeds may swell
> And roots take flesh within her, and men
> Wake naked into harvest-tide.

Soyinka uses the present tense here, a tense which he often uses to express not only what is current but additionally what recurs or is permanent. (The subtle alteration of tenses within a poem is important in the interpretation of all Soyinka's poetry. It is certainly important in a long poem like 'Idanre' where there are frequent changes of tense and hence of significance.) There is thus (because of the use of the present tense in their portrayal) something both in the storm and in the dependence of man on the gods for the harvest that is archetypal – a permanent pattern. When the actual pilgrimage starts in the second stanza of Section II of the poem, the historic past tense is used. Ogun's arrival in what is a recurring pattern – 'again' – is portrayed with the present tense, as distinct from the particular pilgrimage in which the poet joins. First the ritual reappearance:

> He comes who scrapes no earthdung from his feet
> He comes again in Harvest, the first of reapers
> Night is our tryst when sounds are clear
> And silence ring pure notes as the pause
> Of iron bells

For the particular historic walk with which the poem is concerned, the tense changes:

---

[2] For a fuller examination of the harvest image, see E. D. Jones, 'Naked Into Harvest-Tide: The Harvest Image in "Idanre"', *African Literature Today*, 6 (Heinemann, London, 1973).

> . . . We walked
> Silently across a haze of corn, and Ogun
> Teased his ears with tassels, his footprints
> Future furrows for the giant root.

The pilgrimage in the company of a god is preluded by a communion with another human, 'the wine-girl'.

This brief communion with the wine-girl is the poet's last link with his own kind. She is not only human, but woman, and her femininity is highlighted:

> . . . vapours rose
> From sodden bitumen and snaked within
> Her wrap of indigo, her navel misted over
> A sloe bared from the fruit
>
> Darkness veiled her little hills poised
> Twin nights against the night, pensive points
> In the leer of lightning . . .

Earlier her 'womb' had echoed in human terms the rhythm of harvest so important in the symbolism of the poem. There is something archetypal about her too. In his notes to the poem Soyinka endows her with three personalities. Apart from her primary personality as the wine-girl, she is 'Also Oya, once the wife of Ogun, latterly of Sango . . . Also a dead girl killed in a motor accident.' (p. 86.) In the poem itself she is the principle of womanhood; the eternal mother; the human counterpart of Mother Earth, and thus similarly responsive to the elements. As she stands in the rain she too like the earth earlier receives its benevolent influence, her skin bared:

> . . . the thatch
> Ran rivulets between her breasts.

In her elevated role she provides an anchor for the poet in his lonely and hazardous walk among gods and spirits. He is 'earthed' to her:

> *And to the one whose feet were wreathed*
> *In dark vapours from earth's cooling pitch*
> *I earth my being, she who has felt rain's probing*
> *Vines on night's lamp-post, priestess at fresh shrines*
> *Sacred leaf whose hollow gathers rains*

His mind twice returns to the wine-girl during his walk with the god. As an ordinary human she would avoid the hills; she would be prepared to wait 'incurious' for the harvest. She cannot understand why the poet would seek the hills at such a time. In her query she is a representative of the mass:

> . . . what then are you? At such hour
> Why seek what on the hills?

Her query underlies the poet's isolation and the incomprehension with which the society receives his words and actions – even those meant for their benefit. His separation from the wine-girl is symbolic of his separateness from the society he serves. But he is still 'earthed' to her and the society. His relationship is thus fraught with ambiguity. It is this underlying ambiguity that tends to make the lonely poet the victim of his own society which he seeks to save.

The walk with the god takes us through familiar paths at first. The landscape bears the marks of man's inventiveness; high tension cables symbolizing the union of Sango and Ogun, and motor roads strewn with the wrecks of motor vehicles, offerings to the demanding god Ogun. Men have quarried the earth, refined the ores, harnessed electricity, and created marvellous artifacts which in turn destroy them. The irony of this situation intrigues Soyinka as the recurrence of this theme in his works shows. This irony reflects an ambiguity in the nature of the god Ogun who is both creator and destroyer. It is he who inspires the worker in metals; it is also he who demands the sacrifice of the road. Men are Ogun's protégés as well as his victims:

> . . . And we

> Have honeycombed beneath his hills, worked red earth
> Of energies, quarrying rare and urgent ores and paid
> With wrecks of last year's suppers, paved his roads
> With shells, intestines of breathless bones –
> Ogun is a demanding god.

As the poem continues, the irony builds up as not only the wonderful artifacts of man are reduced to 'Playthings for children/For browsing goats', but as man himself, the lord of creation, is reduced to a mere ingredient in the cycle of growth, and his brain, the powerhouse of his inventiveness, is equated with sheep's excrement after his own invention has claimed him as a victim in a car crash:

> . . . growth is greener where
> Rich blood has spilt; brain and marrow make
> Fat manure with sheep's excrement.

But man is more than body: the dead, humiliated in body, rise in essence and join the ranks of the departed ancestors to protect the living and receive their tribute. The cycle, like the cycle of the harvest, is never ending:

> . . . They rose
> The dead whom fruit and oil await
> On doorstep shrine and road, their lips
> Moist from the first flakes of harvest rain –
> Even gods remember dues.

The continuing cycle is represented by various symbols in Soyinka's work. Later in this same poem he uses the image of the snake swallowing its own tail – well known in Yoruba iconography – and the 'Mobius Strip' to represent this principle of cyclical continuity or evolution:

> Evolution of the self-devouring snake to spatials
> New in symbol, banked loop of the 'Mobius Strip'
> And interlock of re-creative rings, one surface
> Yet full combs of angles, uni-plane, yet sensuous with
> Complexities of mind and motion.

The walk is interrupted by a reversion into the poet's childhood and the deliriums and nightmares of his dreams. The reason for the occurrence of this passage here is not immediately clear and has to be worked out. In an inspired moment during the walk, the poet's sensibilities have become heightened and he has seen and felt the presences of the dead:

> Suffused in new powers of night, my skin
> Grew light with eyes; I watched them drift away
> To join the gathering presences.

Two stanzas later the childhood visions are introduced with the lines:

> Vast grows the counterpane of nights since innocence
> Of apocalyptic skies, when thunderous shields clashed
> Across the heights, when bulls leapt cloud humps and
> Thunders opened chasms end to end of fire:
> The sky a slate of scoured lettering.

The change of tense from 'grows' to 'clashed', 'leapt', 'opened', is significant. The growth of the sky since childhood 'innocence' is both a present fact and a continuing experience. The fantasies of childhood had been a confused jumble of the oddments of formal education – the nursery rhyme cow jumping over the moon is just perceptible in 'bulls leapt cloud humps' – and Yoruba lore – later a 'gaunt *ogboni*' vaults on a zebra's back. The point of all this is that the experiences are jumbled and unorganized. Since then the experiences of the night have become vaster. This particular night for example has already yielded an important enlargement of the counterpane of night in the vision of Ogun and the presences. More enlargement is to come by the end of the experience which the poem describes.

The second section of the poem ends with an even further retreat into time – back into fossil time, to the creation of order out of chaos at the beginning; when Ogun, the creator started the 'loop' – the word is significant – of time:

> The night glowed violet about his head
> He reached a large hand to tension wires
> And plucked a string; earth was a surreal bowl
> Of sounds and mystic timbres, his fingers
> Drew warring elements to a union of being
>
> And taught the veins to dance, of earth of rock
> Of tree, sky, of fire and rain, of flesh of man
> And woman. Ogun is the god that ventures first
> His path one loop of time, one iron coil
> Earth's broken rings were healed.

This picture of Ogun as the creator, the first venturer and indeed at this point in time the only god, links up with Section III in which Ogun, now one of many, grieves over the splitting of the single essence by Atunda's act of smashing the godhead with a boulder – a piece of mythology of which Soyinka makes significant use.

> Union they had known until the Boulder
> Rolling down the hill of the Beginning
> Shred the kernel to a million lights.

The sudden creation of a multiple god-head is in contrast to the tortuous path of man's own evolution which is partly fated and partly self-willed:

> Man's passage, pre-ordained, self-ordered winds
> In reconstruction . . .

The present tense signals the continuing nature of the winding path. The search for an undefined goal continues:

> . . . And the monolith of man searches still
> A blind hunger in the road's hidden belly.

Ogun's own pilgrimage (as has been seen earlier) is recurrent. His words make this clear:

> *This road have I trodden in a time beyond*
> *Memory of fallen leaves, beyond*
> *Thread of fossil on the slate, yet I must*
> *This way again . . .*

The poet follows the god, shrouded by night and the suggestive rock complexes of the hill, as Ogun once more seeks 'the season's absolution'.

The relationship between Ogun and men has been seen as being ambiguous. Although man is a creation of the god, he is able to influence his creator even against the creator's better judgement. The men of Ire broke his resolve to separate himself from men once he had hewn a path to earth – itself a reflection of the god's ambiguous nature – and prevailed on him to be their king. The language suggests the persuasiveness of the men of Ire who as representatives of human kind manifest another facet of man's uncanny abilities from which he not only benefits but also suffers. The men of Ire drag the god down by their persuasive arts:

> . . . But Ire
> Laid skilled siege to divine withdrawal. Alas
> For diplomatic arts, the Elders of Ire prevailed;
> He descended, and they crowned him king.

The cost to the men of Ire – more dramatically portrayed in Section V – is dreadful. They had enlisted the aid of ultimate force which, once they had enlisted it, they cannot control –

> . . . O let heaven loose the bolts
> Of last season's dam for him to lave his fingers
> Merely, and in the heady line of blood
> Vultures drown . . .

This is the potential that men have sought to harness for their own petty ends. The harvest they reap is proportionately bloody. Men harness ultimate forces at their peril:

> Who brings a god to supper, guard him well
> And set his place with a long bamboo pole.

The poem here speaks eloquently outside its immediate context in comment on the almost unimaginable capacity in the hands of man – he is able to harness the god himself. Yet man has only his own puny selfish will to control this force. His use of the force then is often perverse and self-destructive because his will is not equal in magnanimity to the magnitude of his material strength.

> We do not burn the woods to trap
> A squirrel; we do not ask the mountain's
> Aid, to crack a walnut.

Yet in defiance of man's own proverbial wisdom, this is what the men of Ire did; this is what men always do. The consequences of the men of Ire's invoking of absolute force is dramatized in Ogun's 'day of error' when the 'lust-blind god' destroys friend and foe alike. Soyinka describes the physical terror of the god's blind rampage in a picture of matching terror. The god dwarfs everyone around him, symbolizing the disproportionate character of the unleashed force:

> . . . Tall he rises to the hills
> His head a rain-cloud has eclipsed the sun
> His nostrils blow visible.
>
> Exhalations as twin-flues through clouds
>
> His sword an outer crescent of the sun
> No eye can follow it, no breath draws
> In wake of burning vapour . . .

Having portrayed the god with the aid of elemental parallels, the only terms which would do – rain-clouds, the sun, burning, vapours etc., Soyinka reduces the scale to portray the consequences to man. He chooses the familiar domestic image of a harvest – a bad harvest:

> There are falling ears of corn
> And ripe melons tumble from the heads
> Of noisy women, crying
>
> Lust-blind god, gore-drunk Hunter
> Monster deity, you destroy your men!

The cost of the devastation is here given in human terms through the image of a reversal of the normal harvest. Confusion replaces order; the songs are turned to wails; the god drinks blood – the blood of his own men – for wine. As the god warms to his work he becomes in turns a butcher and a cannibal. The god who was so susceptible to the 'diplomatic arts' of men is now 'deafened' to their helpless cries. The god does not discriminate (any more than does a nuclear bomb):

> . . . their cry
> For partial succour brought a total hand
> That smothered life on crimson plains
> With too much answering.

As the poet watched the god relive his day of error, understanding – the harvest of his daring – came to him: 'understanding came/Of a fatal condemnation'. The scales fell from his eyes the same moment as in his dramatic agony, the blood-scales fall from the god's eyes, and once again restored to sanity, he sees the error of his deed:

> Too late for joy, the Hunter stayed his hand
> The chute of truth opened from red furnaces
> And Ogun stayed his hand
>
> Truth, a late dawn.

Truth was a late dawn too for the men of Ire:

> . . . Too late came warning that a god
> Is still a god to men, and men are one
> When knowledge comes, of death.

Truth for men alas is too often a late dawn.

The secrets of 'Idanre', yielded to the poet three years and some two hundred miles later than the actual walk up Idanre are revealed in words addressed to the god which the poet overhears. Ogun had grieved over the splitting of the unified godhead. Here what he hears is a celebration of Atunda's act; a celebration of diversity which is the essence of life and growth rather than uniformity which is death. What Ogun heard was:

> . . . not voices whom the hour
> Of death had made all one, nor futile flight
> But the assertive act of Atunda, and he was shamed
> In recognition of the grim particular

> It will be time enough, and space, when we are dead
> To be a spoonful of the protoplasmic broth
> Cold in wind-tunnels, lava flow of nether worlds
> Deaf to thunder blind to light, comatose
> In one omni-sentient cauldron
>
> Time enough to abdicate to astral tidiness
> The all in one, superior annihilation of the poet's
> Diversity . . .

The poet too hears this justification of individuality and the diversity that it brings. It would be an act of renunciation to abandon the individuality which allows the poet to make his lonely pilgrimage. The poem in fact becomes a celebration of the individual will wherever it has appeared and has produced the remarkable individual whose life and thinking has changed the lives of men. Atunda then is no treacherous slave, but a saint in the exalted company of all divine assertions of individual will:

> All hail Saint Atunda, First revolutionary
> Grand iconoclast at genesis – and the rest in logic
> Zeus, Osiris, Jaweh, Christ in trifoliate
> Pact with creation, and the wisdom of Orunmila, Ifa
> Divining eyes, multiform.

This is not a climactic assertion within the poem 'Idanre' alone, but an assertion of the individual will to which much of Soyinka's work points. The dreamer – the lonely visionary – is the potential saviour of his society. Only through him can society be renewed. Only through him can man take one of his forward steps.

After this climactic purgation of his grief, Ogun can depart, and the poet can return to earth. He returns to the symbolic wine-girl. She is still there keeping her lone vigil, and like all of her human kind, looking forward to the harvest; not the perverted harvest of Ogun's day of error but a fruitful natural harvest:

> And Harvest came, responsive
>
> The first fruits rose from subterranean hoards
> First in our vision, corn sheaves rose over hill
> Long before the bearers, domes of eggs and flesh
> Of palm fruit, red, oil black, froth flew in sun bubbles
> Burst over throngs of golden gourds.

This is the harvest for which men pray, but of which all too often by their own contributory actions they are deprived. Such is the latent contradiction in man's nature, a contradiction he shares with Ogun. 'Idanre' is a major poetic expression of some of the pervading themes in Soyinka's work.

'Idanre' is capable of multiple complementary interpretations, and now that in the form of the Civil War Ogun has indeed been wooed once more into the human arena with the predicted devastating effects, the Nigerian political and social applications of the poem would be paramount among such interpretations. While such interpretations are appropriate, Ogun has assumed a greater significance in Soyinka's work than that of a local deity. In *Ogun Abibimang* he is seen in alliance with Chaka from the other side of the continent, but even this is only a partial stride for a capacious metaphor capable of even wider significance. As the ingenuity of man puts him in touch with even greater sources of power, capable of universal destruction as well as of a better prospect of shared happiness, the poet in 'Idanre' should find more companions for his journey.

Poems from Prison[1]

▼▼▼▼▼▼▼▼▼▼▼▼▼▼▼▼▼▼▼▼▼▼▼▼▼▼▼▼▼

WOLE SOYINKA was detained in prison from August 1967 until October 1969. In 1969 Rex Collings published two poems written in prison. There was no doubt in the minds of those who were familiar with Soyinka's work that the poems were his. The characteristic of making the immediate environment yield larger meanings, the ability to light upon the apt fixing image, the economical style were all there. But more important, and to the great relief of his admirers, the ideas were also there – the assertion of the individual will; the lonely figure separate, yet a part of the society – even a victim of the society; the concern for that society even as one groans under it. All these appear in the 'Poems from Prison'.

Totally different in effect though it is, the technique of 'Live Burial' reminds of that of 'Telephone Conversation' – the bantering surface tone lightly spread over the graver implications beneath. Here, however, the surface is more often broken by the sinister undertones. The graver and more sinister suggestions start from the stark first stanza where the narrow confinement 'Sixteen paces/By twenty-three' constitutes a lingering assault – 'siege' – against the prisoner's 'sanity'. The economy of the statement of that first stanza is as good as anything Soyinka produced outside prison. Its starkness is symbolically reflective of the prisoner's deprived state.

The second stanza is based on the Antigone story. The prisoner becomes Haemon who has allied himself with his lover Antigone against his own father Creon. The analogy has aptness. The son allying himself with an outsider becomes even more hated than the outsider. His attempt to 'unearth/Corpses of Yester Year', is doubly embarrassing because he is a member of the family. The sentence in stanza three – 'Seal him Live/In the same necropolis' – is not a literal echo of Antigone where Haemon's entry to Antigone's cave and his later death were voluntary; here the decree is from above. The prisoner is condemned to the same fate as those whose cause he seems to espouse:

> May his ghost mistress
> Point the classic
> Route to Outsiders' Stygian mysteries.

[1] Versions of these poems appear in the later collection *A Shuttle in the Crypt* (Rex Collings/Eyre Methuen, London, 1972).

The prisoner is not killed in our poem, only entombed – 'Sixteen paces/ By twenty-three' – and he is watched by guards who are portrayed with a strong hint of sadism. They 'thrill' at the 'constipated groan' of the under-exercised prisoner whose physical state is thus economically suggested. His suffering is in sharp contrast to the implied sniggers of the 'voyeurs' outside as they listen to the 'Music' singing in a common key, and gloating at their sudden discovery of at least one plane of equality with him. Then comes the almost throw-away tone of the last stanza lightly covering the chilling physical undertones of the last line:[2]

Our plastic surgeons tend his public image.

The line simultaneously suggests good public relations men piecing together clichés to keep the public happy, and more gravely, the damaged physical state of the prisoner being patched up for a public showing.[3]

The poem has far more significance than the plight of any one prisoner. It portrays the plight of the individual who runs up against juggernaut authority – a theme which occurs frequently in Soyinka's work, but particularly in 'The Dreamer', *The Strong Breed*, *Kongi's Harvest*, *The Interpreters*, and with the target enlarged to a small group, *Season of Anomy*. As an author Soyinka has always faced the consequence of such a stance – Eman is sacrificed by the people he tried to save (*The Strong Breed*), Sekoni is driven into insanity, the dreamer is crucified. This poem holds no more optimism for this type of figure in society. It is ironical that Soyinka has suffered in some measure the fate of so many of his 'dreamers'. It is cruel testimony to the integrity of his poetic vision.

At the start of the second poem, 'Flowers For My Land', the poet takes up an anti-war protest song from a distant land. They ask where their flowers have gone, but their distant cry has echoes in the 'here' of the poet's own land where instead of flowers, death is being sown, so that the garlands which result are heavy 'Garlands of Scavengers'. The weight is the weight of guilt; the guilt which arises from man's own act of sowing death for flowers. The application to Nigeria is so obvious that it may blind us to the universality of the kind of guilt which the poem treats. The echo of the protest song is of course a pointer to the world outside Nigeria, and a consequent broadening of the range of application.

[2] In *A Shuttle in the Crypt* a longer version of this poem appears, the addition consisting mainly of further portraits of the guards. The longer version loses the crispness of the original version without adding much of significance.

[3] The subsequent publication *The Man Died* (p. 67) shows, in fact, that this is a very deft use of an actual bulletin issued by the authorities on Soyinka himself.

The analogy between flowers and death is meant to juxtapose the potential for life and beauty, and the opposites for which this is exchanged. This is very starkly brought out in two successive stanzas:

> Seeking
> Voices of rain in sunshine
> Blue kites on ivory-cloud
> Towers
> Smell of passing hands on mountain flowers.

These images of life, beauty, and grace soon become transformed into their opposites (while Soyinka wittily repeats the key words) in:

> I saw
> Four steel kites, riders
> On shrouded towers
> Do you think
> Their arms are spread to scatter mountain flowers?

The kites have grimly become planes; the clouds, protective cover; and the mountain flowers, bombs.

In this situation – of war – voices of dissent (even when they may also be voices of truth) are not tolerated – and this is no specially 'Nigerian' situation. The tares are all too commonly in a position to withhold possession of the lawns from the flowers. In the exigencies of the present, reason and long-term interests are suppressed and crushed. It is against the senselessness of such a situation that the poem makes its ironic call for unity of the weak – 'the mangled kind'. Even the words of the call carry in themselves an anticipatory frustration. The tone of the parody 'Orphans of the world/ignite' is almost self-mocking.

These two poems represent a triumph of the universal mind over the limitations and the frustrations of a purely local situation, even the oppressive, immediate one of solitary confinement. Even from this crabbed environment Soyinka's mind can still reach back into time, and outwards to the rest of the world to view the plight of man, the victim of his own stupidity.

Soyinka's poetry must not be interpreted in too limited a sense. He may be starting from fairly obviously identifiable points – his own imprisonment and the Nigerian war in these two poems – but his concern is with the values he has always been preoccupied with: truth as it is painfully discovered by the individual; the struggle to remain faithful to this truth; the need for self-sacrifice to enhance the truth; the consciousness that even when the mind is resolute, the body sometimes falters when the ultimate price is demanded.

A Shuttle in the Crypt

▼▼▼▼▼▼▼▼▼▼▼▼▼▼▼▼▼▼▼▼▼▼▼▼▼▼▼▼▼▼▼▼▼▼

A Shuttle in the Crypt[1] opens with 'Roots', which acknowledges human vulnerability under intense physical and moral trial and prays for strength. It closes with a memorial to a fellow poet, Christopher Okigbo, who, although he died in the bloom of his manhood, died believing passionately in a cause, his ideals and dreams intact, a circumstance from which Soyinka salvages some consolation:

> Yet kinder this, than a spirit seared
> In violated visions and truths immured
>
> Eternal provender for Time
> Whose wings his boundless thoughts would climb.   (p. 89.)

His untimely death can be accepted, even (though mournfully) celebrated.

There is in the opening poem, when the poet considers his own state – still chained to the rocks, his living body the prey of eagles – a consciousness of vulnerability from which Okigbo is now free; hence the open and *humble* appeal for strength in 'Roots' at the beginning of the collection. The appeal is humble, not abject, for sustaining strength is to come essentially from within himself. If this inner strength cannot withstand the pressures of either physical suffering or official blandishments, then the poet would rather plunge to the peace that Okigbo has achieved.

> O Roots, Roots. If it Shall Not Withstand!
> If it shall cave to wind and choke in sands
>
> Of wilderness, if it shall cinder in flash
> Of the dearth-awaited, your coils unleash
>
> Upon the last defence of sluices! The prow
> Is pointed to a pull of undertows
>
> A grey plunge in pools of silence, peace
> Of bygone voyagers, to the close transforming pass.   (p. 4.)

[1] *A Shuttle in the Crypt* (Rex Collings/Eyre Methuen, London, 1972).

The imagery of 'Roots' moves somewhat uneasily between that of a boat and its anchor and that of a tree and its roots, but the intensity of the feeling comes through. Here death is a prospect of rest and a union with cleansed voyagers who have earlier completed the journey – another link with both the Okigbo and the Victor Banjo tribute at the end.

These three boundary poems all have eventually to do with death; so do the group of poems which for Soyinka is central to the collection, 'Chimes of Silence', which is concerned with 'the passage of five men to and through the travesty of looms, the gallows'. (p. vii.)

Given Soyinka's abiding interest in the nature of death and the possibilities of various approaches to it, his attempt to make something of his proximity to the occurrence of death by hanging at this particular time, when he was also so very much concerned with justice, is only to be expected. The poet's observation point, his 'crypt' in which he is entombed, makes him far from being a detached onlooker; he is a fellow victim of the same tyranny. His search for significance in the events taking place over the wall are thus a search for meaning in his own life through his own suffering, and, though only a watcher, he emerges from the experience 'bedraggled' – 'Mine the bedraggled wings'. (p. 46.) 'Chimes of Silence' are valuable, as we shall see, not so much for any general revelations at the end of the experience but for the experience itself, and since these poems are for the poet central to the whole collection, it is useful to look briefly at their development.

Soyinka first locates his observation post in 'Bearings' before proceeding to the central episode, the death procession, the passage to death. He provides an edited excerpt from the 'record of the actual struggle against a vegetable existence', *The Man Died*, as a special key to this section of *A Shuttle in the Crypt*, which does help by giving the primary stimulus for the poems and their images, though the poems often transcend the immediate experience.

'Wailing Wall' is obviously placed, in its primary sense, by a section in the prefatory passage referred to above. '(I named it that [Wailing Wall] because it overlooks the yard where a voice cried out in agony all of one night and died at dawn, unattended. It is the yard from which hymns and prayers rise with a constancy matched only by the vigil of crows and vultures.)' (p. 32.) The image pattern of the poem gives us a setting, a travesty of religious worship, in which the priests are themselves predators and the trusting congregation their potential victims. The vultures and crows of the prison have become transformed into symbols competing for the exploitation of the congregation:

Wailing Wall
Wall to polar star, wall of prayers
A roof in the blood-rust floats beyond
Stained-glass wounds on wailing walls
Vulture presides in tattered surplice
In schism for collection plates, with –

Crow in white collar, legs
Of toothpick dearth plunged
Deep in a salvaged morsel. Choirmaster
When a hymn is called he conducts,
Baton-beaking their massed discordance;
Invocation to the broken Word
On broken voices.   (p. 34.)

Other suggestions soon transform Evensong into the prelude to a mass burial, not just of the singing prisoners now but, through the introduction of the Plough star, of a much wider universe, so that the defeat of hope affects far more than the immediate province of the vulture and crow:

Cloud drifts across Plough
The share is sunk, and hope
Buried in soil of darkness.   (p. 35.)

The first peal of the 'Chimes of Silence' is one of deep despair. The mood runs into 'Walls of Mists' not only because 'wells/Are the tomb of longings', in which ordinary human feelings are smothered, but also because worse deformations of the human spirit are possible; and in Circean transformations (once again Greek mythology supplies the metaphor) men become swine, their humanity perverted:

Mists of metamorphosis
Men of swine, strength to blows
Grace to lizard prances, honour
To sweetmeats on the tongue of vileness.   (p. 36.)

'Amber Wall', which arises from the poet's observation of a small boy reaching for mangoes and pausing for a bewildered moment to stare at the prisoner, does not step out of the immediate environment, the confined prison and the small patch of the outside world. The closed world of the prisoner is a contrast with the open world of the boy, whose present state of uncaring freedom is bound eventually to give way to apprehension of a

world closer to that now experienced by the prisoner. May this knowledge
– and within the loss there is gain – be bought with less pain than it has
cost the prisoner:

> I would you may discover, mid-morning
> To the man's estate, with lesser pain
> The wall of gain within the outer loss.   (p. 37.)

Already, however, the hopes of the night seem dashed by the experience of
day. Suffering as the price of self-knowledge seems inevitable:

> I hear
> The sun's sad chorus to your starlight songs.

'Purgatory' stays closer, for most of its length, to the primary stimulus –
a glancing look at goings-on behind this particular wall – than the other
poems in 'Bearings'. The opening tone is almost jocular, laughing off even
the sadism of the giant flagellator, until the poem touches those who have
returned from the brink of death, having been reprieved from execution.
In other works, notably *The Road*, Soyinka has sought great revelations
from those who have got so close to death and have returned. What have
they seen? What can they tell us? (He himself is here telling!) These have
seen nothing. They can tell us nothing:

> Weaned from the moment of death, the miracle
> Dulled, their minds dissolved in vagueness, a look
> Empty as all thoughts are featureless which
> Plunge to the lone abyss – And
> Had it all ended? Had it all ended, Here
> Even in the valley of the shadow of night?

The approximation of the poet's solitary confinement to a live burial is
casually reiterated, and once again in 'Vault Centre', where he is the
'Corpse'. The pessimism of the suggestions of that image is soon mitigated,
first through 'thoughts' though 'ghostly', then through the identification
with the less confined birds, with whom he finds an escape in imagination.
The closing image can thus be one which, though still static commanding
only a limited and desolated view, is a vantage point, and with religious
overtones 'An oriel window, eye on chapel ruins'. (p. 41.) From this
limited vantage point the poet experiences the death of five men in the
neighbouring yard. Their hanging yields the image which supplies the title
of this section. They are the 'Bell-ringers on the ropes to chimes/Of silence'.

Once again the poet attempts to probe their death for some revelation, but the result is negative. Their death is no triumph of law, no vindication of justice – as the soundless chimes imply; the real guilt lies outside the prison walls:

> Let no man speak of justice, guilt.
> Far away, blood-stained in their
> Tens of thousands, hands that damned
> These wretches to the pit triumph
> But here, alone the solitary deed.   (p. 42.)

(The imagery is sometimes strained and occasionally distracting through inappropriateness. What, for instance, is the significance of 'owlish fingers' wisdom'?) Throughout the 'Passage' sections the pattern remains the same; there is a search, employing the celebration of death in traditional (and more normal) settings in order to discover some significance in the deaths of the five executed men. Each time the end of the tortuous search is negative.

The opening is almost hopeful, as death and decay are looked on as part of the productive cycle of continuing life, and Earth can be thought 'rich in rottenness of things' (p. 43) and fermentation festive. The poet handled this paradox positively in an earlier poem, 'Rust' in the *Idanre* collection. But here the images change from this optimistic pattern to ones of mere waste, futility and unanswered questions. At the end of the feast what have we got?

> Shade your sight from glare
> Of leavings on the mound. The feast is done.
> A coil of cigarette ribbon recreates
> A violet question on the refuse heap
> A headless serpent arched in fire
> In vibrancy of tinsel light, winding
> To futile answers, barren knowledge.   (p. 43.)

The greedy ant-foragers on the leavings of the feast are symbols of a voracious leadership that has nothing to teach:

> Their hands are closed on emptiness
> And opening shall give nothing out.   (p. 43.)

Tradition is no longer a source of strength. The shuttle with which the old women wove their spells is now stayed. At the end the poet is left in the posture of waiting, his wings bedraggled:

> Waiting for a sound that never comes
> To footfalls long receded, echoing
> In craters newly opened into space
> Listening to a falter of feet
> Upon the dark threshold.   (p. 46.)

The great revelations, whatever they are, can only be known after the threshold has been crossed.

In *The Road* Professor searches for the meaning of death on this side of the threshold, and his search is in vain. There is not much more for the by-stander who watches the last of the five prisoners make his journey to the final reconciliation where 'self/Encounters self'.

The climax of the group of poems is reached at the end of 'Procession I and II'. 'Last Turning' marks an emotional moment as the last of the five men enters 'this last kingdom', where he is 'king/Priest, and subject', but this seems a strangely homely place by comparison, for instance, with the resting place of Okigbo. 'Recession' induces the same reaction, and a feeling of anti-climax ends the section.

One real danger in attempting to write about a situation in which the wit and cunning of an apparently ruthless tyranny is pitted against oneself is that of paranoia. Soyinka avoids this by objectifying the experience through dramatic imagery and through a sense of humour, which never deserts him. One is able to forgive, for instance, the less felicitous of the puns and some of the more arcane images because they allow him to turn his face from the horror (or look above or below it) and make poetry possible. He uses his environment and its denizens – the lizards, cockroaches, spiders, egrets, vultures, ants and so on – but he also liberates himself by scouring for imaginative liberation not only the world outside (Kaura Hills, Obudu Ranges, Idanre, the rivers, the seas) but also biblical and secular history and mythology, particularly Greek mythology.

'Conversation at Night – With a Cockroach' selects a cell-fellow as interlocutor and an apt image of a saboteur of truth, honour, love – indeed, a figure who Soyinka represents as the insidious evil force that threatens to be the country's undoing:

> Oh you have claws
> To leak the day of pity, skin the night
> Within the heart of nature for all
> Of good to seep through unnoticed and unmourned.
> Saw teeth, dribbling a caress
> Of spittle on the wound, you nibbled trust
> From the heart of our concerted bond
> Yet left the seals intact.   (p. 5.)

The cockroach's part of the conversation is a cynical acknowledgement of its activities, while in stark narrative verse some of the consequences of the betrayal – the Northern massacres – are once again chronicled. The poem rolls on with the sheer weight of the horror rather than through any special poetic treatment. The wound is raw; the poet lets the blood flow. Towards the end the interpretive voice asserts itself somewhat in a comment on this 'arid' form of death, unsoftened by tears or mourning. In this kind of death more than the victims die, and silence becomes self-indictment:

> Tears are rainfall in the house of death
> Softening, purging, purifying. Tears
> Are a watering shed to earth's
> Unceasing wounds. This death was arid
> There was no groan, no sorrowing at the wake –
> Only curses. No suffering, for the senses
> Were first to die. We died, the world
> Turned a blank eye to the sky
> And prayed: May Heaven comfort you;
> On earth, our fears must teach us silence.   (p. 13.)

The poem is at its best when it stands back from the naked experience and, as in that last passage, attempts a distillation, or when, as in the beginning, the selected image encapsulates the experience.

In 'Four Archetypes' the selection of the model is crucial to the effective making of the point. With Joseph denying his attribute – patient suffering until time vindicates his position – the original identification also collapses. The new Joseph advocates immediate revolutionary action (this is in keeping with the sharper line taken in *The Man Died* and *Season of Anomy*).[2]

> A time of evils cries
> Renunciation of the saintly vision
> Summons instant hands of truth to tear
> All painted masks   (p. 21.)

'Hamlet' is a perfect fit, again reminding one of Ofeyi, the advocate of non-violence who finds himself with a gun in his hand, picking off his first man in the cause of humanity.[3] The pronoun 'He' (as distinct from the 'I' of 'Joseph') does not suggest total self-identification, and it may perhaps be precipitate to interpret all first-person pronouns as referring to

[2] See above, pp. 21–2.
[3] See below, pp. 206–7.

Soyinka. The temptation to do this in 'Gulliver' is strong, but Soyinka's own prose accounts of his activities in connection with the Civil War are more modestly stated than the image of Gulliver bringing in the enemy fleet single-handed would make appropriate. There are, however, parallels between the anger of the Federal Military Government and that of the Liliputian king at Gulliver's attempts at peace-making.

The comparative ease with which the code of the first three archetypes can be broken contrasts with the near-impenetrability of sections of 'Ulysses'. The image of the lone wanderer, sometimes doubtful of the value of his quest, persists through a succession of elusive images – 'How golden finally is the recovered fleece?'. The nature of the quest – its risks as the wanderer stumbles over unmapped territory – comes out in the last section, where there is also the suggestion that the end of the perilous journeys and quests is knowledge of self, and the reward a return to a pre-natal state; the final port is reached by a passage between vaginal rocks. It is tempting to see here the kind of rest pictured at the end of several explorations of the theme of death – in 'Procession' and the Okigbo poems, for example.

In *Season of Anomy* the leader of the idealized pastoral community, Aiyéro, is given the title 'Custodian of the Grain', grain representing the product of the harmony between man and the earth. Also, grain is the basic source of life and symbolizes life; thus food is sacred in Pa Ahime's creed. Similar suggestions surround 'bread' in the 'Poems of Bread and Earth', where the sacredness of bread should be respected and revered but can also, like life itself, be violated and desecrated.

The measure of a ruler can be taken by his response to his people's need for 'bread' and in Ujamaa, Julius Nyerere's measure is high.

> Your black earth hands unchain
> Hope from death messengers. (p. 80.)

He and his people have become part of the earth's rhythmic cycle and

> Sweat is leaven, bread, Ujamaa
> Bread of the earth, by the earth
> For the earth. Bread is all people.

The cliché formula of the last lines is signficantly used for its undertones of democratic rule. The contrast with 'Relief', the first poem in the group – the title itself is irony enough – is brutally clear. The abandonment of the production of grain for more polluting sources of wealth (oil?) is the point of 'Capital'. (For those who wince at the pun on 'dough', Soyinka turns the knife point by italicizing it!)

While some build seven-storey mansions which their governmental duties keep them from occupying – meanwhile the monstrous edifice conveniently goes on earning rent – others, whole families, starve. Private charity merely bankrupts itself in trying to shoulder burdens which are properly the business of governments – which are too busy making development plans! Soyinka's approach to this grim theme is to laugh in order to keep from crying.

The lightheartedness of the punning opening, which signals the poet's later intentions, belies the grimness that is to come. Even then, the uncomfortable laugh intrudes to point the contrast; 'cuisine' is a wry joke, but it points economically to the fare in mansions like the politician's seven-tiered house. He makes his point with a variation on the opening pun:

> Ever-ready bank accounts
> Are never read where
> Children slay the cockroach for a meal
> Awaiting father-forager's return.
> The mind of hungered innocence must turn
> To strange cuisine – kebab of butterflies . . .   (p. 81.)

The parodic list goes on and on, and the joke becomes more and more sour.

This mixing of jocularity with serious matter – achieved by puns and throwaway lines (the pun has always had as seductive an effect on Soyinka as it had on Shakespeare) – is not only used, as in this example, as a smoke-screen to cover the poet's embarrassment about speaking of his acts of charity, but is also part of Soyinka's recipe for survival in merciless conditions. This was one of the most hopeful signs in the two poems smuggled out of prison, 'Live Burial' and 'Flowers for my Land'.[4] Soyinka carried with him throughout his imprisonment not only his own personal griefs and anxieties but also the visceral concern that he has always exhibited for justice and humanity, particularly but not exclusively as maintained or violated in Nigeria. The poems rage against the violators and celebrate those like Victor Banjo and Okigbo (as in *Idanre* he celebrates Fajuyi) who have had ideals and dreams worth pursuing and have died martyrs, still believing in them. Soyinka's views are not *identical* with those of any one of these; what is important about their lives is that they put ideals higher than temporary self-gratification.

[4] See above, pp. 171–3.

Ogun Abibimang

▼▼▼▼▼▼▼▼▼▼▼▼▼▼▼▼▼▼▼▼▼▼▼▼▼▼▼▼▼

SOYINKA'S CAPTAIN of the soldiers in fiction (*A Dance of the Forests*), and he himself in fact, both suffered for their resistance to what they considered an unjust war. Neither, however, was a pacifist. Under interrogation by 'Mallam D' Soyinka expressed his agreement, 'and always as a last resort', with the proposition 'Any war in defence of liberty'.[1] In Soyinka's judgement, the Federal Military Government in his own country had degenerated into a tyranny which had suppressed liberty and had thus forfeited any claim to loyalty and allegiance. It became a duty to sweep such a tyranny away.

When this attitude is projected into situations outside Nigeria, the author's stance is predictable. The minority regime in Rhodesia was also a tyranny which it was a duty to defeat. Samora Machel's acceptance of this duty therefore found Soyinka responding with enthusiasm in *Ogun Abibimang*,[2] a poem which celebrates Machel's declaration of war against the minority regime of Rhodesia but also attempts an evaluation of the consequences, of the costs. In the celebration of the ideological rightness of the cause, the poet is far from oblivious of the perils of privation and suffering even of those who do not die by the sword. Guns are always got at the cost of bread. While Ogun is at the forge preparing for a just war, his farm must lie neglected:

> Rust and silence fill the thatch
> Of Ogun's farmstead. In corners of neglect –
> Clods of dried earth, sweatrags, kernels,
> A seed-yam's futile springing, a pithless coil
> Sunlight seeking, guide ropes, stakes –
> A planting season lost. Unswept, the woodflakes
> Drift, the carver's craft abandoned. Mute,
> A gesture frozen in ironwood, a shape arrested,
> The adze on arc-point, motionless. Rust
> Possesses cutlass and hoe. But listen . . .   (p. 3.)

It is soon clear that Rhodesia is only a part of the issue – a symptom rather

[1] *The Man Died* (Rex Collings, London, 1973), p. 48.
[2] *Ogun Abibimang* (Rex Collings, London, 1976).

than the disease itself, which involves the whole of southern Africa and has its heart in the Republic of South Africa. Thus it is well to be aware of the enormity of the eventual cost, and later, in 'Sigidi', the poet pauses once again on the brink of action to demonstrate the validity of the cause and the worthiness of the awful sacrifice. The enemy have taken more than just land and physical resources. They have suppressed liberty in the process:

> These, who ill-content with land and trees,
> With pastures, lakes and gems, usurp
> The will to being of man, revile
> The racial fount of stolen habitations.   (p. 9.)

This assertion is made in 'Induction'. There can be no solution other than war. Other so-called solutions are cynical ruses. Dialogue, for instance, with statesmen from far away on behalf of people whose voices cannot be heard because of the inhuman brutality of the South African regime, is starkly imaged:

> Oh distanced statesmen, conciliators
> Soon snared in slight cocoons of words!
> Will you make a gift of gab to swollen tongues
> Broken on the boot, and make their muteness
> Proof of cravings for a Dialogue?   (p. 5.)

The grim aptness of the image rescues a somewhat awkward syntax and the uncharacteristic apostrophe, and the tension is maintained. The result of Soyinka's attempt, in a long-drawn-out pun, to dramatize the 'time-pleading games' – like a dog chasing its own tail – is less happy, in that it distracts and inappropriately lowers the tension. (p. 6.)

The high point of 'Induction' is reached before the particular reference to past betrayals – dialogue, sanctions, Sharpeville – when the struggle has passed into the hands of more than mere men, and the present has become the moment of resolution:

> Let gods contend with gods.
> All claims shall stand, till tested.
> For we shall speak no more of rights
> To the unborn bequeathed, nor will
> To future hopes
> The urgent mandates of our present.   (p. 5.)

The symbol of resistance to the tyranny of white rule in southern Africa is Shaka, the legendary amaZulu king whose great capacity for nation-building has fallen prey to his own human weaknesses, who has had his energies diverted from the real threat to his people. (Soyinka, not for the first time, is able to attribute blame where it is due, black slave traders being as culpable as white – see, for example, *A Dance of the Forests*.) Shaka's failure, in spite of his great abilities, is itself a timely warning to the inheritors of his task, which by this time has exceeded the unaided strength of Shaka's immediate heirs. The rest of black Africa, symbolized by Ogun, must now merge energies with those of Shaka's descendants. The symbols almost choose themselves, Shaka being the outstanding historical figure of his region, and Ogun, the Yoruba warrior god, being the inevitable divine patron for Soyinka in such an enterprise. But the choice has a further aptness. Both Ogun and Shaka, in a moment of lapse, turned on their own men and slaughtered them instead of the real enemy.[3] The coincidence of their histories makes for a common sympathy born of a common consciousness of grave error:

> Our histories meet, the forests merge
> With the savannah.
>
> (p. 11.)

Shaka's remorse when he recovers from his lapse is as deep as Ogun's and gives rise to the burning resolve to complete the unfinished task. First the remorse:

> I woke, a black-etched silhouette of flies
> Swarming to the death my darkness
> Fed upon. Oh my pride of men! Their sparseness
> Was the nation I would build, the earth
> I sought, the dreams of race which beckoned me
> From Slaughter Valley to the Hill of Destiny.
>
> (p. 12.)

Then the resolution:

> The task must gain completion, our fount
> Of being cleansed from termites' spittle –
> In this alone I seek my own completion.
>
> (p. 13.)

Shaka's contrite acknowledgement of his weaknesses, which were the prime causes for his and his people's defeat –

> The termites that would eat the kingdom
> First built their nest,
> In the loin-cloth of the king –
>
> (p. 13.)

[3] For Soyinka's treatment of Ogun's lapse, see *Idanre and other Poems* (Methuen, London, 1967), p. 74ff.

is a part of the purification in preparation for new goals.

As the past had its hazards, so does the future, and the poem warns against false Shakas. In his gloss on Shaka, Soyinka writes: 'The professional apologists of our time have tried to place, uncritically, in the same category of leaders as Shaka, that murderous buffoon who straddles territory where once the great Shaka trod . . .' (p. 23.) In a section of the poem which employs the technique of caricature, and thus achieves a lessened tension, the antics of such a leader are portrayed. At times it seems as though at least two personalities are indicated, but particular identification may be merely distracting.

> Beware of life-usurpers masked in skins
> Flayed from the living forms of amaZulu.
> Beware the jester masks with grinning teeth
> Of the corroded *panga*.   (p. 17.)

As has been indicated above, the poet is conscious of the cost of the war; this is total war – *mfekani*. It will involve the violation of things hitherto held sacred – 'Our sacred graves to yield, in need, thigh-bones/Honed to drinking points'. (p. 9.) The cause, therefore, must be just. This is not a war 'for desire,/Or love, or ease, or craving'. (p. 19.) It is not revenge for any single act like Sharpeville – a mere symptom:

> Remember Sharpeville – not as aberrations
> Of the single hour, but years and generations.   (p. 20.)

Sharpeville should be put in the context of other violations far away from Africa, Guernica and Lidice, symptoms of equally sinister historical tyrannies:

> Our songs acclaim
> Cessation of a long despair, extol the ends
> Of sacrifice born in our will, not weakness.
> We celebrate the end of that compliant
> Innocence of our millennial trees.   (p. 21.)

As the troops of all Abibimang (Black Africa) mass for a cause of whose justice they are now fully convinced, and of whose terrible price they are aware, they pause for a moment of celebration.

Soyinka has never written blank verse with more flowing felicity than in *Ogun Abibimang*. The staple verse is competent, rising to occasional pitches of intensity and lyrical grace. Ogun and Shaka are adequate sources of the imagery, which is always functional. There are momentary nods, but as the poem sweeps to its conclusion, its celebratory tone is assured.

Part 5
Fiction

The Interpreters

▼▼▼▼▼▼▼▼▼▼▼▼▼▼▼▼▼▼▼▼▼▼▼▼▼▼▼▼▼▼▼▼▼▼▼▼

ALTHOUGH *The Interpreters* is a first novel,[1] it comes in Soyinka's work after a number of remarkable plays and a corpus of distinguished poems which had cleared the hurdles of a literary apprenticeship. 1965, the year of the novel's publication, also saw the first production of *The Road* at the Commonwealth Arts Festival in London, and of two radio plays, *Camwood on the Leaves* (March), and *The Detainee* (September) on the B.B.C. By that year, *The Strong Breed, The Swamp Dwellers, Brother Jero, The Lion and the Jewel* and *A Dance of the Forests* had all appeared. The published poetry ranged from the light satirical 'Telephone Conversation' to the sombre probings of life after death in 'Requiem'. The author of this first novel was thus no new writer, and the work shows by its complexity and literary accomplishment the results of a preceding period of intense literary activity.

In a review in *The New African*, Gerald Moore calls the novel 'the first African novel that has a texture of real complexity and depth'. This judgement certainly isolates two of the principal characteristics of the work. The complexity is evident in the actual language – syntax, imagery, etc. – as well as in the dense interlocking of psyches, motives and incidents. Depth is produced by a technique of probing through external manifestations back into preceding histories and backgrounds; to other times and other places. The technique of broken chronology particularly enhances this deepening and widening of the scope of the novel as the author explores below surface appearances. For time clues (of which there are some) he generally substitutes thematic links between sections of the novel to produce seemingly sudden chronological jumps which are however seldom capricious but rather essential and illuminating.

The chronological time covered by sizeable sections of the novel is sometimes on close examination quite brief. As Mrs Anne-Marie Heywood observes in some unpublished notes on the novel, 'The first seven chapters are memories and reflections laced into the events of less than twenty-four hours.' This is the amount of time which elapses between the night-club scene and the two contrasted funerals of Sir Derinola and the elder of Lazarus' Church. This span covers a hundred and thirteen pages of the

[1] *The Interpreters* (André Deutsch, London, 1965).

novel within which the backgrounds and relationships of the friends – 'the new generation of interpreters' – have emerged through flashbacks thematically tied to the contemporary narration. These flashbacks cover whole life spans of some of the characters.

Almost as soon as the novel opens it dives back into time. In the wet, dripping atmosphere of the Lagos night-club, Egbo sits staring at a 'talkative puddle' and his mind goes back to a significant journey by water. The thematic link here is water; the puddle in the night-club receding into 'the still water of the creek' which was the scene of the crucial journey. Through this transition Egbo's significant 'choice' is portrayed. Instead of opting for the traditional pattern of life by which he could succeed (even displace) his maternal grandfather on the throne of Osa – the progressives of the kingdom were all for this – he had opted to go 'with the tide' and continue his routine and comfortable job at the Foreign Office. Egbo's choice is in one sense a personal one – 'the warlord of the creeks against the dull grey filing cabinet faces of the foreign office'. (p. 12.) In another sense it is a more fundamental choice involving a lot more than his personal fortunes, and in this sense it mirrors the changing society in which the novel is set, and the necessity for choice which it presents. Egbo's choice implies a break with the traditional, both its luxuries like polygamy – 'I've thought of that long and seriously' (p. 14) – and its opportunities for unique service which his royal position coupled with his enlightenment would offer him – 'By example to convert the world'. The traditional life has its excitements and rewards, but also its responsibilities; and he is by no means certain that he has the equipment to start from the traditional base, and still convert the world. In a later return to the choice his uncertainties about his fitness for the role of traditional ruler are more clearly revealed. His present job is safe; he can evaluate its demands, and can be reassured by its routine nature. It requires, as he sees it 'less of resources into which a man must needs drill, risky like an oil-well; it could be dry and he would find it out at the moment when his presumption most needed it'. (p. 119.) Egbo's choice, over which he 'broods' continually because he more than suspects it is cowardly, is to 'go with the tide' a phrase which conveniently carries its own criticism.

Egbo's choice involves a struggle; it involves facing issues and taking decisions. Essentially he is on his own, and in this he represents his generation who are all facing a new world with all the weight (but with little of the benefits) of their traditional past. All the young interpreters are individuals trying to make sense of their world. They are hammering out values and codes of conduct in a world which seems to have none ready made. Time and time again the novel portrays the essential isolation of the new generation. Dehinwa the young career girl is alone in the big city, away from the almost oppressive care ('blood cruelty' she calls it) and concern of her family. She has to steer a path through all the opportunities as well as the temptations of the big city without the support of her family. The young unnamed university girl has to bear the consequences of her pregnancy alone. Her message to the father of her expected child – significantly another of her own generation – conveys the loneliness of her position, and the enormous burden of such loneliness. In the words of Bandele the message to Egbo is simple, shorn of all dramatics, but firm: 'When you are sure what you want to do you are to tell me and I will pass it on. And I am supposed to make you understand that you are under no obligation.' (p. 242.) The girl has made what in the social context of the novel is a staggering decision to take full responsibility for her pregnancy and continue to battle with life alone if necessary. She will return to the university.

Similar choices face all the 'interpreters' and it is this necessity to make choices, to carve paths – even wrong or uncomfortable ones – which distinguishes them from other members of the society who float along without any real values, or whose choices have been made for them. No doubt Egbo's agony is born of the recognition that he too seems merely to be going with the tide. But, just to conclude these remarks on Egbo, he has further choices. He has to make a decision to accept his responsibilities and desert Simi – whose physical charms are still undiminished. He has to give something up since it is clearly impossible for him to go on satisfying his body with Simi and his mind with 'this . . . the new woman of my generation' (p. 235). He is shown on the brink of a decision with the scales delicately tipped in favour of the new woman who, ironically is absent at the crucial time. Egbo's plight is representative of that of all the interpreters.

There is stress and tension in the lives of the friends who make up the group of interpreters, but in none is this more clearly shown than in Sekoni's life which after all is the only one which is complete in that he dies in the course of the novel. The portrayal of Sekoni is extraordinarily compact and powerful. One intense passage covering about five pages (pp. 26–31) sweeps him dramatically from the deck of the ship bringing him home bursting with dreams, to a mental hospital, while his dreams – symbolized by his ingenious power station – lie in ruins, battered by his own frustrated hands. Sekoni's inner intensity – he is the most religious of the interpreters – is effectively conveyed by the stutter which his creator gives him. There always seems to be more inside him than the stutter permits to come out. He is better when he is not speaking, and Soyinka's prose rises to a peak of intensity as he portrays Sekoni's dreams:

Sekoni, qualified engineer, had looked over the railings every day of his sea voyage home. And the sea sprays built him bridges and hospitals, and the large trailing furrow became a deafening waterfall defying human will until he gathered it between his fingers, made the water run in the lower channels of his palm, directing it against the primeval giants on the forest banks. And he closed his palms again, cradling the surge of power. Once he sat on a tall water spout high above the tallest trees and beyond low clouds. Across his sight in endless mammoth rolls, columns of rock, petrifactions of divine droppings from eternity. If the mountain won't come, if the mountain won't come, then let us to the mountain now, in the name of Mohammed! So he opened his palm to the gurgle of power from the charging prisoner, shafts of power nudged the monolith along the fissures, little gasps of organic ecstasy and paths were opened, and the brooding matriarchs surrendered all their strength, lay in neat geometric patterns at his feet . . .   (p. 26.)

The language here combines reality with fantasy. The energy of the prose suitably conveys the dimensions of the work to be accomplished. It also dramatizes the matching imagination of Sekoni for the task. The effect is one of a creation myth with Sekoni in the position of the all-powerful creator. Both the vast potential of the land and the vast strength needed to harness it are present. The contrast between this size and strength on the one hand and the puniness and triviality of the tasks Sekoni is assigned when he actually takes up his post – 'applications for leave', 'bicycle advance', etc. – are a quick recipe for disaster. Five pages or so later, Sekoni is, and convincingly so, in a mental hospital. A mental breakdown is almost inevitable in the circumstances. Because Sekoni is the most intense, his frustrations are of greater dimensions. He really goes through the furnace.

It is significant that when he turns to art, his masterpiece is a sinewy manifestation of inner strength and intensity: 'Taut sinews, nearly agonising in excess tension, a bunched python caught at the instant of easing out, the balance of strangulation before release, it was all electricity and strain.' (p. 99.) It is produced in a frenzy of activity 'as if time stood in his way' (p. 100.) As indeed it did, for he died soon after. Both Sekoni and his 'wrestler' in their way are symbolic of the struggle in which the generation is involved (if it cares to be involved). The inspiration for the statue had indeed been conflict – a night-club brawl. Sekoni had created an abiding masterpiece out of a fairly trivial piece of mundane experience. In a similar way, the total meaning of life for Soyinka's young men is to be painfully pieced together out of the trivia and the routines of existence –

sexual encounters, riotous nights at the night-club, cocktail parties, inter-views for jobs, encounters with corrupt politicians, witnessing the chasing of thieves, attempts at formal philosophical formulations, attempts at artistic expression, teaching university classes and marking uninspired essays, witnessing gory road accidents, being bereft of friends by death, looking for the residual presences of the ancient gods in their midst, trying to make sense of the claims of new religious manifestations. Through all these, men are to make a coherence of the jumble that is life. Egbo in particular, because he has this special feeling that he has opted for a purposeless life, feels the need for the contemplation of life's experiences. This is why his nature shrine is so valuable to him:

> I come here often to draw upon that gift and be reprieved. I find I need it more than all my friends, they are all busy doing something, but I seem to go only from one event to the other. As if life was nothing but experience. (p. 133.)

Whether through art or through meaningful relationships, each of the young people is to work out some sort of resolution – even in death – of their experiences.

Kola looks to art for his fulfilment, and comes to the painful realization that, unlike Sekoni, he is no artist; this in itself is a valuable if painful piece of self-knowledge: 'I am not really an artist. I never set out to be one. But I understand the nature of art and so I make an excellent teacher of art.' (p. 227.) Beside the wrestler, his Pantheon is mere 'weight'. His face saving 'I never set out to be one' is rather belied by his jealousy (which he honestly admits) at the obvious superiority of Sekoni's work. (p. 100.) His realization of his limitations in spite of his hard work is yet another manifestation of the basic honesty of the interpreters. His admission of his feelings for Monica brings with it a new decision, a choice which holds some promise of the fulfilment which he has failed to find in art.

Sagoe eventually finds a similar anchor in Dehinwa whom he will marry. In return for Dehinwa's surrender he has promised to burn his 'Books of Enlightenment'. Sagoe had elevated his rather superficial thoughts on Voidancy into a philosophy in which he sought escape from the trials of existence. His resort to these 'Books' on one difficult occasion is instruc-tive. Soyinka uses their different reactions to the death of Sekoni as a significant index to the character of each of the young men. Sagoe had drenched himself in beer and vomit for a week and had then sought refuge in a random page from this book. It is clear that this is mere escapism, and this Sagoe implicitly acknowledges when he trades his book and its philosophy for a settled relationship with Dehinwa.

Bandele functions among his friends as a prod for their consciences. It is significant that it was in response to his question 'which way?' that Egbo made his choice: 'with the tide'. (p. 14.) He is generally reticent but springs into action when this is necessary. In the opening night-club scene he had used his prehensile limbs most effectively to rescue chairs and tables from the rain (p. 7) and in a later brawl, it was he who had almost miraculously felled and trussed up the threatening thug. (p. 219.) He is the consoler; this is his role, significantly, at the death of Sekoni. Egbo escaped to his shrine, Sagoe into drink, but 'To Bandele fell the agony of consoling Alhaji Sekoni.' (p. 156.) This is typical. He tries to reconcile Egbo with his choice, (p. 120) and is always something of a reconciler. His ability to tolerate the company of uncongenial people surprises his friends. (p. 203.) Even to the objectionable Faseyi he is 'guardian uncle' (p. 206) and 'god-father'. However his probings and even his silences sometimes make his friends bristle or feel uneasy. (This is the role of a conscience.) He certainly affects Kola in this way when the latter is struggling not only with his Pantheon but with his feelings for Monica, and a possible decision to step in and take her away from her husband Ayo Faseyi. Bandele's entry throws him on the defensive: 'The door opened again and Bandele entered, throwing Kola instantly on his guard, almost belligerent, "If you have come to start . . ."' (p. 218.)

As the various relationships move uncomfortably to some sort of resolution, this tall towering man becomes increasingly detached from his companions, and seems to assume the role of a divine judge. Some of Soyinka's descriptions of him at the end clearly suggest this: 'Bandele came in again, a palace housepost carved of iron-wood.' The detached aloofness of a carving reflects his new role of touchstone and objective point of reference. Metal casting and carving supply other significant pictures of him, symbolizing some sort of ultimate reality against which acts and decisions have to be measured: 'It was as if he had neither pity nor indulgence, and yet the opposite was true . . . And Bandele held himself unyielding, like the staff of Ogboni, rigid in a single casting. . . . Bandele sat like a timeless image brooding over lesser beings.' (p. 244.) It is through the eyes of this timeless arbiter which Bandele seems to have become, that events like the death of Noah (which Golder seems to be getting away with), the desertion of Simi by Egbo for 'the new woman of my generation'. (p. 235.), the eventual equities of this girl's own case, have to be eventually viewed. It is he who with the full authority of his new position proclaims the final curse on the sneering, uncompassionate old guard – old and young, 'Bandele, old and immutable as the royal mothers of Benin throne, old and cruel as the *ogboni* in conclave pronouncing the Word.

"I hope you all live to bury your daughters."'   (p. 251.)

The group which Bandele so solemnly curses represents (with other characters) the establishment against which the young interpreters continually bruise themselves in their individualistic adventures in the society. Ayo Faseyi who is almost pathologically anxious to establish himself as a member of this power group gives a reasonable sample of its membership as he complains of the damage his wife has done to his candidature: 'Do you know a Minister was present. Yes, and one or two other VIPs. Oguazor knows people, you know. I saw four corporation chairmen there, and some Permanent Secretaries.' (p. 202.) Faseyi here characteristically lists people by their titles. In this society, this is all that matters – the front that is presented to the world. So long as this front is starched and ironed, it does not seem to matter what lies behind. It is this lack of concern for essentials, this substitution of an appearance of honour and morality for the thing itself, that the novel continually satirizes.

Professor Oguazor, the novel's main satirical butt of the Ibadan establishment, is symbolically placed in a house decorated with plastic fruit and flowers, in which these objects take the place of real ones. The house is, in a phrase which aptly presents the novel's attitude, 'The Petrified Forest'. Sagoe enthusiastically approaches the inviting basket of fruit – 'there is no fruit in the world to beat the European apple' – only to discover its phoniness. (This is a variation of a favourite Soyinka image for the negation of the forces of life – the aborted harvest.) The falsity of the façade is imaged as an unnatural substitution of death for life: 'A glaze for the warmth of life and succulence'. (p. 140.) This unnaturalness suggested by the image of the plastic fruit is exemplified by Professor Oguazor's act of unnaturally hiding away his illegitimate daughter – 'the plastic apple of his eye' – in a private school in Islington. ('Plastic' once again devalues any natural feelings that Oguazor as father might have had for the child.) Having neatly tucked his natural child away, Oguazor can now present to the respectable world a nicely laundered façade of virtue. He can take the most uncompromising line of 'meral' rectitude against the young university girl and her partner if he can be found: 'Well, see that he is expelled of course. He deserves nothing less . . . The college cannot affort to herve its name dragged down by the meral terpitude of irresponsible young men. The younger generation is too merally corrupt.' (p. 250.) Oguazor's real unfitness to make judgements of this kind contrasted with his power to do so because of his position in the society, is at the heart of the satire in the novel.

This is also the basis of the satire implied in the treatment of Sir Derinola, the judge. On the bench he is a pillar of rectitude but he is not above taking petty bribes, hiding behind the more obviously corrupt front of the crooked politician Chief Winsala. The demolition of the façade is accomplished in the novel by both fantasy and fact. In fantasy, Sir Derinola appears in Sagoe's hangover daydream, symbolically naked, stripped of all his respectable facade of robes and wig, but, to make the picture truly comic, dressed in a pair of Dehinwa's brassieres – 'For the medals young man. The medals. They pin something on you when they give you a knighthood you know.' The incongruity of the medals against the nakedness of Sir Derinola is a physical image of his unfitness for the honour that the medals imply. In another episode, the exposure in fantasy is dramatized in fact when Sir Derinola is confronted by Sagoe in circumstances which establish conclusively his involvement in Chief Winsala's attempt to extract a bribe. The public image suffers a crushing blow: 'But above all, Sir Derinola was truly paralysed at the confrontation of a future image, and could not move to help. Now he saw Sagoe move forward, and tried to shrink back behind the palm. They gazed into each other, all subterfuge pointless. It was Sagoe who took his eyes away.' (p. 92.)

The satire, particularized here through Sir Derinola, is more general. It is the whole society which is characterized by this hypocrisy and moral confusion. The chase of the young thief Noah, in chapter eight, becomes a farce in which the crowd which in the name of virtue bears down on the young thief is itself made up of thieves: 'So the crowd bore through him, swarmed into the car park, slipped on wet tar and rose muddy and gay, snatched a handbag or two from sheer opportunity and blacked the grounds before the squat lumpy factory that was Hotel Excelsior.' (p. 114.) The whole business of justice has become a game in which the sword is in the hands of thieves. As the passage goes on, the whole society becomes involved in the satire on this particular crowd: 'Run, you little thief or the bigger thieves will pass a law against your existence as a menace to society . . . run, Barabbas from the same crowd which will reform tomorrow and cheer the larger thief returning from his twentieth Economic Mission and pluck his train from the mud, dog-wise, in their teeth.' (p. 114.) The values of the whole society have become inverted; morality has become redefined, a point which is bitingly made when the chase of the thief is ironically called 'a moral demonstration'. (p. 114.)

The inhumanity displayed by Oguazor and his company towards the young pregnant girl is paralleled by the chase of the thief. It is this same essential inhumanity that characterizes the treatment of Sekoni. He is reduced to a state of mental collapse while the cynical Chairman of the Electricity Board actually makes money out of his condemned power station. The sheer comedy of some of the episodes through which society is satirized – the Oguazor party for example – should not obscure the basic inhumanity which the attitude involves. To protect the phony façade, those who do not conform are crushed – 'expelled', sentenced, driven to insanity. The satire is indeed serious, and *The Interpreters* is a most serious novel in spite of its cloak of comedy. This is a characteristic which it shares with Soyinka's comic plays.

The primary society with which the novel is concerned is contemporary Nigeria in which, although the ancient traditional life still makes its appearance, the predominant impression is of a society in the grips of a turbulent modernity. Its institutions – universities, hotels, churches, night-clubs, newspapers, etc. – show an uneasy blend of influences. Somewhere in the background linger the numinous presences of the old gods, manifesting themselves intangibly but still effectively by the banks of the Oshun and Ogun, and, as though the new generation is straining back to something to hold on to, in the Pantheon of Kola's canvas. The *apala* band asserts itself in the Lagos night-club when the western saxophones and trumpets have succumbed to the rain, but the night-club itself – the Cambana – is a curiously uncertain place. It is a pale imitation of an American evocation of Africa – 'in the States they really go to town'. (p. 157.) The paints of the fire-eater are done in 'designs which he had perhaps copied from the film of Tarzan's adventures with the Authentic Cobra Maidens of Kokokabura' (p. 158.) Lazarus' church, while showing perhaps a little more independence with its defiantly African rhythms, manifests its uncertainties in the sub-standard English of the Elder: 'Brother Ezra was our oldest man. On his wise head we rely on for so many advices, so many of our problem that we have to deal with.' (p. 170.) When Chief Winsala is caught without the price of the schnapps he has been guzzling in the Hotel Excelsior, it is in the words of traditional wisdom that he mirrors his position to himself and implicitly reproves himself for thus exposing himself: '*Agba n't'ara* . . . it is no matter for rejoicing when a child sees his father naked, *l'ogolonto. Agba n't'ara.* The wise eunuch keeps from women; the hungry clerk dons coat over his narrow belt and who will say his belly is flat? But when *elegungun* is unmasked in the market, can he then ask *egbe* to snatch him into the safety of *igbale*? Won't they tell him the grove is meant only for keepers of mystery?' (pp. 91–2.) The point here is that Winsala has been caught in a modern situation – a company director fishing for a bribe – but in the moment of stress he recalls the ancient rules of conduct which he has violated in the process. It is interesting that the Chief seems to regret only his temporary disgrace, not the basic reason for it, namely, his dishonesty.

Sometimes there is little mutual comprehension between the old and the new. Dehinwa's mother and aunt are in a totally incomprehensible world when they visit her in her flat in the city, and she turns up with a drunken man who proceeds to go to sleep on her bed. Dehinwa too, having absorbed the detached attitudes of the city, has forgotten that in traditional life everybody's business is everybody's business as this exchange shows:

> 'But, mamma, you shouldn't listen to that kind of talk. Next time tell them to mind their business.'
>
> The aunt left her mouth open in mid-swallow. 'What did the child say? Tell people to mind their own business when it is their love for your mother that prompts them to speak?'   (p. 37.)

In such ways do the old and the new Africa in this fluid society sometimes confront, sometimes uneasily blend with each other in the novel.

In the lives of individuals in the new Africa, the old Africa could never be totally ignored. Even the young interpreters find that they have to take old Africa into account in the formulation of their new values. The old refuses to be bodily jettisoned. Sagoe fondly hoped that he could shed his family and carve out a life for himself as an individual in the city. His plan on his return from his studies abroad was to settle himself first, then 'a brief courtesy visit and then finish. Every man to his own business.' Bandele, the wise one, had promptly indicated that this was not as easy as it sounded. Bandele shook his head, 'That is not so easy.' (p. 90.) (That courtesy visit would have undone him anyway.) Egbo's attempt to wrench himself free of the past is no more successful. The past, history, tradition, and the dead will never let him go, even when he has seemingly decided against committing himself to his traditional role as king of Osa. The tyranny of the past hangs over him and he is irritated by it: 'It [the past] should be dead. And I don't just mean bodily extinction. No, what I refer to is the existing fossil within society, the dead branches on a living tree, the dead runs on the bole. When people die, in one sense or in the other, it should not matter what they were to us. They owe the living a duty to be forgotten quickly, usefully. Believe me, the dead should have no faces.' (p. 120.) The fact is, as the novel reminds us, they have.

Egbo's irritation reflects the uneasy quality of a society which has not completely come to terms with itself. It is in this unsettled atmosphere that corruption, tribalism, window-dressing hypocrisy, and moral uncertainty flourish. It is through all these uncertainties that the interpreters seek a path; it is in formal recognition of the fact that the past cannot be disregarded in this search that they slaughter a black goat at the dedication of Sekoni's work.

The primary society treated is Nigeria, but the society is shown in bustling contact with the wider world. Not only do managing directors circle the world on economic missions, but Germans, Americans,

Englishmen flow in and out of the society, and widen the area of experience which the novel covers. The interpreters themselves have studied abroad. Artifacts from the outside world are introduced, sometimes satirically, throughout the novel. The Managing Director's 'pachydermous radiogram' (p. 78) is not only an index of his own faulty taste and misplaced values – 'only the radio was ever used, and that just for the news' (p. 75) – but the circumstances of its purchase in Germany when the Director tries to lure the sales girl to his hotel, underlines the satire. The executive toilet ornately furnished with fittings from Switzerland but housed in a decayed building in the middle of a slum, the large American cars, are all used to point to a certain vulgar ostentation against which Sagoe protests by perversely riding only a bicycle.

Not only the artifacts, but people from other places widen the novel's canvas. Joe Golder, Pinkshore, Peter the German American, even Monica (who however becomes a part of the Nigerian scene) function in this way. Pinkshore is an Englishman who has accepted the fact of political independence, and realizes that things have changed and that black men now have to be humoured by white men: 'It was a good thing to perform small services for this new black élite which he secretly despised but damn it all if the asses are susceptible to fawning and flattery let's give it them and get what we can out of them while the going is good.' (p. 149.) The satire is double-edged, cutting both the black élite and the insincere foreigners.

Joe Golder is even more fruitfully used as a vehicle of double-edged satire. He becomes a representative of the American dilemma. He himself is of a complexion that could pass for white, but having Negro blood in him, he is, in American terms, black. Golder overcompensates by being passionately and aggressively black. He tortures himself in the sun trying to darken his stubborn complexion, and urges Kola to represent him in the Pantheon in the blackest black: 'For God's sake, blacken me. Make me the blackest black blackness in your pantheon.' (p. 217.) Golder's predicament is compounded by the fact that he is also a homosexual. This conflict of races and of sexes in the one man produces a figure who hovers between comedy and tragedy. His hideous attempts to blacken himself may be comic, but it is comedy born out of the victim's real pain. There is real tragedy also. The racial conflict within him had turned him against his father whom he drove to suicide. His sexual deviation leads directly to the death of Noah. From this background of tragedy Golder's voice rises in the apt Negro spiritual whose lines – with which Soyinka punctuates his presentation of other matters – symbolize not only Golder's own personal isolation, but also the essential loneliness of each of the seekers: 'sometimes I feel like a motherless child . . .'

A list of topics which the novel covers either substantially or glancingly would almost match the number of its pages. Through glancing allusions, the canvas stretches from America to Chiang Kai Shek's 'American China'. In the realm of human relations, racialism, tribalism (Dehinwa's mother is scandalized at the idea of her daughter going out with a Gambari), religious intolerance (Sekoni and his father), homosexuality, different kinds of sexual relations, various kinds of monogamy, polygamy, love, are all explored. The satire encompasses corruption, political thuggery, bribery, universities (undergraduates as well as their teachers), religion, war, and a host of other topics. All this Soyinka harmonizes into a novel of true artistic distinction. It mirrors in its energy the vitality of its setting, and, in its restless style, the agonies through which the immediate society (and the world) must go if it is to produce some kind of solution to its myriad problems. The novel makes few assertions, but it probes and exposes themes for judgement.

The young interpreters, as distinct from others in the novel who are self-satisfied and complacent, are engaged in a search for individual solutions without the automatic props of the old sheltered way of life or any substitute for it in the modern world. They have to cut their way through a maze consisting of their own personal resources and limitations and the opportunities offered by their immediate environment of Nigeria, but ultimately of the whole modern world, through friendship and love, through hatred, intolerance, and corruption. The novel is an artistic realization of the opportunities as well as the awful responsibilities of being an individual on his own in a maze of a world.

Season of Anomy

IN HIS dedication of *The Man Died* 'to the unacknowledged', Soyinka notes how between the lines of books smuggled to him in prison 'are scribbled fragments of plays, poems, a novel and portions of the prison notes which make up this book.'[1] Their striking similarity of prevailing mood and matter makes it easy to suppose that the poems which appeared as *Shuttle in the Crypt*,[2] including the two which, having been earlier smuggled out, had appeared in a broadsheet,[3] and the novel *Season of Anomy* were among the works which were at least partly delivered between the lines of Paul Radin's *Primitive Religion* and Soyinka's own 'Idanre'.

The three works form a trio of mutually elucidatory material, of which *The Man Died* provides the basic documentary recording (though frequently in very highly charged language), while the other two give, one in poetry and the other in prose, more imaginative realizations of the basic experiences. The provenance of these three works and their relationship (not only to each other but also to an episode as traumatic as Soyinka's imprisonment) make it artificial to separate a discussion of their content from the real-life circumstances of the author, *The Man Died* being the factual point of reference. Thus the direct statement of the threat to the sanity of the victim appears in the documentary, *The Man Died*: 'I testify to the strange sinister byways of the mind in solitary confinement, to the strange monsters it begets. It is certain that all captors and gaolers know it; that they create such conditions especially for those whose minds they fear. Then confidently they await the rupture.' (p. 12.) The poetic transmutation of the experience is given expression in the opening of 'Live Burial', where the Greek myth of Antigone provides the dominant metaphor:

> Sixteen paces
> By twenty-three. They hold
> Siege against humanity
> And truth
> Employing time to drill through to his sanity

[1] *The Man Died*, 2nd edn., (Rex Collings, London, 1973).

[2] *Shuttle in the Crypt* (Rex Collings/Eyre Methuen, London, 1972).

[3] *Poems From Prison*, containing 'Live Burial' and 'Flowers For My Land' (Rex Collings, London, 1969).

Schismatic
Lover of Antigone
You will? You will unearth
Corpses of yester-
Year? Expose manure of present birth?

Seal him live
In that same necropolis.
May his ghost mistress
Point the classic
Route to Outsiders' Stygian Mysteries.[4]

There are similarly frequent reminiscences of the prison memoir in *Season of Anomy*. In *The Man Died* the author recalls the introduction of unqualified foreigners into the Civil Service through irresponsible patronage, giving quite briefly a summary of the case of a Pakistani medical orderly translated into a surgeon:

> In one of his many moments of expansiveness at the expense of the nation, the Sardauna guaranteed this orderly a top job in Northern Nigeria if he chose to return with him. He did and was created Medical Officer. He practised surgery with predictable results. Finally, in 1963, alarmed at the phenomenal rate of deaths under the surgeon's knife, an inquiry was ordered and the minion's antecedents were uncovered. Even so the final decision was merely: Forbidden further surgery. This butcher retained his post as Senior Medical Officer and held regular clinics.   (p. 192.)

This brief factual recollection is fictionalized in *Season of Anomy* (pp. 230–2), in which an Indian doctor, Chalil, is the main narrator, with Ofeyi and Zaccheus as his scandalized interlocutors, the episode being strung out with dialogue to a greater length. The words of Dante's *Inferno*, 'All hope abandon, ye who enter here' are recalled at the entrance to both the real-life Kaduna prison and the fictional Temoko; in the former by Soyinka himself[5] and in the latter by the dimunitive Acting Superintendent.

Such correspondences are particularly interesting as illustrations of the techniques by which fact becomes fiction, but they do not bring *Season of Anomy* into the category of documentary presentation of real life now known (quite unblushingly) as 'faction'. It is a work of imagination which

[4] *Shuttle in the Crypt*, p. 60.
[5] *The Man Died*, p. 129; 'Abandon hope all who enter here'; *Season of Anomy*: p. 282, 'abandon hope all who enter.'

is informed by occurrences, some of which the author himself experienced. There is no doubt that the circumstances leading to the Nigerian Civil War and his involvement in them are the skeleton of *Season of Anomy*.

The novel can be seen as a development in, rather than a break with, Soyinka's earlier work. The emphasis in the earlier work is on the 'dreamer', the lone visionary, but the implication is always that the dreamer is a dreamer *for society*; there is always a community in which he works. In some works this is more than an implication; both the leader and the led are clearly visible. The community behind the Daodu/Segi reformist alliance (*Kongi's Harvest*) is not left as an implication, to give just one example.

The situation is not very different in *Season of Anomy*, where the men of Aiyéro provide an already developed community, with ideals derived from isolated thought and experiment now ready to be exported into the larger society. But they too have their dreamers, who have occasionally to retreat and, in isolation, to recover their sense of direction. Ahime introduces Ofeyi to the secluded pool to which the leaders of Aiyéro resort in order to solve, within its almost magical isolation, their individual problems of leadership:

> So Ahime led him to the pool. 'Whatever bones lie beneath the water, the spirits that left from them must be beneficient ones, of that I am certain. Just sitting on the shore I drift off sometimes for an entire day. At the end I feel restored, rejuvenated. No matter what trials drove me there to seek its peace, they are resolved, as if an oracle had whispered in my ear.' (p. 105.)

Aiyéro is built up as a counter-force to the rest of the corrupt society, represented by the Cartel (the dominating alliance of the army, big business, corrupt politics, both new-style and traditional), the Cocoa Corporation, Jeku (the political party) and Zaki Anuri, the effete, venal traditional ruler. The contrast is variously underlined. The peace implicit in the pool of Aiyéro described in the quotation above is available nowhere in the rest of the country – but this is only an implication. More explicit contrasts are suggested by both imagery and incident, of which the ceremonies attending the burial of the late Founder of Aiyéro and those surrounding the unveiling of the Cocoa Corporation chairman's fish-pond are fairly illustrative.

In the pastoral paradise of Aiyéro the climax of the funeral rites is the ceremonial slaying of the bulls for the subsequent feast.[6] The language

[6] For the symbolic significance of feasting, see my 'Naked into Harvest-tide', *African Literature Today*, 6, (Heinemann, London, 1973), pp. 145–51.

very carefully relates the blood-letting to natural processes and the release
of pent-up emotions for socially beneficent purposes. A short excerpt
should convey this essence:

> Ahime moved with feline balance, his hand poured back the drapes
> which fell away from his shoulder as he bent over the bull nearest
> the alcove. The cloth fell again so he caught it over the left arm and
> kept it there pressed against his waist. His knife hand moved once,
> slashed deep and drew across the throat. The taut skin parted easily,
> opening to a layer of translucent membrane, yielding in turn to
> tendons and a commencement of red mists. Suddenly the white
> afternoon was showered in a crimson fountain, rising higher and
> higher, pumping ever upwards to a sun-scorched sky. Ahime
> stepped back quickly but not so far that the falling spray should not
> find him. His white vestments bloomed suddenly with small red
> petals and a long sigh rose, fell and filled the air with whispers of
> wind and the opening of buds. He moved swiftly now, the sighs of
> release were woven among the spreading mists, a thousand eyes
> followed the motions of the priest whose flutist blade was laid again
> and again to ivory pipes, tuned to invocations of renewal. Opening
> the vents of a rich elixir, he of the masseur's fingers stooped at each
> succeeding sluice-gate, a fountain head covered in rime, his arms
> were supple streams in a knowing course through ridges bathed in a
> sun's downwash. He nudged the ridges' streams awake and they
> joined their tributaries to his fountain-head. A deep beneficence
> rested over the motions of his hands, opening red sluices for the
> land's replenishment.   (pp. 16–17.)

The whole process is a cycle, arising out of the surrounding earth and
subsequently replenishing it.

In contrast to this, Chief Batoki's fountain and fish-pond, surmounted
by an equestrian St George slaying the dragon, is an excrescence, 'a
Florentine moment in the heart of the festering continent'. Soyinka's
parody of heraldic prose (not to mention the Arthurian glance with
Excalibur)–'an armoured knight equestrian'–and archaic clichés ('noble
steed') hit the appropriate register of caricature, counterpointing the
reverence of the Aiyéro passage:

> Only the Chairman's running commentary jarred from time to time
> the viewer's contemplation of a Florentine moment in the heart of
> the festering continent.
> White-coated servants gathered up the dust-sheets and pulled them

slowly backwards. The fountain pool, itself a fish-pond was indeed scooped out of the shape of the cocoa-pod, floor and sides laid in tiny tiles of amber. From the centre of the pod rose a noble plinth, a marble arm from the enchanted lake, which for Excalibur upheld a blue marble platform upon which sat an armoured knight, equestrian. At the horse's feet writhed a monstrous dragon, scales of silver, tongue of bronze, fiery, fire-flashing eyes of onyx. It was transfixed by a ponderous silver spear and pounded by steel hooves of the noble steed. (p. 44.)

Aiyéro is authentic Africa. Indeed, it had broken from its parent community Aiyetomo because its founder wish to opt out of 'the teachings of this white god', whose followers 'kill, burn, loot, maim, and enslave our people', turning rather to 'the religion of our fathers'. (p. 10.) Aiyéro is a given. Its special, almost magical, qualities have to be accepted. Its young men go to all parts of the world but are not seduced by the bright lights of cities. They return to their 'quaint anomaly' and resume their contact with the rhythms of nature. (There is an interesting contrast here with the village in the swamps in an early play, *The Swamp-Dwellers*, whose young men never come back.) The complete recipe for this idyllic existence is not given, any more than are many mechanical details of the general plot, the escape from Temoko prison being a notable example of a skimming over of details. Pa Ahime, confronted with a straight request to reveal the magic of Aiyéro, replies that the question is like asking 'why we came, why we are still here, why we live. The answer is, I do not know.' (p. 3.) The answer is not totally negative. The secret of Aiyéro is to be found in its whole history, and in its philosophy, and in its total way of life. This is not fully depicted in a novel which often employs the shorthand techniques of a parable or a folktale side by side – in the descriptions of atrocities, for instance – with techniques of stark realism. In the Aiyéro sections the techniques of suggestion and symbolism are dominant. We do not have clear pictures of any of the native inhabitants except Pa Ahime, the priestly leader. The 'men of Aiyéro' are a mass manifestation of an ideal which the rest of the country needs.

Those who come into contact with the Aiyéro way of life are for ever ennobled by it and are never the same again. Thus three of the novel's principal characters, Isola Demakin (the Dentist), Iriyise and Ofeyi, visit Aiyéro for their own limited purposes and emerge with a fateful evangelical zeal. The transformation if Iriyise, who abandons her life of soft pleasure, takes place to the astonishment even of her lover Ofeyi, himself not impervious to the charms of Aiyéro:

Iriyise returned mid-morning in the midst of the old women. She came in a white-and-ochre wrapper, antimony round her eyes, a solid bangle of ivory on her neck – how did they get those heavy things on to a woman's neck! Ofeyi felt himself excluded by such transparent numinous excitement as flushed her face . . . how little I know of her, how very little after all. When they were at last alone she would only say, it filled me, Ofé, it filled me completely where I had felt so empty. I know I am now complete. Who on earth, what on earth could have taught her to say that, whose only knowledge of fulfilment till now had been the aftermath of love!   (p. 7.)

Iriyise rises almost to divine heights. She becomes so much part of the earth rhythms that 'Her presence, the women boasted, inspired the rains.' (p. 20.)

Ofeyi is a servant of the Cocoa Corporation and is thus a part of the organization of whose vicious influence he is so conscious. In Aiyéro he recognizes a quality of life with which to counteract the evil influence of the military/commercial/political alliance which dominates the country, and the moral dilemma of this central character, and of the novel as a whole, is whether the change should be wrought peacefully, through careful dissemination of the Aiyéro way, or violently, through assassination of the top figures of the establishment and their instruments in the administration.

Ofeyi's conviction is that the change should be made through education and peaceful infiltration. Against him, Soyinka pitches the Dentist, who believes that Ofeyi's methods are the result of woolly thinking and are bound to fail. Only 'violence – selective assassination' – could purge the land of the festering evil of the Cartel and its supporting forces – could, in the imagery of his soubriquet, 'extract the carious tooth'. The debate takes place in Ofeyi's own mind and in discussions with Pa Ahime, but reaches flashpoint when the two collaborators meet, the one pleading, on the side of moderation, for time; 'Time to educate on a truly comprehensive scale. Nothing can be achieved by isolated acts, we have to organize.' (p. 104.) There are moments when the debate, like the two characters themselves, seems artificial.

Ofeyi's aim is originally the limited but daring one of using the facilities of the Cocoa Corporation to undermine the Cartel.[7] But the Cartel is not entirely brainless, and Ofeyi's attempts at moral sabotage are discovered. As the novel proceeds, he is pushed further and further away from such indirect methods and, especially after his confrontation with the horrors

[7] One thinks wryly of brave men who invade radio stations and transmit pirate broadcasts censuring the owners of the facility!

perpetrated by the alliance, into a position little different from that of the Dentist. At such crucial moments – as when the house of the mining engineer, 'Semi-Dozen', is beseiged and he kills his first man (p. 252) – an invincible sense of justice takes over, and he becomes a man of action. Ofeyi, like other Soyinka heroes, is an artist and intellectual, a creator and thinker. His talents have been given to creating promotional material for the Cocoa Corporation – stage spectaculars, films, music, words aud lyrics – but art in the service of corruption has proved merely frustrating; it soon becomes clear that he cannot serve Art and the Corporation in good conscience. The break with the Corporation means also a hounded life. The brutalities of the regime make his choice clear. He has been offered the leadership of Aiyéro (the position of Custodian of the Grain), a choice reminiscent of that offered to Egbo in *The Interpreters*[8] – his grandfather's chieftaincy or the retention of his Foreign Office job. Ofeyi does not formally accept the position, but he uses his privileged status in the community to recruit the men of Aiyéro as evangelists of his new ideas: they are to form 'New affinities, working-class kinships as opposed to the tribal' (p. 170). The horrible slaughter of this dedicated band of men in particular, and of strangers in general, in the fictional Cross River State dramatizes the horrors of tribalism, another of the novel's themes.

In *The Man Died* Soyinka has recorded episodes in the Northern Nigerian massacres of strangers, some of the evidence of which he saw. Those accounts in the documentary book are more or less straight reportage. There is a difference between the techniques used in recording events in *The Man Died* and in fictionalizing them in *Season of Anomy*, the main one being a more conscious patterning. When this method succeeds, the author gives us some extraordinarily compelling pictures of senseless mass slaughter, whose effect, but tor man's dogged perversity, should itself be therapeutic. Among the many images of death is one which haunts Ofeyi, that of a nursing mother machine-gunned as her infant sucks at her breast, life-giving milk mingling with untimely blood in wanton destruction:

Among a welter of images one that constantly monopolized evocation was the mystery of a woman dead of machine-gun bullets, whose hand still tightly clutched an infant's legs. The infant's head was a pulp of brain and bone. Did madness enter her with that same bullet

[8] In the first edition of *Season of Anomy* (Rex Collings, London, 1973), a curious mistake occurs by which 'Egbo' is used for 'Ofeyi'. For a discussion of the relationship between the two novels, see Juliet Okonkwo, 'The Essential Unity of Soyinka's *The Interpreters* and *Season of Anomy*', *African Literature Today*, 11 (Heinemann, London, 1980), pp. 110–21.

which first passed through the child that was feeding at her breast? The breast hung free and her milk had mingled in blood to paint a testament of damnation on earth, beside spilled peppers, an upturned stool and a bowl of pap. Even the soldiers had been afraid to touch her where she lay.   (p. 141.)

The experience has come out of Ofeyi's mind with a qualitative definition suggesting the senselessness of desecration and a hint of the curse that attends such casual disregard for the sacredness of human life.

In another passage Soyinka confers on another such scene a hint of larger perspective by seeing it through the eyes of archaeologists happening on the site of a massacre many years later, but here adopting the technique of caricature. The scientists' breezy excitement over their interesting find parodies the full human degradation portrayed in passages like that last quoted or, for that matter, in the scenes surrounding the observer's imaginary flight into the future. (pp. 271–2.)

The hunting down and subsequent killing and degrading mutilation of a single emaciated fugitive by a pack of hostile villagers (pp. 160–5) provides a sustained illustration of Soyinka's artistic handling of incidents of ghoulish cruelty. The dominant impression left by the narration is, once again, the dehumanization of both perpetrators and victims of such acts. The incident itself is placed after a short passage of which the central feature is a nightmare in which Ofeyi, pursued by a pack of rabid dogs, finds himself miraculously (and, in the circumstances, luckily) turned into a long-toothed, blood-dribbling dog. Awakened from this dream, he seeks in it an explanation of the plague of bestiality which sweeps through whole groups of people:

Was this the truth of man-wrought plagues, and was it the secret of their confidence, those men who unleashed such terror on the innocent? Was it the certainty that once the pack began to hunt, after the first selective base of a night of Long Knives the instruments achieved a transformation in their own nature and even innocents donned a mask of the jackal to ensure safety from the hunting pack?
                                                            (p. 160.)

The image of hunting has already been introduced in the passage quoted. This is sustained in the narration of the killing which takes place next, of which only a few features can be singled out here. What Ofeyi swerves wildly to avoid is not immediately clear. He and Zaccheus strain to identify 'a brown matted bundle that now lay motionless in the middle of the road', and which to both of them looks like a monkey. But the 'monkey' is wearing clothes, and something of the grotesqueness of the object is suggested by its jocular association by Zaccheus with a circus. The image of a non-human object, a hunted prey, persists; the hunters too, when they appear, behave atypically and give the whole scene an eerie air. Only gradually does it become clear that what Ofeyi and Zaccheus are witnessing are the final moments in the cold-blooded pursuit and killing of a man by other men who at this stage, like the 'monkey' they have finally killed, have also become dehumanized: 'Their faces betrayed neither thought nor feeling.' The total effect is captured in a passage in which the possible course of the stalking of the hapless prey is reconstructed in Ofeyi's mind as he tries to reconcile himself to the full horror of men hunting down and killing another man:

A scene of stalking had surely preceded this. It took animation from the disintegrating tableau on the deserted road: the measured pace of beaters on their own grounds in pursuit of a quarry that went round in circles. They would herd him patiently, beat the sparse ground on the perimeter of successive lairs towards the waiting line of hunters, primed for the despatch. The group had listened to his self-deluding cunning, his furtive breaks and exhausted crawl on all fours among the stunted camouflage of this scrubland. Feeding on roots, leaves, worms, retching as he ran, convulsing from unaccustomed juices and poisonous barks . . . how many days had they pursued this game? It grew clearer every minute, the passage of this fugitive who had sought safety in an isolated village, untouched (so he hoped) by the madness that had broken in the cities but in truth alerted for the prospect of such diversions where the cities had left off. From one arid death then, to this other, in a forest which cushioned its betrayal with springy earth, decaying wood and leaves that deadened the hunters' footsteps.

Finding the road at last, listening to the roar of cars and leaping madly towards that sound of safety and encountering only the real line of his killers, had he in desperation flung himself in the path of a far [more] humane death? (p. 163.)

Indeed, a far more inhuman death and dismemberment was to follow.

Against the massive plague which has been let loose on the land neither the counter-force of education through the men of Aiyéro nor that of violence led by the Dentist achieves anything of significance. The Dentist's plan to assassinate the terrible guards of the Cartel fails, and the total score of victims in the programme of selected assassination is one corrupt judge. Except as a foil to Ofeyi (and Ofeyi seems capable of

putting arguments for violence himself), the Dentist seems rather
unnecessary and sometimes rather artificial. His ride through Curfew City
(even though he comes from the area), in the circumstances of
surrounding treachery, has an unreal, Scarlet Pimpernel aura. His
speeches too are occasionally theatrical, and at least once even he is
conscious of that. After one of his more posturing outbursts, both the
authorial narrative voice and the more balanced Ofeyi intervene:

> Increasingly disturbed, swirling his drink round and round his glass,
> wondering how much of the personal emotion would go into settle-
> ment of the score of betrayal. The youth appeared to read his
> thoughts: 'Don't worry about me,' he said. 'I speak like this only
> from frustration at my long inaction.' The boyish grin returned. 'And
> the effect of the whisky. That is why I never drink on duty. At the
> point of action the machine takes over. The decisions are made in
> advance because I must avoid the luxury of doubts. Don't worry
> about me.' He repeated.   (p. 104.)

Indeed, the posturing does not really stop; the picture of the machine in
action is as much a self-deluding image as that of martyr.

The Dentist's 'history' – not his character – is drawn from the fate of the
'Action Group stalwarts' mentioned as fellow prisoners with Soyinka in
The Man Died.[9] Like them, he was in training for revolution in a
neighbouring state but, after a change of regime, he and his companions
were betrayed. He, unlike Soyinka's fellow prisoners, escaped before he
could be bodily repatriated.

The Dentist's 'troops' in the novel are even less well defined than the
men of Aiyéro. Even though he was an earlier convert to Aiyéro and,
incredible as it seems, had deliberately set out to recruit Ofeyi on the
instructions of Pa Ahime, he finds the men too peaceful for his tastes. His
positive achievements do not match his promise, but he does join in the
rescue of Ofeyi and Iriyise from Temoko and in the return to Aiyéro to
regroup and continue the fight. (It is difficult to imagine that the Cartel,
having identified Aiyéro as a source of dissidence, with its power still
intact and its appetite for blood stimulated, would make this easy!)

The general malevolence of the Cartel, given the grim reality of the
massacre of innocents, converts most of the country outside Aiyéro, but
particularly Cross River, into hell. The bridge over Cross River thus
becomes 'the formal doorway to the territory of hell'; crossing it to rescue
the abducted Iriyise marks the beginning of Ofeyi's journey into hell. The
parallel with Orpheus' mythical rescue of Eurydice has been often pointed

---

[9] *The Man Died* (Rex Collings, London, 1972), pp. 45–6.

out, but it is a general one and should not be expected to yield exact correspondences. The Cross River hell becomes pin-pointed in Temoko prison; the analogy of prison with hell is also made in *The Man Died*.[10]

Iriyise's conversion to the ways of Aiyéro has already been discussed. For all her fiery temper and her reputation as a veritable Cleopatra when it comes to men's affections, in the novel her role is rather limited; she acts out roles defined for her by Ofeyi and is the victim of the abduction and the object of the rescue at the end of the novel. Unconscious, she becomes a symbol of the helpless suffering of the country under the Cartel. There is no certainty that she will recover or that, even imbued with the Aiyéro idea and her journey through hell, she will be part of an effective counter-force to the Cartel.

The momentum of this novel is provided not so much by the characters or what they do, as by the power of the evil force loosed on the country. The reader is left with an uneasy consciousness of the weakness of the individuals as such and that of the strength of the forces that they can generate; the overwhelming force here is evil. Beside the evil of the Cartel, the beauty of the humane Aiyéro indeed is crushed. It is interesting that the impression of the puniness of the individual is implied as much by the evil characters when they are shown individually as by the virtuous ones – perhaps even more so.

Chief Batoki, huddled in one of his luxury sofas to escape the wrath of his wife, hardly looks, in that shoddy domestic scene, like one of the nation's powerhouses of evil. After witnessing his humiliation and the utter triviality of the man's personality, Ofeyi does not rate him worthy even of assassination: 'don't waste your time on Batoki. He is not worth killing.' This, however, is the man with a cold-blooded recipe for subduing his people to his will: 'When you have killed a couple of them and put away some tens behind bars, the rest will behave themselves and toe the line. If they don't, add a zero to the numbers . . .' (p. 137.) The simple recipe, with its multiplier principle, is addressed particularly to Zaki Anuri, 'the all-powerful tyrant of Cross River', whose territory is soon converted into the hell of the metaphor. Out of the mouth of the henpecked Batoki comes this simple, savage formula for dealing with 'cowards'; from the family man, the prescription for eliminating whole families. Beside the force that he unleashes, the man himself is insignificant.

Zaki Anuri, the other leg of the Cartel of whom we are given a picture, emerges as an almost passionless evil force, directing his sadistic activities with hardly open eyelids and mere gestures to his minions. The generative force of the influence of Zaki Anuri is well expressed through the image of

[10] See above, p. 202.

poisoned growth, and a poisoning of the source of growth, in a passage depicting the massacres in Shaage in the Zaki's jurisdiction:

> Ofeyi felt its essence as the protrusion through a slanted ridge of a toxic tuber. A man stubbed his toe on it and maybe dies; death as sowed by these false farmers, the power-men, was planned to burgeon under the soil. The offensive outcrop was only a wilful, incidental wart, a mere tip of the iceberg that might warn or kill. The real death from under, the long creeping paralysis of flesh and spirit that seized upon them as the poison tuber might spread through bowels of earth. Those noisy individual deaths were merely incidents. The real extermination went on below.   (pp. 128–9.)

A principle which recurs in Soyinka's portrayal of good characters – its converse can sometimes be seen in his portrayal of evil ones – is neatly summarized by the Dentist, albeit in a rather theatrical and almost effusively patronizing speech: 'we must acknowledge the fact – pimps, whores, thieves and a thousand other felons are the familiar vanguard of the army of change.' (p. 218.) The implied irony could be applied not only to Iriyise, to whom it directly refers, but to the anonymous 'men of Aiyéro' as well, such as the loyal and (in his own minor way) heroic Zaccheus; Aliyu, the deformed 'Lion of the Tabernacle'; and even the dumb, trusty of Temoko, in whom, in however unlikely terms, Ofeyi seems to have sparked off some human response. Pa Ahime also appears in the middle of the fray, far away from the peace of Aiyéro, to organize the rallying and ordered retreat of his defeated followers, while in isolated churches in the bush unsung priests and catechists perform wonders of physical and mental rehabilitation.

Tailla, together with her brother and their mother, flit across the scene to introduce a broader perspective into a sordid internecine affair. In a situation in which men of essentially the same race slaughter each other with mindless indifference, the possibility of love and caring which seem to know no borders is introduced. Thus the macabre vision of an Indian's strange bone structure among the skeletons in some future archeological dig offers some comfort, however cold, in the surrounding gloom, just as in the present reality of the dark, dismal church, its windows barricaded against further onslaughts of violent killers, some can still mumble, 'The Lord is my Shepherd . . .'

Bibliography

▼▼▼▼▼▼▼▼▼▼▼▼▼▼▼▼▼▼▼▼▼▼▼▼▼▼▼▼▼▼

(A) PRIMARY MATERIAL

(i) Poetry

'Two in London': 'The Immigrant' and 'The Other Immigrant'.
African Treasury, ed. Langston Hughes, Gollancz, London, 1961.
'Telephone Conversation'
'Death in the Dawn'
'Requiem'
'Prisoner'
'I think it Rains'
'Season'
'Night'
'Abiku'
Modern Poetry from Africa, Penguin, London, 1963
'For now the sun moves'
'Lament for the rains'
'Oriku Emu'/'Praise of Palm Wine'
'Egun'/'Maledictions'
'Alimotu adengbe'/'Alimotu of the golden gourd'.
Proceedings of the first rites of the Harmattan Solstice, (mimeograph), Lagos, 1966.
Poems from Prison, Rex Collings Ltd., London, 1969.
Idanre and Other Poems, Methuen, London, 1967

(ii) Short Stories

'Madame Etienne's Establishment', *Gryphon* (Leeds University journal), March 1957.
'A Tale of Two Cities', *Gryphon*, Autumn 1957.
'A Tale of Two Cities' (a different story), *New Nigerian Forum*, London, no. 2, 1958.

(iii) Essays and Articles

'Salutations to the Gut', *Reflections*, ed. Francess Ademola, African Universities Press, Lagos, 1962.
'The Fourth Stage', *The Morality of Art*, ed. J. W. Jefferson, Routledge and Kegan Paul, 1965.
Nigeria's International Films, Festival, 1962', *Nigeria Magazine*, no. 79, Dec. 1963
'And After the Narcissist?', *African Forum*, I, vi, 1966, pp. 53–64.
'Towards a True Nigerian Theatre', *Nigerian Magazine*, no. 75, Dec. 1962, pp. 58–60.
'The Writer in a Modern African State', *The Writer In Modern Africa*, ed. Per Wästberg, Uppsala, 1968.

(iv) Plays

The Lion and the Jewel, Oxford University Press, 1963.
A Dance of the Forests, Oxford University Press, 1963.
Three Plays, Mbari Publications, Nigeria (includes *The Swamp Dwellers, The Trial of Brother Jero, The Strong Breed*), 1963.
Five Plays (includes *A Dance of the Forests, The Lion and the Jewel, The Swamp-Dwellers, The Trials of Brother Jero*, and *The Strong Breed*), Oxford University Press, London, 1964.
The Road, Oxford University Press, 1965. (Had appeared earlier in *Gambit*).
Kongi's Harvest, Oxford University Press, 1967.

The Strong Breed, Orisun Acting Editions, Ibadan, 1970.

Three Short Plays (includes *The Swamp-Dwellers*, *The Trials of Brother Jero* and *The Strong Breed*), Oxford University Press, 1969.

Opera Wonyosi, Rex Collings, London, 1981.

Requiem for a Futurologist, Rex Collings, London, 1985.

(v) Revues
Before the Blackout, Orisun Acting Editions, Ibadan, 1971.

(vi) Novels
The Forest of a Thousand Daemons (translation of D. O. Fagunwa's *Ogboju ode ninu Igbo Irunmale*), Nelson, 1968.

The Interpreters, Andre Deutsch, 1965.

Season of Anomy, Rex Collings Ltd., London, 1973.

(vii) Autobiography
The Man Died, Rex Collings Ltd., London, 1973.

Aké: The Years of Childhood, Rex Collings Ltd., London, 1981.

(B) SECONDARY MATERIAL
(i) Books
Beier, Ulli (ed) *Introduction to African Literature*, Longmans, 1967.

Beier, Ulli *The Story of Sacred Wood Carvings From One Small Yoruba Town*, Nigeria Magazine, 1957, 1959.

Beier, Ulli *A Year of Sacred Festivals in One Yoruba Town*, Nigeria Magazine, 1959.

Cartey, Wilfred J. *Whispers From a Continent*, Random House, 1969.

Esslin, Martin *Brecht: A Choice of Evils*, Eyre and Spottiswoode, 1959.

Gibbs, James ed. *Critical Perspectives on Wole Soyinka*, Heinemann, London, 1981.

Gibbs, James *Wole Soyinka*, Macmillan London, 1986.

Gibbs, James *Wole Soyinka: A Select Bibliography* (in progress) mimeograph undated.

Gleason, Judith I *This Africa*, Northwestern University Press, 1965.

Hughes, Langston *An African Treasury*, Crown Publishers, 1960.

Idowu, Bolaji *Oladumare: God in Yoruba Belief*, London.

Jahn, Jahnheinz *A History of Neo-African Literature*, tr. Oliver Coburn and Ursula Lehrburger, Faber and Faber, 1966.

Laurence, Margaret *Long Drums and Cannons*, Macmillan, 1968.

Moore, Gerald *The Chosen Tongue*, Longmans, 1969.

Moore, Gerald *Wole Soyinka*, Evans, London, 1978.

Ogunba, Oyin *The Movement of Transition: a study of the plays of Wole Soyinka*, Ibadan University Press, Ibadan, 1975.

Ojo, J. Afolabi *Yoruba Culture*, University of Ife Press and London University Press, 1966.

Ramsaran, John *New Approaches To African Literature*, Ibadan University Press, 1965.

Taylor, John Russell *Anger and After: A Guide to the New British Drama*, Methuen, 1963.

Tibble, Anne *African-English Literature*, P. Owen *c.*1965.

Tucker, Martin *Africa in Modern Literature*, Frederick Ungar, 1967.

(ii) Critical Articles
Adedeji, J. A. 'The Place of Drama in Yoruba Religious Observance', *Odu*, III, i (July 1966), pp. 88–94.

Adedeji, J. A. 'Form and Function of Satire in Yoruba Drama', *Odu*, IV, i (July 1967), pp. 61–72.

Akaraogun, Alan 'Wole Soyinka' (Interview), *Spear Magazine*, May 1966, pp. 13–19.

Banham, Martin 'African Literature II: Nigerian Dramatists in English and the Traditional Nigerian Theatre', *Journal of Commonwealth Literature*,

III, 1967, pp. 97–102.

Banham, Martin 'Notes on Nigerian Theatre: 1966', *Bulletin of the Association for African Literature in English*, IV, March 1966, pp. 31–6.

Beier, Ulli 'Review of *A Dance of the Forests*', *Black Orpheus*, no. 8, 1960.

Berry, Boyd M. 'Review of *Kongi's Harvest*', *Ibadan*, no. 27, Oct. 1966, pp. 53–5.

Esslin, Martin 'Two African Playwrights', *Black Orpheus*, no. 19, March 1966, pp. 33–9.

Also in *Introduction to African Literature*, ed. Ulli Beier, Longman, 1967.

Esslin, Martin 'The Theatre of the Absurd', *Essays in Modern Drama*, ed Morris Freedman, D. C. Heath & Co., Boston, 1964.

Jones, Eldred D. '*The Interpreters*, Reading Notes', *African Literature Today*, No. 2, 1969, pp. 42–50.

(No author given) 'Our Authors and Performing Artists I', *Nigeria Magazine*, no. 88 (March 1966), pp. 57–64.

Maclean, Una 'Wole Soyinka', *Black Orpheus*, no. 15, August 1964, pp. 46–51.

Nkosi, Lewis 'Soyinka's Plays Produced by South Africans', *South Africa*, May 1966.

Ogunba, Oyin 'The Traditional Content of the Plays of Wole Soyinka', *African Literature Today*, nos. 4 & 5.

Ogundipe-Leslie, 'Molara 'Review of *Ake*', *African Literature Today*, Heinemann, London, no. 14, 1984.

Watson, Ian 'Soyinka's International Drama', *Transition*, no. 27. 1966.

West Africa 'Portrait: A National Dramatist', *West Africa*, December 19, 1964.

Westcott, Joan 'The Sculpture and Myths of Eshu-Elegba, The Yoruba Trickster', *Africa*, vol. 32, 1962.

Yankowitz Susan 'The Plays of Wole Soyinka', *African Forum*, I (Spring 1966), pp. 129–133.

Index